YOUNG CHILDREN, PEDAGOGY AND THE ARTS

Ways of Seeing

Edited by Felicity McArdle and Gail Boldt

Routledge
Taylor & Francis Group

NEW YORK AND LONDON

First published 2013
by Routledge
711 Third Avenue, New York, NY 10017

Simultaneously published in the UK
by Routledge
2 Park Square, Milton Park, Abingdon, Oxon OX14 4RN

Routledge is an imprint of the Taylor & Francis Group, an informa business

Library of Congress Cataloging in Publication Data
Young children, pedagogy and the arts : ways of seeing / edited by Felicity
McArdle and Gail Boldt.
    p. cm. – (Changing images of early childhood)
Includes bibliographical references and index.
    1. Arts–Study and teaching (Elementary)   I. McArdle, Felicity, editor of
compilation.   II. Boldt, Gail, editor of compilation.   III. Knight, Linda.
Small acts of resistance.

LB1591.Y68 2013
372.5–dc23
                                                              2012040297

ISBN: 978–0–415–62698–9 (hbk)
ISBN: 978–0–415–62699–6 (pbk)
ISBN: 978–0–203–09583–6 (ebk)

Typeset in Bembo
by RefineCatch Limited, Bungay, Suffolk

SUSTAINABLE FORESTRY INITIATIVE   Certified Sourcing
www.sfiprogram.org
SFI-01234
SFI label applies to the text stock

Printed and bound in the United States of
America by IBT Global

YO UNG CHILDREN, PEDAGOGY AN D THE ARTS

Young Children, Pedagogy and the Arts is an innovative text that describes practices and research that cross all five strands of the arts—visual, drama, music, dance, and media—and illuminates ways of understanding children and their arts practices that go beyond the common traditions. The book:

- offers practical and rich illustrations of teachers' and children's work based on international research that integrates theory with practice;
- brings a critical lens to arts education;
- includes reflective questions and recommended further readings with every chapter.

Young Children, Pedagogy and the Arts provides a more nuanced understanding of the arts through an exploration of specific instances in which committed teachers and researchers are discovering what contemporary multimodal tools offer to young children. Chapters contain examples of 'doing' the arts in the early years, new ways of teaching, and how to use emerging technologies to develop multiliteracies, equity, agency, social and cultural capital, and enhance the learning and engagement of marginalized children.

Felicity McArdle is Associate Professor at Queensland University of Technology, Australia.

Gail Boldt is Associate Professor at The Pennsylvania State University, USA.

Series Title: *Changing Images of Early Childhood*

Series Editor: Nicola Yelland

Books in this forward-thinking series challenge existing practices in early childhood education and reflect the changing images of the field. The series enables readers to engage with contemporary ideas and practices of alternative perspectives which deviate from those theories traditionally associated with the education of young children and their families. Not only do these books make complex theory accessible, they provide early childhood educators with the tools to ensure their practices are backed by appropriate theoretical frameworks and strong empirical evidence.

Titles in the *Changing Images of Early Childhood* series include:

Young Children, Pedagogy and the Arts: Ways of Seeing edited by Felicity McArdle and Gail Boldt

Diversities in Early Childhood Education: Rethinking and Doing edited by Celia Genishi and A. Lin Goodwin

Early Childhood Qualitative Research edited by J. Amos Hatch

Shift to the Future: Rethinking Learning with new Technologies in Education by Nicola Yelland

Playing it Straight: Uncovering Gender Discourse in the Early Childhood Classroom by Mindy Blaise

Childhood and Postcolonization: Power, Education, and Contemporary Practice by Gaile S. Cannella and Radhika Viruru

Rethinking Parent and Child Conflict by Susan Grieshaber

Felicity dedicates this collection of conversations to her mates in the 'Art Club'—On Fridays, we draw, paint, share wide-ranging ideas and opinions, look out for each other, marvel about our beautiful children, and share the most delicious lunches.

Gail dedicates this book to all of those kids who have filled her brain for the past twenty-five years.

CONTENTS

SERIES EDITOR'S INTRODUCTION

The terrain of education has been significantly remodeled since the new millennium. Conservative and neo-liberal forces have constructed and implemented an agenda that attempts to reduce educational outcomes to the minutiae of observable outcomes that can be demonstrated in simple tasks that require routine responses, rather than viewing the educational experience as engagement with people and ideas. Today we find ourselves in a situation where *whole* education *systems* are judged on how their students perform in an international test—the Program for International Student Assessment (PISA). In fact, teachers are also being assessed by how well their students perform in national and international tests, despite the obvious disadvantage this places on those teachers who work in challenging locations. Assessment is focused on measuring what are regarded as basic skills in Literacy and Numeracy, while PISA also claims to assess problem solving. The level of importance placed on high achievement in these tests has meant an increased focus on Literacy and Numeracy and in many cases a narrowing of teaching and learning experiences to accommodate their domination of curricula.

The paradox that is contemporary education reflects a confusion about the kind of citizens we want to help to mature in the twenty-first century against a desire to have individuals perform specific tasks that a few consider to be universal indicators of being a successful student at any given point in time. The former context is complex and messy while the latter is contained and specific. The former requires research that attempts to explore the nature of our existence and challenges our belief systems while the latter reduces performance to specified criteria with observable outcomes and derives generalizations that attempt to describe universal phenomena that bear resemblance to a limited population of aggregated averages.

Yet, in the contemporary field of early childhood, despite the efforts of conservative forces to reduce performance to a set of observable behaviors, the impact of developmental psychology has been reduced. Early childhood education has been enriched with ideas that have emerged from other disciplines such as anthropology, cultural studies, sociology, and philosophy. This has broadened the capacity of early childhood educators to respond to the new demands of contemporary times with pedagogies and practices that are appropriate to the various changing needs and interests of young children and their families.

The books in this series have been a response to this phenomenon and consider contemporary and alternative theoretical perspectives in the field. Their relevance to everyday practices is continually highlighted, thus enabling educators to create learning environments which are underpinned by a respect for all, equity and social justice. The *Changing Images of Early Childhood* books challenge and confront educators with a wide range of topics. They reflect the *complex* nature of our lives in a postmodern world where issues around globalism and the multifaceted nature of our experiences are not easily resolved. Secondly, they *respect* the participants in research by giving them voice. Finally, they provide us with *rich* descriptions of classrooms, teachers' experiences and decision making, and engage us in conversations around intricate sets of circumstances.

The books that constitute the series were included because they enable early childhood professionals to engage with contemporary ideas and practices from alternative perspectives rather than those which have been traditionally associated with the education of young children and their families. They provide opportunities to critique aspects of the field that many early childhood educators have accepted as being beyond question as well as act as catalysts for contemporary interrogations and investigations. The ideas contained in the books incorporate a wide range of theoretical perspectives that are particularly appropriate to life in the postmodern world. In this way, this latest addition is vital since it provides a rationale, exemplars and discussions about the complex range of issues and dilemmas related to the Arts in Early Childhood. Most specifically it encourages thinking about new *ways of seeing* children who come to learn in our public schools.

The *ways of seeing* children can be considered from multiple perspectives, but here they coalesce into three parts. The initial chapters in the book focus on Ways of Seeing—The Arts. They then shift to Ways of Seeing—Children, before finally considering, Ways of Seeing—Curriculum and Pedagogy, in the Arts. As the Editors state in the opening chapter, "seeing comes before knowing . . . and knowing comes before seeing . . ."—it is not a linear relationship. The chapters in this book were written by authors who work with young children. They had a desire to re-think their practices in light of contemporary research. The Editors note that they "recognize the contradictory pressures facing teachers . . ." and that they hope that this volume will enable them to gain a greater insight into arts practices and the ways in which providing contexts for encouraging the arts in education will, in fact, benefit the total educational experience for the child. The authors in the book share with us teaching and learning experiences that span traditional subject divisions in the curriculum and consider learning in multimodal contexts. Their work makes a valuable contribution to our understandings about contemporary schooling, pedagogies and issues of equity and social justice.

Young Children, Pedagogy and the Arts: Ways of seeing enables the reader to gain insights into the pedagogical practices that are derived from a deep consideration of children's interests, needs and dispositions. This is a complex process and requires teachers to shift their view of children as subjects to one in which they are regarded as vibrant and creative individuals who are partners in this learning journey. The chapters illustrate how the arts can expand ways of experiencing, knowing and communicating in our lifeworlds. They highlight and legitimize the arts as a vehicle for learning which begins with the essential component of engagement and a variety of ways of seeing and understanding our world. Effective teaching in the arts has the potential to provide contexts for demonstration of competencies and capabilities that go much further than simplistic demonstrations of performance in tests. *Ways of Seeing* encourages you to think, rethink, explore and be imaginative – it is stimulating reading.

Nicola Yelland
Victoria University, Melbourne

ACKNOWLEDGMENTS

Felicity and Gail would like to acknowledge the invaluable support of Julie Nickerson, whose special talents have been integral to the compiling of this collection of ideas. It takes a particular set of skills to manage what Julie has done, and we respect and appreciate her support and advice, the provision of which goes beyond the mechanics of bringing a book together. Thanks Julie, a wonderful Capricorn!

Introduction

1

YOUNG CHILDREN, PEDAGOGY AND THE ARTS

Ways of Seeing

Gail Boldt and Felicity McArdle

Seeing comes before knowing (Berger, 1990). A child sees a cat before knowing it is named 'cat', and before knowing its furry, four-legged ways of being. And knowing comes before seeing. We see what we know. We buy a new car, and although we had never noticed it before, suddenly it seems like the roads are filled with that brand of car. If we know children as inherently 'naughty', we see their faults and deficits. If we know children as immature, we see them as possibly cute, but certainly not serious or capable in their interactions with people and things. If we know children as skilful and creative negotiators of their social worlds, we are prepared to see and appreciate what they can do. This book aims to suggest new ways of seeing young children through discussing new ways of thinking about children's engagements in the arts.

In this book, we have brought together work by scholar-practitioners who are all interested in rethinking the arts and young children. The authors, coming from a number of different countries and institutions, bring their own cultural and contextual lenses to their work, and provide a range of approaches to practice and theorizing. They share a commitment to research that enriches the curriculum and the learning experiences of all young children and their teachers. And they share the conviction that learning is enhanced through a curriculum that has a strong focus on the arts. In this book, that commitment takes two primary forms: 1) working with the arts as central in early childhood classrooms; and 2) particular pedagogic approaches for working with children and the arts. These pedagogic approaches foreground collaborative relationships between teachers and children, relationships in which children are seen as capable participants, co-players, co-artists, and co-learners with the adults who work and play alongside them.

Both of these commitments feel particularly urgent in the contemporary education climate. In our home nations—the United States and Australia—as in many countries worldwide, increasingly the curriculum is narrowing to consider only what are regarded as the 'academic' subjects and courses. Success is measured by test scores that are, by their very nature, confined to knowledge and activities that are 'measurable'.[1] In many cases, this means a distinct focus on 'literacy' and 'numeracy'. Ironically, the narrowing of focus in education is occurring at the same time that words like 'creativity' and 'innovation' have come to the forefront in the lexicon of industry and even business and management whose employment advertisements recruit for innovative and collaborative workers for the twenty-first century.

One response to the 'back to basics' push and data-driven teaching is to make the arts fit the mold, and create rubrics and measuring tools for arts pedagogies. Another response is to take up the arts in a 'multiliteracies' approach to literacy. This book is not an argument between literacy and the arts, but rather, contains the thinking of early childhood scholars in art education and in literacy education. We recognize that while strategies like Discipline Based Art Education (DBAE), 'whole language' and multiliteracies have proven successful in at least enabling a space for the arts to endure in curricula, they have also constrained arts education and our understanding of what the arts can do, and what children can do with the arts. Designing a rubric for 'measuring' Picasso's 'Weeping Woman' would seem absurd. Equating the arts with a 'language' undersells much of what the arts can achieve beyond words. And having to view both the arts and literacy through lenses of quantifiable productivity stymies our ability to see beyond measurable outcomes—let alone see what children are up to in their classroom engagements (Leander & Boldt, 2013).

Teachers can be forgiven for shaking their heads when they are simultaneously urged to get 'back to basics' and put test scores for literacy and numeracy above all else, at the same time as curriculum and policy documents insist on creativity, collaborative partnerships, and future oriented education. Ambivalence about the arts is reflected in many parts of society, and support for the arts has historically vacillated in response to this institutionalized ambiguity. For example, in England, the Creative Partnerships project (House of Commons Education and Skills Committee, 2007) recognized the value of creativity and the arts for children's success, not only in schools, but in wider society. Two successive Labour governments supported the development of the arts in schooling, curriculum, and beyond in communities. Many teachers worked with artists in collaborative partnerships, based on beliefs about the value and importance of the arts. Most recently, with a new coalition government of the Conservatives and Liberal Democrats, all funding to these projects

---

1 For an incisive analysis of the economic and political interests driving this reform movement in the United States, see Taubman (2009).

has been stopped. In Queensland, Australia, the State education department declared 2009 the 'Year of Creativity', the year after the first national literacy and numeracy (NAPLAN) tests were conducted. The so-called Year of Creativity passed almost un-remarked. In the USA, in 2001, the No Child Left Behind Act was introduced, which more than any other policy in the USA has driven the arts to the margins of American education. In 2009, the Staying in School Report, by the Center for Arts Education, established direct links between graduation rates in New York City high schools, and the degree of access to the arts for students.

We recognize the contradictory pressures facing teachers and we hope this book will provide ways of articulating more nuanced understandings of the arts. If diverse learners and their teachers are to negotiate the promises and challenges of educational access and success afforded by schooling today, then the arts are essential. When the arts are pushed to the periphery of education policies and practices, then students are denied artistic methods and modes to develop and articulate their understandings, feelings, knowledges, experiences and perceptions. Teachers are denied artistic ways of teaching and learning that can, if you like, in fact enhance literacy and numeracy outcomes. More importantly, at the same time, the arts can provide teachers with ways to challenge the assumptions of those diminished, standardized ways of seeing the world.

As a research method, the arts can offer a means of building relationships and connections between the researcher and the 'researched'. As will be evident in many of the chapters to follow, arts experiences can prove a powerful means for generating rich data usable by teachers and researchers alike. Interviews, surveys, and other forms of testing become particularly problematic when teachers or researchers and children do not share a language or core experiences and assumptions. As several chapters in this book will demonstrate, working with children engaged in artistic modes of exploration, expression or production sometimes makes learning and thinking visible in a direct and immediate way not available through more traditional research methods.

Yet, the use of the arts as method is not without its complexities. In order to be able to facilitate and analyze artistic processes and products, researchers too need rigor, and a sound foundation in the discipline knowledge of the arts. Naïve 'interpretation' (or analysis) of artistic products can lead to shallow, false or misleading conclusions. The authors in this book have documented specific instances in which committed teachers and researchers are exploring what contemporary multimodal tools offer to young children. This collection contributes to a growing body of empirical knowledge about the potential and problematics of twenty-first century pedagogy, schooling and educational equity.

More specifically, the authors describe arts practices and research involving young children. Commonly, young children's art is valued for its 'novelty', or is taken for granted as 'natural' and 'free', or is placed within developmental age/stage schemas that are constructed as universals. Others use the arts as a means for gaining entrée into the secret and the subconscious of children's minds and 'souls'. The authors share examples of 'doing' the arts in the early years that challenge these ways of understanding children's art and illuminate more complex and nuanced ways of understanding children, their arts practices and the arts that go beyond the traditions.

In this book, we invite the reader to think again about the arts in the early years. Throughout the chapters, readers will find a focus on pedagogical practices that are based on complex understandings of children. Achieving this complexity demands that, as teachers and researchers, we learn to see children not primarily as objects of our teaching, as understood in standardized and back-to-basics approaches to curriculum. Rather, the authors begin with the assumption that children are best viewed as creative and capable subjects in their own right, as the most valuable collaborators in teaching and learning. Additionally, many of the chapters demonstrate ways in which the arts can expand ways of experiencing, knowing and communicating the world and ourselves, and can challenge more traditional notions of literacy, learning and learners. In the chapters that follow, the contributors to this book argue for the legitimacy and promise of art as a powerful means of engaging children, beginning with their strengths, capacities and capabilities, not their deficits, shortcomings, and what they cannot yet do.

Organization of the Book

In this era of curriculum standardization and narrowing, there is no shortage of materials that advocate for 'quality', that list 'activities and plans' or 'benchmarks and standards' for the art classroom, and that argue over what is art and what is not. We leave those undertakings to others. Instead, we have searched for different questions. Generally, a book such as this will be organized to cover each strand of the arts—music, dance, drama, visual arts and media. While the recognition of these distinct and different strands of the arts is important, it is not how we have organized the thinking in this book. Rather, we have grouped the chapters into three sections. The first section of the book is:

- Ways of Seeing—The Arts

Here, we ask questions about how a privileging of the arts might allow us to see teaching, learning and research differently.

The next section is:

- Ways of Seeing—Children

We are interested here in seeing children first, and how this might affect our understanding of what matters in curriculum and classrooms.

Finally, the third section is:

- Ways of Seeing—Curriculum and Pedagogy

Here we have considered promising ways to think about teaching that will contribute to children's powerful engagements in the arts.

This approach to organizing the book is meant to disrupt traditional discipline based approaches to the arts. Our organization of the chapters and themes embodies alternative ways for seeing and thinking the arts, arts education, and children. Beginning with this current chapter, we develop the idea of looking for alternative frameworks for thinking through seemingly contradictory constructions of children and schooling. Our aim is to set up possibilities for other ways of thinking, speaking and enacting arts rich programs with young children. These new ways of thinking enable new possibilities for working with young children in the early years. We suggest various ways to rethink young children's experiences and learning in the arts.

The matching of chapters with sections was not easy. The authors in this volume share some fundamental beliefs about children and the arts, and in several instances, chapters fit with two if not all three section headings. Therefore, while we invite readers to consider the particular ways in which a chapter connects with the theme of its section, we also encourage readers to read across the chapters to identify and contemplate the shared values of contributors from such far-flung locales and experiences. In what follows, we describe our conceptualization of each theme, why it matters, and how the assigned chapters take up the questions of that theme.

Ways of Seeing—The Arts

In the contemporary era in which learning is reduced to a simplified accounting of easy quantifiability, it is more crucial than ever to insist that privileging the arts can lead to important ways of exploring, knowing and expressing the world and one's place in it. By 'privileging the arts', we do not mean that all subject matter should be understood and undertaken through an arts lens. We are making a simple argument for the value of the arts—both integrated into general education classrooms, and as a set of practices and skills that require their own place in the curriculum, in the form of art education. There is a real risk that comes with an era when the arts are marginalized to 'specialist classes' if not eliminated from schools altogether as luxuries that cannot be afforded in lean financial times. The risk is that access to the arts becomes available only to those who can afford this, and those where linguistic, cultural and/or social barriers or differences exist are increasingly disadvantaged.

Although it may be hard to recognize this when looking at contemporary educational priorities, learning and knowing are not confined to letters and numbers. Across many millennia, human civilizations have recorded their knowledges and ways of living in ways that remain meaningful today. Recent understandings of intelligence and competency have challenged the dominance given to traditional text-based forms of literacy as culturally constructed. This work proffers many other ways of knowing (for example, Pink, 2005). Indigenous and embodied knowledges, for example, can be transmitted directly through dance, music, spatial orientations, gesture and the creation of images. Knowledges are not limited to, nor even necessarily best communicated through, the compilation of rubrics or benchmarks, lists of developmental markers, written or spoken narrations of 'what I learned', meta-analyses of processes or parts, the mediation of anthropologists or other specialists, or other means of 'translation'. Enabling children to learn through the arts can open multiple kinds of communication channels, resulting in deeper learning across all curriculum areas, including enhanced literacy outcomes (see Fiske, 1999; Vaughan, Harris, & Caldwell, 2011).

Across its history, theories of literacy have suffered from the same sins of colonial arrogance that have characterized the human and natural sciences. The 'literacy myth', as Gee (2008) describes it, is that literacy is what makes humans civilized. In the 1960s, anthropologists John Goody and Ian Watt, as well as British classicist Eric Havelock, argued that literacy leads to the development of cognitive capacity for analytical, critical, and rational thinking. According to these theorists, these traits mark cultures that are more highly developed or advanced. Such development was described as facilitating the ability of the literate culture to distinguish between myth and rationality thus initiating the capacity for scientific advancements, increasingly complex forms of government, and care for the rights and needs of individuals (Gee, 2008, p. 50).

Although the connection between text based literacy and individual or cultural sophistication has long since been disproven (see for example Scribner & Cole, 1981), the assumed developmental superiority of written over pictorial texts persists. As Linda Knight argues in Chapter Two, many primary grades teachers enforce the mistaken belief that drawing may be acceptable for the youngest of children, but that the replacement of drawing by written texts, both in children's writing and in their reading materials, is a mark of intellectual development.

The arts are not the developmental precursor to becoming literate but are, in fact, their own forms of making meaning that allow children unique opportunities for experiencing potential and engaging in interpersonal relations. Writing and reading written texts must be placed alongside, not above or in competition with, other sound, movement, and image based ways of knowing and expressing meaning. Art (via sound, image and movement) conveys and captures moods, feelings and meaning, including times when words are not available or when they are inadequate (Wright, 2012). In Chapter Two, Knight points out that 'complex inter-textual practices necessitate receptive pedagogies that help the teacher to make sense of a child's way of communicating, to help tap into a child's engagement with education effectively' (p. 23). She writes that if teachers are to 'change their approaches to drawing in their classrooms', then this requires critical examination of 'their personal definitions of artistic practice and competency, and their understandings of popular developmental paradigms' (p. 25).

Our argument is not with the importance of children developing text based reading and writing fluency. Rather, we are concerned with the privileging of this above or to the exclusion of all else. Traditional and taken-for-granted conventional approaches to teaching language and literacy work to privilege print-based alphabetic literacy over other forms of cognitive and multimodal engagement. With this strong emphasis on the word, artistic forms of expression and communication are often undervalued, with the arts relegated to the margins of education and research. The bias towards valuing text-based competency leads to a perception that those who are not proficient with language skills are somehow less than, or deficient. Equally troubling, it narrows the ways that humans are able to perceive and interact with our world.

Indeed, research has demonstrated across multiple settings that arts-rich programs assist with building capacity and understanding, not only for the children but for the involved adults as well (McArdle & Spina, 2007; McArdle & Tan, 2012). In her exploration of dance in early years classes in Chapter Three, Adrienne Sansom begins with Māori (Aotearoa/New Zealand) dance pedagogy to think about what happens when we consider dance as a cultural practice. Arguing that all children come to school with experiences of dance that reflect their cultural experiences, Sansom sets about making the case that dance offers an opportunity for teachers to recognize the strengths that children bring into the classroom. She goes further, however, arguing for teachers to dance alongside children. This, she maintains, forces teachers to step beyond the safe parameters of control and venture where uncertainty lies. In her thinking about the power of such an event, Sansom argues, 'These discoveries led to more than just the creation of dance; they were also about the relationships that occurred between the child and the adult, the child and other children, as well as a deeper understanding of the self for both the child and the teacher' (p. 40). For Sansom, dancing alongside children makes possible a reciprocity that changes the way teachers and children understand themselves and their places in the classroom in important ways.

While we do not make a naïve claim that the arts can solve all the educational ills of today, we believe that the arts contribute important materials and ways of working. In addition, the arts allow for experiences and expressions that are unique to each art form. In Chapter Four, Christina MacRae shows the worth of fighting to preserve space in the school day and education budgets for the arts and artists, and art classrooms. Curriculum built around dance, drama, music, digital and visual arts is not the same as, and does not do the same things as, other—more usual—forms of curriculum. In her chapter, MacRae describes her work as an artist in residence in an early years classroom. She holds on to differences in her identities and ways of work—as an artist, a university researcher and a trained and experienced early years teacher. This has not always been easy, nor clear cut for her, but her reflections have enabled blurrings and creative recombinings that allowed her to see all three roles anew. For MacRae, the specificity of the materials made a difference. She writes, 'My focus was always on the objects themselves; the power they might exert, and what they might show me about the part they play in our lives' (p. 61). She goes on to say that this focus on the materials meant that she did not always know how things would unfold. This led to ways of working that are different from what is more usual in schools. She argues that it is this 'not knowing' which is central to her practice as an artist. This not knowing opened up productive discussions with the teachers with whom she worked, and promoted a pedagogy of listening when she was working with the children. McArdle takes up this point again in the final chapter of the book, in relation to preparing teachers who can appreciate Leadbeater's (2000) concept of 'useful ignorance'.

Ways of Seeing—Children

To many, it may seem counterintuitive or even nonsensical to argue that adults need to learn to *see* children. After all, we were all once children and have memories of being children. Many of us, and especially teachers, caregivers and parents, spend a great deal of time around children. Supervising their play and learning, providing for their many needs, planning and purchasing and working for their welfare, children are constantly in our sights.

In spite of this, we argue that children remain invisible to many, even those who spend long hours each day with them. This is so for many reasons. Our own memories fool us into believing that we know what childhood is like and that, therefore, we know the children in our care. There is, however, much research that demonstrates how faulty and stereotyped our memories of childhood actually are (Jenkins, 1997; Mitchell & Reid-Walsh, 2002). Our memories are far more connected to the person we see ourselves as or wish to be today than to the actual historic record of what happened. We remember selectively and our remembering is heavily mediated by our own desires—half truth and half myth.

It is common when speaking about our beliefs about contemporary childhood to tell nostalgic or tragic stories about our own childhoods that either exult childhood or condemn 'kids these days'. Our nostalgia for what childhood used to be like is less about remembering life as it actually was and largely about what we *wish it was*. We may fail to recognize that through stories we tell about contemporary 'good' and 'bad' childhoods, we reveal our stereotypes of what other people's lives are like. These stories are often raced and classed—the people who raise their children 'right' and those who 'don't care'. Memory serves us up the stories that we want to tell.

Myths of childhood innocence, which have dominated Western conceptions of childhood since the seventeenth century (Higonnet, 1998), intermingle with and depend upon stories of family depravity and innocence lost. When we imagine children as naturally innocent, what we are really doing is imagining them as empty (Kincaid, 1992). Such a perspective, Kincaid argues, allows us to project our own interests or desires or agenda onto children. If we see children as lacking their own desires, interests, complexities, ambivalences, social ambitions, sexual energies and so on, we can see them as simply products of a good or bad society, as victims, or as the products of heroic child rearing. This requires less of us than if we see children as people who are entitled to rights, whose actions, wants, and agency we have to take seriously. Whether we imagine children as either innocents to be protected at all costs, or as already 'contaminated' (by poor parenting, a bad society, poor education, or popular culture), these are two sides of the same coin, and the effect on our actions is similar. In either instance, we imagine that we are justified in our interventions into children's lives in the name of protecting, fixing or saving them. Regardless of how we enact our beliefs in 'the innocent child', children are subject to the constant policing and disciplining of their interests, behaviors, speech, and desires and rarely are asked to speak for themselves about their lives.

In schools—and especially in the contemporary era of standardization and 'accountability'—children are most often treated as the object of teaching rather than collaborators with teachers in their learning. Developmental theory offers teachers stories of what children are like or should be like. If we think of children as driven by 'natural' development to be a certain way, we fail to take into account how culture shapes a child's way of being. Children learn to interact and be in the world within the specific contexts or cultures of their home and community. Failure to see this means that, generally, the children who are favored and who succeed in school, are those who are most like the teacher, administration, and curriculum makers. Judgments of what is 'normal' or 'expected' are based on cultural experiences, which are taken as 'normal' (Dyson, 2003). Children (and their families) whose speech pattern, experience, language, pre-existing knowledge, interests and behaviors are different from what is valued for school children will be seen as 'not right'. From this perspective, it is the child and family who are supposed to change and adapt the school norms, rather than understanding that the school norms are limited and need to be expanded.

Even for children whose cultures are similar to those favored in schools, 'one size fits all' is simply bad teaching. Ironically, approaches to curriculum and pedagogy that are based on standardized and disembodied beliefs about what *all* children must be taught in the name of 'equality', actually produce the very differences in learning outcomes that they claim to be addressing. It is a mistake, in other words, to believe that just because we have taught something, a child can and will learn it. Standardized approaches to learning begin with curriculum and measure children through their success or failure to learn it. Our focus in this section of the book is on the importance of beginning with children, seeing what is happening as they are creating, learning, and being.

Children have their own lifeworlds, separate from adults, and in many classrooms the curriculum and the day to day planned experiences fail to take this into account. For instance, their interests in popular culture are trivialized or policed. The belief in education and high art as civilizing or liberating forces has found its way into many contemporary classrooms in the form of a disdain for commercial or popular children's culture. This collection goes some way to highlighting the affordances of the arts, contemporary technologies, and children's culture for enhancing learning engagement—and perhaps most importantly, for marginalized children in terms of their developing literacies, equity, agency, social and cultural capital. The authors in this collection do not view children's culture, which is often in close relationship with popular and commercial culture, as a scourge to be stamped out by the 'purist' art teacher. Our interest is in what children do with the multiple cultures and identities they bring with them into the classroom, and how these can be built upon as children develop their artistry. Here we acknowledge Dyson's (2003) notion of the 'permeable curriculum' in which home and school cultures can work together to create more inclusive classrooms.

The chapters in this section include accounts of research that began with questions of what it is that children are doing when they are engaging with the arts. In Chapter Five, Kortney Sherbine and Gail Boldt look into a second grade classroom. Sherbine's vision of teaching and learning changed along with her close attention to her students' passion for an online multiplayer game, *Poptropica*. Sherbine's students used drawing, writing, painting, singing and dancing to express their intense engagement with the classroom *Poptropica* project. Sherbine and Boldt argue, however, that to focus on what happened in this (or any) classroom solely or primarily as examples of arts or literacy pedagogy would be to miss what it was about for the children. They argue that more than anything, the children used the affordances of the classroom, of popular culture materials, of art and literacy practices, of previous experiences and of relationships to one another to feed their experiences of passionate intensity. For Sherbine, following the children's energy led to the recognition that intensity and desire were central forces in the classroom. When she realized this, her stances on curriculum and pedagogy changed.

Christine Marmé Thompson, in her beautifully titled Chapter Six, shares with Sherbine and Boldt the desire to use relationships with children, research and teaching as opportunities to 'understand children with greater clarity and specificity, as individuals, as members of multiple social groups within the classroom, and as participants in and producers of cultures beyond the classroom' (p. 95). Thompson describes her research project, observing and talking with children who chose to use sketchbooks as a part of their time in preschool. Like MacRae (Chapter Four), Thompson describes this as a 'pedagogy of listening' which she takes from the work of Carla Rinaldi (2006). In particular, Thompson follows Andrew, a child potentially seen on the one hand as a gifted artist and on the other, as moody, stubborn, uncooperative in activities that did not interest him, and overly immersed in the world of cartoon superheros. Thompson unfixes Andrew from these common classroom descriptors, and asks what happens to our understanding of teaching if we see Andrew, and indeed all children, differently. Thompson suggests seeing Andrew as a child whose identity is not and should not be fixed, but who is rather both open to the world around him and is, through his very being and becoming, adding to the abundance, beauty, and surprise of our shared world.

In Chapter Seven, Eeva Anttila argues that modern dance curriculum offers a continuation of a romantic conception of art as separate from everyday life and a search for exceptional talent to cultivate. Anttila demonstrates how dance can be understood instead as a form of creative play. She turns developmental narratives on their heads, rejecting descriptions of children as simply the receivers of existing molds and patterns when it comes to dance. She draws from her own research and that of others who see children's rich capacities for making and expression meaning. Quoting Corsaro (1997), Anttila describes children as 'active, creative social agents who produce their own unique children's cultures while simultaneously contributing to the production of adult societies' (Corsaro, 1997, p. 4, quoted by Anttila, p. 112). Anttila calls for a way of seeing children and the world that allows for imagining teaching as a form of co-creative choreography.

Ways of Seeing—Curriculum and Pedagogy

It would be easy to misread our commitment to formulating pedagogy and curriculum as solely about seeing the children. On the contrary, we suggest that there is an important place for teacher direction in the classroom. When it comes to teaching and the arts, liberal humanist discourses about individual freedom and creativity produce taboos about structure, copying, and 'stifling creativity' that makes teachers reluctant to 'teach'.

This is especially an issue for art teachers, who may perceive their classrooms as one of the last bastions for students to pursue their interests or to engage in learning in idiosyncratic ways. There are a number of possible explanations for this. Art teachers often inherit a personally significant mythology about art as the cool space on the outer fringes (see McArdle, 2008). There can be an expectation of a stereotype of a 'cool and groovy' art teacher (Burnaford, Aprill, & Weiss, 2001), existing on the edge of the mainstream, proudly claiming and being permitted 'difference', and enjoying the power that comes with being on the margins (hooks, 1984). Or, because of the close links between modernist art and psychology, art teachers are sometimes fervent believers in the art emerging from the subconscious or unconscious discourse, and its therapeutic self-expression purposes, making it best left alone, un-taught. Or, like many other early childhood educators, they may see children's artistic productions as simply an expression of a developmental trajectory, and thus not in need of direction.

With mantras, then, of self-expression, freedom and creativity, art teachers may avoid providing much direct instruction about art making to children, all the while having 'rules for breaking the rules' and to 'teach without teaching' (McArdle, 2008, p. 367) which go unspoken and taken for granted. Many preservice teachers, having themselves been left in primary and secondary school to develop 'naturally', give the lie to this notion of 'natural unfolding', when they arrive at university with little or no skills or artistry and without artistic language or insight. The discourse of 'natural unfolding' is attractive to those who know nothing about art, and it is convenient in the contemporary era of bare bones educational funding. If there is no teaching to be done in the arts, then there is no need for an art teacher.

Pedagogically, good intentions and therapeutic models of engagement with the arts are not sufficient to meet children's learning needs. Teachers of literacy and numeracy do not eschew intentional teaching. Children are not told: '*I am not going to teach you how to read and write. You make up your own words. That will be much better than any words I can tell you*'. There is no suggestion, for example, that the development of spelling is a natural accomplishment, somehow biologically driven. Children are encouraged to attempt approximations, invent, and there is a recognition that errors will occur, but that this is part of the learning process. Spelling is encouraged in an environment in which spelling is necessary and appreciated, where exemplars are modeled, feedback and support provided, rules explained, 'tricks' and techniques are taught (Cambourne, 1995). This approach acknowledges that children will become far more powerful and flexible spellers if they understand the principles and patterns that guide spelling. This is in contrast to a memorization approach. When children have an understanding of phonemic principles, then this allows them to apply the schema they have already developed about how spelling works to making increasingly accurate inferences about how to spell new words.

In this approach, teachers do not spell for children, but neither do they ignore spelling. Rather, they fill classrooms with words, read frequently to children from text the children are able to see, talk with the children about rules and patterns in spelling, ask children to talk about spelling issues they are noticing and connections they are making as they read and write, and give the children many opportunities to write as best they are able. In this as-best-they-are-able writing, teachers expect that the child's writing will be filled with approximated spellings. Teachers accept these spellings not because they are cute, but because they are expressions of the child's current understanding of how spelling works. The strength and value of these approximations are recognized and appreciated. At the same time, teachers look for opportunities through feedback, modeling, and discussion to scaffold the child into ever more sophisticated understandings of spelling. The pace at which this occurs cannot be pre-ordained, but it is important that the child does not become overwhelmed, confused or frustrated. Ultimately, the teacher has to recognize that the pace and specifics of learning will be different from child to child, simply because neither the teacher nor the child has conscious control over the child's schema building.

It is easy to draw parallels in art education. It is difficult to imagine a class-room with a teacher who cannot and does not care to read. If young children are to learn to construct and compose and create, they need to be in the company of people who believe that the arts are worthwhile and important. They need to be able to work alongside adults and peers who are themselves engaged in art practices. They need opportunities to work in environments rich with examples of the arts. Children need supportive environments with teachers who respect how an individual child's artistry, creativity and under-standing unfold. Children need teachers who believe that there is something to be learned when it comes to the arts. And children need teachers who under-stand that they must themselves first learn about the child and their interests and their thinking. According to the authors in this section of the book, effective teaching in the arts requires a combination of knowledge about the arts with an understanding of how to see children—how to tune in and learn from children what it is that they need.

Many preservice teachers arrive in generalist early years teacher education programs with shallow knowledge, skills and practices in the arts. This often brings with it 'art anxiety' (Genever, 1996) and 'baggage' left over from their own often partial and incomplete memories of school (Britzman, 1997). Without background knowledge and understandings, these teachers may provide arts activities that can possibly have therapeutic value. The arts curriculum might allow young children the time and space to explore themes or images that disturb or puzzle them. Or the arts activities might simply provide respite from the main 'business' of the more academic curriculum. However, arts activities can just as easily become surface 'busy' work, with little or no evidence of effective learning.

The chapters in this section focus on arts based experiences that are made available to young children and what children can and may do with those opportunities. The goal here is not to provide an exhaustive list of classroom how-to's and, indeed, these few chapters barely scratch the surface of arts education curriculum and pedagogy. Rather, we have placed them in this section because they offer models of ways to think about curriculum and pedagogy that can be applied by readers more broadly.

In Chapter Eight, Karen E. Wohlwend and Kylie Peppler describe the affordances of children's popular media, in particular *Barbie* transmedia, which provide children with rich opportunities for play and design. Wohlwend and Peppler point to design (clothing, furniture and interior) as an area that is typically ignored in arts education. They suggest that this is not only to miss an opportunity to explore design theories and skills, but also that 'widespread dismissing of the value of Barbie play comes at additional costs, given the complicated positioning and potential marginalization that comes with critiquing a toy so strongly associated with girlhood' (p. 132). Wohlwend and Peppler note the disappearance of play time in multiple settings, and argue for the value of making space for children to play with design in early classrooms. They conclude with multiple suggestions for strategically expanding opportunities for such artistic play.

Amy Pfeiler-Wunder, in Chapter Nine, offers a critical reading of how a standardized arts education curriculum is understood and instituted in two schools within a single district. One of the commonly touted reasons supporting standardizing curricula is democracy—the idea that all children are on a 'level playing field', when curriculum is set and centralized. Pfeiler-Wunder's inquiries suggest a different story. The differences she notes can be connected with social class, and how the arts are understood and enacted in relation to class. Pfeiler-Wunder looks not only at differences in how teachers and administrators think about the role that arts education plays in the curriculum and the lives of the children, but at how the children themselves use the arts to express their relations to social class. This chapter is intriguing, and an especially cautionary tale for those who consider the arts to be a matter for the individual, for a free and un-mediated, untaught self-expression. This chapter suggests that even the loftiest goals in a curriculum plan are always interpreted and enacted in a social context. Not all children and families have access to discourses of art that celebrate notions of 'self-expression' or 'personal freedom' or a space where there is 'no right or wrong'.

In Chapter Ten, Jan Sverre Knudsen describes intercultural events—concerts that are made available to children in Norway. Knudsen's analysis looks at the differences in what the organizers believe children's experiences of music are or should be. In his research undertakings, he has interviewed young children about their experiences of the events. Knudsen argues that in relation to the concert experience, children in fact attended to things that were very different from what was often expected by adults. This becomes even more interesting when taking into account that the concerts were designed to introduce children to unfamiliar music styles from cultures other than their own. Knudsen identifies several unexpected ways in which the children insert themselves into concert experiences. He suggests that concert programs which fail to provide children with opportunities to connect in ways that are meaningful to them will not achieve anything deeper than being an entertaining 'happening'.

Throughout this book, there is an insistence on the importance of the teacher when it comes to the arts in the early years. While stressing the primacy of seeing children first, our voices are the voices of teachers, artists, researchers.

In the final chapter of this book, for Felicity McArdle, the work begins with preparing teachers. Like much of this book, the thinking in this chapter is sometimes about art specifically, sometimes about pedagogy and curriculum (in this case, tertiary pedagogies), and sometimes about ways of seeing learners and learning—in this case, university students, preparing to be the teachers of the future. McArdle begins with acknowledging the Indigenous people of her home country, and the powerful role that the arts played and continue to play in the oldest continuous culture on the planet. In the final part of her chapter she discusses the usefulness of models for preservice teachers, but cautions that models of excellence such as the Reggio Emilia 'phenomenon' of recent years can work to both enable and constrain when it comes to ways of seeing young children, pedagogies and the arts.

We hope that this book provokes readers to see the arts differently when it comes to young children. In each chapter, the reader will find questions, designed as discussion starters or prompts for reflection. Each author has paused at different points in their discussions, to invite the reader to pause, ponder and take the time to consider the author's ideas, and their own standpoints in response to the provocations. This book is not an argument for one way of thinking about the arts over another. For us, the arts can be fun and serious, and social and cultural, and therapy and nonsense, and taught and learned, and free and structured, and high and low, and, and, and . . . At the very least, if you work with young children, we hope this book prompts you to try it yourself—dance, and sing, and draw, and paint, and imagine, and perform, and make, and play, and, if you make a mistake, try it again.

References

Berger, J. (1990). *Ways of seeing: Based on the BBC television series with John Berger.* London: British Broadcasting Corporation and Penguin Books.

Britzman, D. (1997). The tangles of implication. *Qualitative Studies in Education, 10*(1), 31–37.

Burnaford, G., Aprill, A., & Weiss, C. (2001). *Renaissance in the classroom: Arts integration and meaningful learning.* Mahwah, NJ: Lawrence Erlbaum Associates.

Cambourne, B. (1995). Toward an educationally relevant theory of literacy learning: Twenty years of inquiry. *The Reading Teacher, 49*(3), 182–190.

Corsaro, W. A. (1997). *The sociology of childhood.* Thousand Oaks, CA: Pine Forge Press.

Dyson, A. (2003). *The brothers and sisters learn to write: Popular literacies in childhood and school cultures.* New York: Teachers College Press.

Fiske, E. (Ed.) (1999). *Champions of change: The impact of the arts on learning.* Washington, DC: The Arts Education Partnership and the President's Committee on the Arts and Humanities.

Gee, J. (2008). *Social linguistics and literacies: Ideologies in discourses.* New York: Routledge.

Genever, M. (1996). Art anxiety: Framing some responses. In S. McGinty & L. A. Fitzpatrick (Eds.), *Tertiary teaching: Models of innovative practice* (pp. 63–69). Townsville, QLD: Centre for Social and Welfare Research, James Cook University.

Higonnet, A. (1998). *Pictures of innocence: The history and crisis of ideal childhood.* New York: Thames and Hudson.

hooks, b. (1984). *Feminist theory: From margin to center.* Boston: South End Press.

House of Commons Education and Skills Committee. (2007). *Creative partnerships and the curriculum: Eleventh report of Session 2006–07.* London: The Stationery Office.

Jenkins, H. (1997). *The innocent child and other modern myths.* Retrieved from http://web.mit.edu/cms/People/henry3/innocentchild.html.

Kincaid, J. (1992). *Child-loving: The erotic child and Victorian culture.* New York: Routledge.

Leadbeater, C. (2000). *Living on thin air: The new economy.* New York: Viking.

Leander, K., & Boldt, G. (2013). Rereading 'A pedagogy of multiliteracies': Bodies, texts and emergence. *Journal of Literacy Research, 45*(1), 22–46.

McArdle, F. (2008). The arts and staying cool. *Contemporary Issues in Early Childhood, 9*(4), 365–374.

McArdle, F., & Spina, N. (2007). Children of refugee families as artists: Bridging the past, present and future. *Australian Journal of Early Childhood, 32*(4), 50–53.

McArdle, F., & Tan, J. (2012). Art as language, pedagogy and method: Promoting learning engagement for young African refugee migrant students in urban Australia. In A. Yeung, E. Brown & C. Lee (Eds.), *Communication and language: Surmounting the barriers to cross-cultural understanding.* Charlotte, NC: Information Age Publishing.

Mitchell, C., & Reid-Walsh, J. (2002). *Researching children's popular culture.* New York: Routledge.

Pink, D. H. (2005). *A whole new mind: Moving from the information age to the conceptual age.* New York: Riverhead Books.

Rinaldi, C. (2006). *In dialogue with Reggio Emilia: Listening, researching and learning.* New York: Routledge.

Scribner, S., & Cole, M. (1981). *The psychology of literacy.* Cambridge, MA: Harvard University Press.

Taubman, P. (2009). *Teaching by the numbers: Deconstructing the discourse of standards and accountability in education.* New York: Routledge.

Vaughan, T., Harris, J. L., & Caldwell, B. J. (2011) *Bridging the gap in school achievement through the arts.* Summary Report of Project commissioned by The Song Room. Melbourne: The Song Room.

Wright, S. (Ed.) (2012). *Children, meaning-making and the arts* (2nd edition). Frenchs Forest, NSW: Pearson.

PART I

Ways of Seeing—The Arts

2

SMALL ACTS OF RESISTANCE

The Role of Intergenerational Collaborative Drawing in Early Childhood Teaching and Learning

Linda Knight

This chapter focuses on 'intergenerational collaborative drawing', a particular process of drawing whereby adults and children draw at the same time on a blank paper space. Such drawings can be produced for a range of purposes, and based on different curriculum or stimulus subjects. Children of all ages, and with a range of physical and intellectual abilities, are able to draw with parents, carers and teachers. Intergenerational collaborative drawing is a highly potent method for drawing in early childhood contexts because it brings adults and children together in the process of thinking and theorizing in order to create visual imagery and this exposes in deep ways, to adults and children, the ideas and concepts being learned about. For adults, this exposure to a child's thinking is a far more effective assessment tool than when they are presented with a finished drawing they know little about.

This chapter focuses on drawings to examine wider issues of learning independence and how in drawing, preferred schema in the form of hand-out worksheets, the suggestive drawings provided by adults, and visual material seen in everyday life all serve to co-opt a young child into making particular schematic choices. I suggest that intergenerational collaborative drawing therefore serves to work as a small act of resistance to that of co-opting, in that it helps adults and children to collectively challenge popular creativity and learning discourses.

What Drawings Can Perform

The three- and four-year-old children sit and wait to begin drawing. The teacher recalls an environmental story they had read earlier. She asks the children about components of the story via recall questions, which they answer. They then begin their collaborative drawing. Each child and the adult sit by a space of a large sheet of paper. They have brushes and bamboo skewers and India ink. One child and the adult experiment with the media, three children begin drawing flowers (Figure 2.1).

There is a lot of activity elsewhere in the classroom. A small group of children are standing around the table of drawers, watching them, however the four children that are drawing are very quiet, hardly speaking.

One child paints a black shape, which he enlarges during the course of the drawing episode. Another child carefully draws a schematic flower then proceeds to obliterate it with the ink and a large brush. This child demonstrates some unexpected change of direction by covering over their initial drawing.

The teacher then asks the four children to move around the paper so they are now forced to work on top of, or around an existing drawing. Interestingly, the child who painted the large black shape proceeds to paint over the prior drawer's efforts by obliterating their flower with large black ink strokes.

This collaborative drawing episode can be interpreted in different ways; one interpretation is to suggest that the group is working compatibly on a group task—no-one complained of having their drawings covered over or changed. Another interpretation is to say that each person made different drawings and also responded to others' drawings differently. They did not simply continue the drawing that someone else had begun.

(Field observation notes from an intergenerational collaborative drawing episode, September 17, 2008)

FIGURE 2.1 Ink on cartridge paper.

Intergenerational collaborative drawing (Knight 2008, 2009a, 2009b) enables adults and children to make drawings on the same paper surface at the same time. This is not the same as making a drawing 'together' because 'Different dialogues co-exist and feed into the drawing event as a collection of multiple literacies' (Knight, 2009a, p. 55). Each contributor works alongside, but not identically with the other drawers. As the field observation above suggests, a teacher can sit with a child or small groups of children and they can work on producing visualized evidence of what they each think about or comprehend on a particular issue or subject. They might produce one large collaborative drawing but the ideas contained within it are not identical.

This form of drawing is an important method for teachers and other educators to consider because it enhances opportunities for communication between adults and children in educational and other integenerational contexts. Intergenerational collaborative drawing is highly useful then because it helps adults and young children to work together in grasping diverse concepts across all areas of learning. It also helps to attest that drawing is an intellectual, academic activity, assisting children and adults to encounter and understand a range of concepts and ideas across subject areas.

It is important to embed drawing into everyday learning because children use drawing to help them realize their thoughts and actions (Pillar, 1998; Weber & Mitchell, 1995). Children are regarded in this chapter as meaning-makers, in that they pull on a diverse collection of ideas, experiences, imaginings, and information to form their opinions, learning and relationships with the world. Drawing is a central repository for this so children should have high-quality opportunities to use drawing to assist in their thinking and imagination.

Children utilize combinations of movement, dialogue, and sound while they draw (Coates, 2002; Wright, 2007). These complex inter-textual practices necessitate receptive pedagogies that help the teacher to make sense of a child's way of communicating, to help tap into a child's engagement with education effectively. Without this, 'the rootedness of texts in visual imagery is neglected' (Weber & Mitchell, 1995, p. 33) and children's drawings can be simply passed off as formative attempts at art making.

When adults and children use drawing as a way of exploring and conceptualizing diverse aspects of learning, they often use different symbols and marks. Drawing collaboratively actively liberates adult and child drawers from creating 'pictures' laden with the conventional schema that often flood children's drawings. It also engages drawers, and importantly, adult drawers, in an expanded process of cognitive discovery. For adults who do not draw regularly, not only does this engage them in far more authentic drawing practices, it also helps to avoid situations whereby a child presents a completed drawing to the adult for them to interpret. Visual interpretation of completed drawings is a problematized task for educators who may not grasp that the marks in a young child's drawing pay attention to specifics such as emotion, movement, smell, taste, etc.

(Bodrova & Leong, 2003; Braswell & Callanan, 2003; Matthews, 1999), or that the image of a figure or detail may not represent a particular meaning. Interpretations therefore leave sizeable gaps between the perceived meaning of the drawing and the actual meanings the child wove into it. This has significant implications if those interpretations form part of a developmental snapshot or report on the child.

Collaborative drawing is a dynamic enactment whereby drawers find out how much they and others know because it initiates deep exploration of cognitive concepts. Educators can undertake collaborative drawings to initiate dialogue about curriculum-based or diverse learning concepts. Working in collaboration on drawings can give educators a greater insight into their students than they may have otherwise.

The Drawing as Valorized Object

The complex nature of what children draw and the reasons why they draw is theorized upon via a number of philosophical paradigms. Developmental psychologists used children's drawings to help define various aspects of childhood growth (Nicholls & Kennedy, 1992; Porath, 1993; Ring, 2006; Toomela, 1999), including examining drawings produced by gifted children to gain further understandings into the nature of their giftedness (Harrison, 1999). Sociocultural investigations have focused on wider contexts, such as whether world societies influence a child's communication development as they progress through early childhood (Ivashkevich, 2006; Rogoff, 2003; Seidman & Beilin, 1984), or why drawing is discarded as a key literacy as children move 'from nursery to the top of the infant school' (Coates, 2002, p. 25). Cultural studies texts also focus on drawing in its wider contexts and suggest that drawn images refer to actual things, or to things experienced, and these can affect the expectations of what schema might appear in drawings, particularly if developmental analyses are used (Weber & Mitchell, 1995).

Research texts can be incredibly influential on pedagogy, and can quickly embed into daily practices and become 'truths'. Developmental theories particularly have had significant impact on how drawings are regarded. For example: 'By age 5, boys and girls tend to develop separate styles and preferences for their graphic expression' (Weber & Mitchell, 1995, p. 36). Such statements are loaded as they reveal how drawings might be selectively searched for particular symbolic indicators to help uphold the theory.

Because adults often utilize such paradigmatic theories to help define children's learning (Ball, 1994; Braswell & Callanan, 2003; Matthews, 1999) it is important to raise awareness that children's drawings often serve a wider purpose than asserted in those popular theories. It is useful to take a metaphysical step back at this point and cast a wider look at the relationships between drawing and visual art, and particularly, children's drawings in relation to children's art. This is important because, along with popular learning theories, educator beliefs about art can often direct how and why drawing is undertaken in a classroom. The beliefs and valorizations that help to define what 'is' art are often informed by wider societal contexts about what is art, what is 'good' art, and how to create 'good' art. For many non-Indigenous Australian adults, making art is likely to be about creating something that looks pleasing to the eye in terms of its color, line, composition, and balance. It must fulfill the criteria established by Modernist aesthetics scholars such as Bell who asserted that art must have 'significant form' (cited in Warburton, 2003, p. 10); meaning what is produced must incite a strong emotional response in the viewer due to its aesthetic powers. Aesthetics in this context relates to a form of pleasing beauty. In drawing, one common but significant preconception about being a 'good drawer' extends on Modernist aesthetics of making something that has pleasing beauty, and includes an assumption that artists conjure up and then set about replicating a pre-existing image or idea seen in the mind's eye. The skill of the drawer is seen to rest on their ability to accurately replicate this complete, imagined vision. However, interviews with artist drawers tend instead to tell of accounts of working toward a vague idea (Ambrus & Aston, 2009; Simblet, 2004), or just working without any idea of what might emerge (Tan, 2010).

I suggest that approaches to arts and drawing practice are what most clearly differ between artists and non-artists. While artists certainly push their artistic capacities all the time, they can be a lot easier on themselves, in terms of what they want to finish up with, than non-artists. I have heard plenty of non-artists (in this case, student teachers) declare, 'My drawing hasn't turned out how I wanted—I'm no good at drawing.' This seems to suggest how differently non-artists and artists approach their work.

There is a clear need to provide educators with explicit information about the importance of drawing and the role it plays in a child's mental growth and in their intellectual development, as well as the more experimental and less product driven attitude that artists take toward their work. If educators can critically examine their personal definitions of artistic practice and competency, and their understandings of popular developmental paradigms, they can change their approaches to drawing in their classrooms. Such critical examination can help educators realize that what children draw cannot be accounted for simply by imagining it to be primarily an expression of a particular developmental stage or that their drawings aren't always beautiful and aesthetic. Educators can begin to understand that children's drawings are produced for many reasons and purposes and that they emerge from a range of sources including stories, metaphysical constructions, and non-human factors such as spaces, locations, atmosphere, time, etc., and are not always about something the child has actually experienced.

Educators need appropriate guidance about the importance of drawing in relation to all aspects of learning. If drawing can be regarded as a process for thinking, understanding, communicating, and transforming, it can be thought of as a process whereby children bring random experiences and references to their visualizing, irrespective of their age or culture. The child's processes for visualizing may be better understood if adults can discard culturally driven perceptions of stage development and gain greater understanding about the intellectual capacities required for drawing.

Effecting change *is* difficult if it requires a significant dismantling of development/art theories that have held persuasive power over curriculum and pedagogy for some time. If educators always view children's scribbles primarily through the expectation that a scribble is creeping slowly toward a recognizable thing rather than being significant in its own right, then this is what the child is seen to produce. This is often because other symbols and marks are overlooked or disregarded because they are not pertinent to the analysis that is dominated by the search for indicators of development. Better understandings of how and why children draw should be nurtured, so the need to form good pedagogical practices around drawing and their purposes is of paramount importance.

Drawing and the Curriculum

I look at drawing as a mode of practice. I am interested in promoting drawing as a way to explore cognitive concepts across the curriculum, as I am keen for educators to try to halt the slow decline in drawing as a key activity for children as they progress through school. Across-curriculum drawing is often sidelined even though children engage in rich learning as they create these drawings. One possible explanation for this in the Australian context is that Australian children now undertake their education in 'an age of unparalleled government, discipline and control' that professes conversely to offer the greatest liberation through 'choice and freedom' (Dahlberg & Moss, 2005, p. 50). Control occurs via what is prioritized in the school timetable, the rationale being to ensure that fewer children fall through the gaps in terms of being illiterate and innumerate by the time they graduate. How does this play out in schools? Currently, Australian schoolchildren are driven to achieve competencies via minutely governed steps, particularly in literacy and numeracy. In this way, teaching and learning is highly pressurized, and both liberating and repressing for teachers as well as students.

An example of how this plays out is seen in recent shifts to schools using a greater number of template handouts/workbooks across subjects. This has resulted in a 'lost curriculum' of teacher driven content; children are now 'essentially' educated, and teachers are less relied upon to plan independently. The effect this has on across-curriculum drawing is that children are now often given pre-drawn templates or worksheets to color/fill in. This removes imaginative learning for the child and reduces opportunities for a teacher to initiate independent, high-quality lesson ideas.

FIGURE 2.2   Oil pastel, pencil on cartridge paper.

To illustrate what is possible for young children to produce, I will compare an example of science-based learning via collaborative drawing (Figure 2.2) with an account of a science-based worksheet recall task. The worksheet recall task consists of a labeling activity of aligning some key statements: 'The Sun makes plants grow', 'The Sun makes us warm', and 'The Sun makes light' to relevant simple illustrations. Figure 2.2 is an intergenerational collaborative drawing that was produced after some stimulus activity undertaken in the classroom.

The worksheet contains pre-existing writing and images, so there is less opportunity for a child to put their own mark on the activity. The primary purpose is to ensure the correct statement accompanies the correct image. The child is able to color over parts of the illustrations; however, they already contain grey-scale tones so there is less for a child to do in terms of considering how they might want to visually think through some of the meanings or concepts in the statements. Completing a worksheet like this is also essentially a solitary task and requires a predicted sequence of activity to complete it: read the statements, cut them out, place them under the illustrations, glue them down, color in the images. Any deviation from that, or any discussion on the activity, is minimized. Further, the statements read as truths, which leave little room for exploring alternative possibilities, or different concepts/facts/beliefs about the sun.

The drawing in Figure 2.2 is the result of a class of four-year-old children and their teacher undertaking a collaborative drawing about water. Initially the preschool class of children explored water as liquid matter and how it is different to solid or gas matter. They were able to investigate the water in large clear plastic tanks and with various pouring and sifting containers. Their activity was focused on looking at how water behaved and what happened when they looked through the water. Their discussions as they did this focused on how water can run through their fingers, be either heavy or light, and can become solid when frozen then return to liquid form as it melts. A child and his parent then worked with water-soluble oil pastels, water and brushes on A2 sized white paper to draw what had been observed and discussed. As they drew they continued to discuss water as a liquid matter as well as recall the experience of playing with the water.

During the collaborative drawing of Figure 2.2, the child expressed far more elaborate knowledge about the topic than could be initiated in the worksheet task. For example, he asked questions about the shape of bubbles, and why they were always round in shape, and how the water 'sparkled' when the sunlight hit it. These questions were directly affected by him having to think of particular details as the children and adults began to draw what they had seen. These two short descriptions highlight the clear differences in the richness of each consolidation; however, looking at Figure 2.2 it would be easier to read the information contained in a text rich worksheet than in this drawing. But this is why intergenerational collaborative drawing is such an important teaching and learning method. A completed drawing that you haven't produced yourself is much harder to understand than one you have produced. The drawing contains no writing, so of course to a busy teacher, a worksheet seems more functional in terms of understanding (and assessing)—but this is the case only when the educator is not involved in the activity.

Using drawing as a communication literacy within heavily structured curriculum models is problematic if the adult is not involved in the drawing activity. However, if educators know they can undertake collaborative drawing across many areas of school learning they can participate more fully with children as they learn about a diverse range of concepts, and they can build and expand on their understandings of the potential of drawing and feel confident in using it more readily across the whole curriculum.

It is possible for teachers to initiate change in their classrooms, 'to confront dominant discourses that claim to transmit a true body of knowledge' (Dahlberg & Moss, 2005, p. 2). A child who draws to 'know', for instance, might be identified as having particular strengths (such as being artistic) that do not accurately reflect the wider range of her interests, competencies or why she draws. When their drawings are viewed apart from understanding the knowledge or ideas they communicate, such children can be seen as lacking in written skills, in rational or systematic thinking, concentration skills, etc. In short, they are often not regarded as being 'academic' students. Intergenerational collaborative drawing offers a particular challenge to these dominant education discourses because it contests well-established beliefs about young children and their drawings. Intergenerational collaborative drawing is important, then, because it exposes to adults the multiple ways by which children disseminate their thoughts and connections to their learning, and it does this by bringing adults and children together as they theorize and visualize their world.

Definitions of what is art seem to rely upon factors external to the art object: human gaze, contextual knowledge, philosophic belief, culture, and society. Works of art then require this extra knowledge to bring them into being. Drawings are often thought about as art too, even if the producer has made them for a different purpose.

○ What would be the main reasons why early childhood educators avoid using drawings for across-curriculum learning?

○ Do you think early childhood educators should use drawing for across-curriculum learning?

Small Acts of Resistance

Cultural studies consider educational environments as 'a cultural site within which performances take place' (Weber & Mitchell, 1995, p. 10). Such performances are many and complex but predominantly include the behaviors and beliefs of the educator as pedagogue, and of the child as learner. A critical/poststructural reading of educational spaces acknowledges that bigger forces such as history, culture, politics, etc. impact upon and govern how these performances are taken on, and explore why they might occur in the first instance. Critical readings also suggest that to perform differently from what usually takes place forces a disruption to notions of teaching and learning. Critical examinations of teaching and learning, then, highlight some of the conventions around the adult/child relationship and its contexts, and they also help to consider alternative means by which adults and children can communicate. Critical approaches broadly allow challenges to constructed education 'truths' (Grierson, 2003), who establishes those 'truths', and to what end.

In relation to drawing, critical examinations highlight that drawing is not often regarded as a central, primary literacy once written and oral literacies are learned. Educators are mostly convinced to use other modes of communicating as children progress through school despite evidence that suggests young children particularly prefer drawn, over written expression (Weber & Mitchell, 1995). The sway of influence that developmental stage theories have held prompts teachers to expect that around the end of early childhood, children 'have become critical of their attempts at representation, aware they fall short of the real object' (Coates, 2002, p. 31) and therefore adopt writing as a more competent literacy. Development theory upholds a view that children become 'naturally' disillusioned with their drawing skills.

If educators are unable to challenge this, they unwittingly contribute to a trend of using writing over drawing. If educators can, however, re-evaluate 'truths' about drawing, they may be less likely to push it aside as children learn to write. Drawing collaboratively, as part of a range of learning activities can assist in regarding drawing as a learning tool because it exposes how children make rigorous use of visual production. Adults can undertake this activity with children, rather than observe it or report on a completed drawing. The act of drawing with children can reconnect adults with the physical, emotional and critical requirements of the task, which in turn reconnects them to the value in drawing for learning.

A challenge facing educators who might want to draw collaboratively with their students is how to produce drawings as curriculum-based assessment pieces. A possible way to use drawings for assessment is for educators to resist their usual routine and change what they would normally do. An example might be to draw collaboratively with children about their thinking on the digestive system—as the primary documentation on that learning experience. Not only does this provide fertile opportunities for children to communicate their learning in more diverse ways, because the educator is interacting closely and richly with children as they all draw together, she can report on the children's learning outcomes just as effectively as if reading written work or viewing completed worksheets. Additionally, because she has participated in the drawing, she can use the drawing to effectively remind herself of what was discussed, drawn, questioned, and theorized upon. The educator here does not judge the drawing as a piece of art so the focus is on using the drawing to consider each of the intended learning outcomes rather than writing about it for its beauty and/or aesthetic qualities.

Educators don't need to make big-scale shifts (i.e., change the whole curriculum) to bring drawing into their curriculum learning. These small 'acts of resistance' to using worksheets and templates can have a huge impact on a child's experience of formal education. Small acts of resistance can also bring about critical reflection of one's normal teaching practices, and show that altering them in some way can often bring about higher quality teaching and learning.

Conventions and Symbolizing Frictions

This chapter has suggested that the ways by which drawing occurs in educational contexts are shaped by wider forces, and that critical examinations of early childhood education enable interrogations of 'educator', 'learner', and 'curriculum' definitions (Kilderry, Nolan, & Noble, 2004). With respect to children's drawing, critical investigations into the purposes of drawing are needed because ideologies about art and culture, such as what kind of art is produced by whom and where, still permeate through education; this can be particularly evident in an early childhood classroom. For example, the assumptions and conventions about children's childhood art experiences are cyclical: as a young child grows up to become an educator, the reactions given by adults to his early drawings go on to form pedagogic truths in him as an adult. This perpetual cycle thus brings about a 'tendency toward stasis' (Moore, 1999, p. 306) around the regulation of materials, contexts and aesthetics.

Curriculum expectations can fuel why educators resist applying more responsive practices that more effectively connect with a child's learning. Using schematic template worksheets that are regarded as 'appropriate' for young children disconnects from their preoccupations and instead rotates around a perception of what a child will expect to complete, and what is appropriately a school task. If a child is required to constantly complete the simple schema and regulated answers in activity worksheets, however, these almost certainly will not correlate with the rich and diverse experiences and references actually being made by that child on the world around them.

Anning's (1999) observation that 'it would be an unusual act for an adult to respond to a child's drawing by drawing an image themselves' (p. 166) suggests that there is some way to go before educators regard and use drawing as a continuing central communicating process in the early childhood learning space. If they can resist an urge to search for certain forms of signification in children's drawings they may be able to consider the child's abstract visual processes as credible, and avoid the expectation that a child should name or draw a recognizable 'thing' in a drawing. Challenging deep-seated approaches to drawing is paramount in helping to break down a perpetual cycle of visual conformity. A child's creative potential should be explored to its fullest, so alternatives to simplistic templates are vitally needed to encourage contemporary early childhood educators to engage with learning in meaningful and rigorous ways. Without research and implementation of collaborative teaching and learning strategies, restrictive approaches to children's learning will inevitably continue.

Young children can, in their formative drawings, make detailed and intelligent observations of things and objects. Opportunities to randomly reference should not be reduced through conventional signs. If adults can acknowledge and then positively foster difference and diversity there is a chance of breaking down some of those conventions.

Conclusion

It is necessary to present challenges to education discourses which 'have force of authority that goes beyond the tutor' (Cheyne & Tarulli, 2005, p. 136). Intergenerational collaborative drawing undermines governed activity in various ways; through expectation, response and direction. If adults can be persuaded to enter into democratic and reciprocal ways of drawing they serve the child better in terms of providing opportunities for a rich, meaningful and intellectually stimulating education.

---

o   Can children's visual works be considered art within the definitions that are applied to adult artists' works?

o   Do you think that educators value drawings primarily as art, despite the intention of the producer?

o   What 'is' children's art, then, if not their drawings?

References

Ambrus, V., & Aston, M. (2009). *Recreating the past.* Stroud, UK: The History Press.

Anning, A. (1999). Learning to draw and drawing to learn. *Journal of Art and Design Education, 18*(2), 163–172.

Ball, S. (1994). *Education reform: A critical and post-structural approach.* Bristol, PA: Open University Press.

Bodrova, E., & Leong, D. J. (2003). Learning and development of preschool children from the Vygotskian perspective. In A. Kozulin, B. Gindis, V. S. Ageyev & S. M. Miller (Eds.), *Vygotsky's educational theory in cultural context* (pp. 156–176). New York: Cambridge University Press.

Braswell, G. S., & Callanan, M. A. (2003). Learning to draw recognizable graphic representations during mother–child interactions. *Merrill-Palmer Quarterly, 49*(4), 471–494.

Cheyne, J. A., & Tarulli, D. (2005). Dialogue, difference and voice in the Zone of Proximal Development. In H. Daniels (Ed.), *An introduction to Vygotsky* (2nd ed.) (pp. 125–147). London: Routledge.

Coates, E. (2002). 'I forgot the sky!' Children's stories contained within their drawings. *International Journal of Early Years Education, 10*(1), 21–35.

Dahlberg, G., & Moss, P. (2005). *Ethics and politics in early childhood education.* London: RoutledgeFalmer.

Grierson, E. (2003). Framing the arts in education: What is really at stake? In E. M. Grierson & J. E. Mansfield (Eds.), *The arts in education: Critical perspectives from Aotearoa New Zealand* (pp. 93–117). Palmerston North, New Zealand: Dunmore Press.

Harrison, C. (1999). Visual representation of the young gifted child. *Roeper Review, 21*(3), 189–194.

Ivashkevich, O. (2006). Drawing in children's lives. In J. Fineberg (Ed.), *When we were young: New perspectives on the art of the child* (pp. 49–59). Berkeley: University of California Press.

Kilderry, A., Nolan, A., & Noble, K. (2004). Multiple ways of knowing and seeing. *Australian Journal of Early Childhood, 29*(2), 24–28.

Knight, L. (2008). Communication and transformation through collaboration: Rethinking drawing activities in early childhood. *Contemporary Issues in Early Childhood, 9*(4), 306–316.

Knight, L. (2009a). Desire and rhizome: Affective literacies in early childhood. In D. Masny & D. R. Cole (Eds.), *Multiple literacies theory: A Deleuzian perspective* (pp. 51–62). Rotterdam: Sense Publishers.

Knight, L. (2009b). Dreaming of other spaces: What do we think about when we draw? *The Psychology of Education Review, 33*(1), 10–17.

Matthews, J. (1999). *The art of childhood and adolescence: The construction of meaning.* London: Falmer Press.

Moore, A. (1999). Unmixing messages: A Bourdieusian approach to tensions and helping-strategies in initial teacher education. In M. Grenfell & M. Kelly (Eds.), *Pierre Bourdieu: Language, culture and education* (pp. 301–312). Bern: Peter Lang.

Nicholls, A. L., & Kennedy, J. M. (1992). Drawing development: From similarity of features to direction. *Child Development, 63*, 227–241.

Pillar, A. D. (1998). What do children think about the drawing process? *Journal of Art and Design Education, 17*(1), 81–86.

Porath, M. (1993). Gifted young artists: Developmental and individual differences. *Roeper Review, 16*(1), 29–33.

Ring, K. (2006). What mothers do: Everyday routines and rituals and their impact upon young children's use of drawing for meaning making. *International Journal of Early Years Education, 14*(1), 63–84.

Rogoff, B. (2003). *The cultural nature of human development.* Oxford: Oxford University Press.

Seidman, S., & Beilin, H. (1984). Effects of media on picturing by children and adults. *Developmental Psychology, 20*(4), 667–672.

Simblet, S. (2004). *The drawing book.* London: Dorling Kindersley.

Tan, S. (2010). *The Bird King and other sketches.* East Kew, VIC: Windy Hollow Books.

Toomela, A. (1999). Drawing development: Stages in the representation of a cube and a cylinder. *Child Development, 70*(5), 1141–1150.

Warburton, N. (2003). *The art question.* London: RoutledgeFalmer.

Weber, S., & Mitchell, C. (1995). *'That's funny, you don't look like a teacher': Interrogating images and identity in popular culture.* London: RoutledgeFalmer.

Wright, S. (2007). Young children's meaning-making through drawing and 'telling'. *Australian Journal of Early Childhood, 32*(4), 22–30.

3

DARING TO DANCE

Making a Case for the Place of Dance in Children's and Teachers' Lives within Early Childhood Settings

Adrienne Sansom

It is the Rugby World Cup final—New Zealand versus France—and expectations are high. The stadium is packed. There is an international television audience of tens of millions all expecting to see a game of rugby at top level. The spectacle promises to be thrilling, where athletes with muscles of steel are about to pulverize each other for 80 minutes. There is the likelihood of injuries and extreme athleticism. But first, the fifteen New Zealand men, dressed in their national uniform of black, perform a dance.

The mighty New Zealand All Blacks line up in rows facing their opposing team. They look ominous as they commence the exhilarating performance of the haka Kapa o Pango. With the initial chants of:

> *Taringa whakarongo!*
> *Kia rite! Kia rite! Kia mau! Hī!*
> *Kia whakawhenua au i ahau!*
> *Hī aue, hī!*[1]

Fifteen muscle-bound men standing with their knees bent in the deep plié pose of the haka, crouch down on bended knees and punch toward the ground with forceful fists. They rise slowly—beat their chests, slap their thighs, strike their forearms and advance toward the opposing team with arms outstretched. They perform the pukana using menacing facial expressions, extruding their tongues and exposing the whites of their eyes. In complete unison the All Blacks' bodies move rhythmically, exuding the power and energy (ihi) that is universally recognized as the essence of the haka. The dance concludes with a slash across the throat which is a symbolic gesture that signifies the vital energy entering the body (literally meaning drawing the breath of life into the heart and the lungs—hauora) in

---

1 Kapa o Pango lyrics retrieved September 8, 2012, from http://en.wikipedia.org/wiki/Haka

readiness for the All Blacks to engage in the game. The All Blacks are now fully prepared both physically and mentally for the ensuing battle they face with the opposing team.

The haka electrifies the crowd. The sound of the chant is deafening and resonates throughout the stadium. It is a terrifying but also awesome sight to behold. The crowd loves it! The haka is a form of communication but you don't have to know the language to 'get' what is happening—everybody understands it—and feels it! The energy or power of the haka is spine-tingling—a beautiful full-bodied rendition of a historical Māori warrior dance.

The performance has been taught and rehearsed in consultation with Māori experts, including the composer of the new haka Kapa o Pango, which was specifically created for the All Blacks. A leader, who is chosen by the team, makes the initial calls, and the rest respond. Part of the pageantry includes the opposing team's reaction. The opposing team stare steadfastly back at the All Blacks but the challenge has been laid down in no uncertain terms.

The haka is a part of the culture of the Māori people, the Indigenous people of Aotearoa, the Māori name for the land that is known internationally as New Zealand. It has become recognized across the world as a national dance because the men who perform this dance carry a certain *mana* or prestige. The status of the All Blacks as a rugby team of international standing provides a platform and a level of acceptance for the youth of Aotearoa New Zealand to engage in learning and performing the haka. The dance carries the history and tradition of the Māori people but it also represents the national pride of Aotearoa New Zealand.

The haka reflects a component of the Māori culture where dance, in a variety of forms, was embedded in everyday life. Dance was not separated from the life world of Māori *kaupapa* (cultural customs and protocol) and Māori *tikanga* (cultural values and beliefs) (Pere, 1994; Ritchie, 2008). The provisions of culturally meaningful activities such as dance are learned and shared alongside one another in the spirit of *ako*—the Māori concept for reciprocity between the learner and teacher (Pere, 1994).

The 'learning' of dance for Māori children is not divorced from learning about life but comes about as part of being alongside adults and immersed in their culture. The young child learns to dance, together with other cultural inheritances, by being present among expert others. The learning had special intent and purpose. The experienced others instill learning by sharing their cultural *taonga* (treasures) with the inheritors of these precious gifts, the *tamariki* (children) (White, Ellis, O'Malley, Rockel, Stover, & Toso, 2009). The presence of the child is honored and so too, the dance the child performs and shares.

As Risner and Stinson (2010, p. 14) point out, 'Bourdieu (1986) reminds us that every child enters the classroom *[or early childhood setting]* with plentiful cultural capital including languages, symbols, knowledges, aesthetic preferences, and other cultural assets.' Before children learn that the knowledge they possess and exhibit is discounted, this cultural capital must be acknowledged and nourished. Young children in many early childhood environs come from a multiplicity of different cultural backgrounds—their dance offerings will invariably consist of multicultural nuances. As stated by Risner and Stinson (2010, p. 6) '*all* dance should be considered "ethnic" or cultural dance' (original emphasis).

Dancing Lives

This chapter makes a case for the vital presence of dance in the lives of both children and teachers within early childhood settings. Drawing on the concept of dance as a component of the cultural capital we all possess, the argument here is for the recognition of dance as a way of knowing and as a reflection of culture. There are two central aspects to the discussion in this chapter. Firstly, the position of dance in the early years curriculum can be an indicator of the disregard for the rich historical, cultural and intellectual ways of knowing and understanding that can be embodied in dance. The marginalization of dance underestimates its potential and its place in learning and holistic development. Secondly, this chapter raises some questions around the notion of a 'child-centered' curriculum. While professions of drawing on the children's interests appeal to discourses of freedom, democracy and children's rights, when it comes to dance, the curriculum ultimately becomes dependent upon the teacher's interest and confidence. A close scrutiny of the teaching of dance in the early years might well reveal that the so-called 'child-centered' approach has its limitations. The chapter also acknowledges the fears and associated risks that can be found to accompany teachers' attitudes about dance. Ultimately, due consideration is given to how these factors related to dance impact the children in our care.

To begin with, all that we know and do exists in our bodies. This makes them consciously thinking bodies. According to Malaguzzi (1992), 'School and the culture separate the head from the body' (cited in Edwards, Gandini, & Forman, 1993, p. vi). Education, as Malaguzzi further points out, seems to be concerned with the rational and abstract rather than with the expressive, the traditional or the cultural (in Schiller & Meiners, 2012). In their examination of dance in education, Schiller and Meiners (2012) insist that dance can act as a conduit to express our thoughts and feelings, as well as our humanity, identity and culture. At first glance, this understanding of dance might seem a far cry from the forms of dance that have come to be associated with early childhood settings—for example, action songs such as 'Heads, Shoulders, Knees and Toes', simple folk-loric dances, the popular culture and movement styles of singing groups such as 'The Wiggles', or even the 'free-form' moving to music favored by others. The aim of this chapter is to prompt a rethinking and perhaps destabilizing of the way dance is perceived as education in both children's and teachers' lives.

Dance which is considered appropriate for young children is most often referred to as creative dance or creative movement (Stinson, 1988). However, while '*dance* always involves *movement*—*movement* is not always *dance*' (Stinson, 1988, p. 11). What makes the difference is that 'dance is about—making movement *itself* significant' (Stinson, 1988, p. 2). Through the use of our kinesthetic sense—'involving full engagement and awareness, attending to the inside' (Stinson, 2002, p. 158)—dance is a conscious process of communicating what we understand about ourselves, and the world. The purpose of dance in education, as Koff (2000) suggests, is to explore the creation of dance with regard to what one knows, our relationships with others and the environment, and to learn to dance as a means of understanding our own and others' expression of culture. If young children are to learn to use the techniques of dance in both expressive and functional ways, then the starting point is to understand what dance is. The fundamental elements of dance such as time, space and energy act as the rudimentary language of dance, and young children can use these non-verbal forms of expression to communicate how they think and feel.

If we are to respond to the young child's desire to dance, and honor the rich cultural capital we all possess, then dance can be an event that both the child and adult create and do together. This dance is not something that only a chosen few do, separated from life and culture. Rather, the dance space can be a site that engenders an evolution of human interrelationships.

Dance Pedagogy: Honoring the Child's Dance

If this type of interrelationship is to occur, teachers who work and play with young children may find it necessary to shed some of their prior perceptions or attitudes about dance. These things that influence teaching may be 'enmeshed within and at times shackled by the past' (Jones, Holmes, MacRae, & MacLure, 2010, p. 291). A glimpse into the past echoes Pinar's (1975, 1994, 2004) *currere*, where those things that have influenced our very being had their genesis in times long ago. For a range of reasons, teachers might be reluctant to respond to a child's dance, and might be unwilling to embrace the unfamiliar. Jones et al. (2010) adopt the concept of Foucault's (1967) heterotopias. They use the example of 'the mirror' (Foucault, 1998), as well as echoes and shadows, which can distort time and place. For dancers, the mirror is a particularly important piece of equipment. It provides a reflection of the dancer's outer or objectified body, and the dancer learns to use the mirror for critique, in order to achieve a pleasing aesthetic body line or form. Metaphorically, teachers can hold a mirror to the self to critically reflect on what they do.

For teachers, contemplative reflection is an important element of analysis. Foucault's (1998) concept of 'the mirror' calls for exposing 'the original' and its reflections, echoes and shadows, that in turn, enable teachers to 'throw back and contest' (Jones et al., 2010, p. 294). The mirror can act as a reflection of what has been as well as a reflection of the self. Drawing on Foucault's thinking, the mirror enables a form of reflection where one can stand outside the mirror to look at the self, and interrupt what is familiar or taken-for-granted.

An emergent curriculum such as the New Zealand early childhood curriculum *Te Whāriki* (Ministry of Education, 1996), is an open-ended non-content-specific curriculum. The choices available to both adults and children within this curriculum are only limited, to a large degree, by the adults and children themselves. However, there is a paradox here. It is the adult who structures the program, albeit guided by the child's interest. And it is the adult who chooses when to follow through, what to leave entirely to the child, what to ignore, or what to omit altogether. The adult's decision is often dictated by a level of familiarity or comfort with the activity or learning experiences. It is not uncommon for early years teachers to lack confidence and/or have limited knowledge about dance. Many teachers are products of poor dance education themselves and this, combined with body inhibitions, can lead to an uneasiness with dance as part of the curriculum. If dance is not mandated in the curriculum it may become less of a priority for those teachers who are unfamiliar or uncomfortable with dance.

Several young children had gathered together in an open carpeted area to dance. The majority of the children were Pacific Islanders (Tongan, Niuean, and Samoan). One young child, Sione,[2] was new to the early childhood center and his language was Samoan. The main language spoken by the teachers in the center was English, and consequently Sione was having difficulty navigating his way around various routines and events. For example, when it was time to eat Sione was unsure about the procedures to follow and unless given guidance he sometimes did not get a snack. A student teacher, Ava, who also had Samoan heritage and could speak Samoan, was able to converse with Sione. Ava spent time talking to Sione to ensure he understood those things he needed to know to help him settle into the kindergarten's routines. On this occasion, Sione noticed the other children who were dancing and decided to join them in the carpeted area. Sione started dancing and Ava joined in alongside Sione and the other children. Initially the dance they performed together was the Samoan sasa. Other dances followed such as Niuean and Tongan dances, as well as Māori poi dances. Sione suddenly began performing the haka. His movements were strong and forceful and it was clearly evident that he knew how to do the haka. Ava, together with the other children, joined in being guided by Sione and the strength and commitment he conveyed while doing the dance. Sione was definitely central to the dance experience. The other children recognized his energy and began imitating his actions as they danced together. Sione's face lit up as he knew his dance was being acknowledged and he was clearly making new friends.

Just as the haka by the All Blacks is as much about how the other team responds, Sione's dance was about reciprocity and interrelationships. When Ava responded to Sione's dance she was recognizing and acknowledging Sione's identity,

2 All names have been changed to pseudonyms.

background, culture and lived experience. The other children's involvement in these self-created and directed dance experiences captured their knowledge, energy and vitality. The children were confident with their cultural inheritance and also understood the nuances of other cultures' dances. Much of this dance experience occurred because Ava recognized the children's interest in dancing, and especially Sione's spontaneous performance of the haka. It is the teacher who can make the difference when it comes to young children's engagement and continuing development in the arts.

In the first place, Ava had planned for possibilities, and provided recorded music that was culturally appropriate, which invited the children to choose to dance their dances. Additionally, in the moment, she paid attention to the dances the children were performing and danced alongside them as a guest invited into their space. As noted in the opening paragraphs of this chapter, to dance with young children in a reciprocal fashion is to honor the dance of the child, and the way they are 'dancing'. Ava mirrored Sione's bodily actions, and copied some of the movements he created. She re-created these movements in a dialogue with him. This type of interrelationship could be seen as a form of movement conversation brought about through spontaneous and improvisational exchanges in response to the child's movements. Or the dance may evolve as a form of cultural interchange when the child and the teacher dance alongside each other.

Not all teachers, however, have Ava's confidence to respond to Sione's wish to dance as she did. For one thing, Ava was familiar with the dances from Sione's culture. Ava also appeared to have confidence to dance, while for others, this might be outside their realm of comfort or expertise. Exposing what one does not know is not always comfortable.

However, taking risks in dance can give rise to new potentialities in the dance-making process. Risk can be positive and a 'willingness to take risks' can be important to effective teaching in the early years (Grieshaber & McArdle, 2010, p. 61). If the teacher is authentically present to receive the dance a young child shares, then it is inevitable that the adult will be entering the unknown. But if teachers take those risks in dance, they can be open to children's interests and current dance trends. Risk-taking is one component that helps creativity, and this includes the processes involved in the creation of dance (Chappell, Rolfe, Craft, & Jobbins, 2011). Together with uncertainty and entering the unknown, risk-taking contributes to the production of new dynamics and offers novel ideas to the creative process that evolves. Embracing risk can help to sustain dance in children's and teachers' lives.

In the toddler group at an early childhood center, one of the teachers, Fae, who was from India, had brought some Indian music into the center. When the music played, Sid, a two-year-old Indian boy, responded to the music and began dancing. Sid's young body became a muscle-bound moving machine as he immersed himself in his dance. His special movements consisted of performing an inverted action by placing both hands on the floor and raising one leg up in the air; he would then repeat this action using the other leg followed by a roll incorporating some twisting actions on the floor. It was obvious from Sid's responses that he was very familiar with this song. Fae shared Sid's interest in the song by singing along, but she did not dance with him.

Sally, another teacher in the center, noticed Sid's dancing but because she was not familiar with the song she was hesitant in responding to the music with Sid. Sally had immigrated to New Zealand from Eastern Europe, and had not been exposed to Indian music or dance before. She was not familiar with the song and it simply did not have the same meaning to her as it did for Sid. Nevertheless, Sally did consider it was important to acknowledge Sid's dancing. Her struggle was engaging with the unfamiliar Indian music, and having very little knowledge of Indian dance, or of how to move with Sid.

At the same time, some of the parents of other children had walked into the center and it was noticeable that these adults, particularly those who were not from India, were somewhat uncomfortable with the loud Indian music playing. They registered surprise and uneasiness on their faces. Sally understood how the parents felt and took this into account, but she also recognized just how much Sid was becoming engrossed in his dance, and enjoying himself. She started to respond to Sid's dancing by mirroring his movements, and soon found herself being 'taught' his special ways of moving.

When young children's dance enters our early childhood centers so do young children's lives, their families, and communities. It was clear that Sally had come to understand some of the dilemmas she had been facing about responding to children's interests—when these were outside her realm of experience, both aesthetically and culturally. By choosing to participate in the dance experience and learning different ways of moving from Sid, Sally was able to enter the unfamiliar or the unknown. She understood that it was important to support Sid's interests and accept him for who he was. For as long as Sid showed this interest, Sally shared in and supported his dance, together with a number of other children who regularly joined in the dancing.

When Sally noticed and responded to a young child's emergent interests in dance, she was also unearthing new-found discoveries, not just about dance but also about the child's background and culture. In addition, this is a story of the teacher who was making her own discovery of becoming more comfortable in herself and her dance, guided by the self-directed dancing of a two-year-old Indian boy. For this young child the significance of familiar Indian music gave impetus to the creation of dance and reminded the teachers that the links between the early childhood center and the child's home and culture were truly important. These discoveries led to more than just the creation of dance; they were also about the relationships that occurred between the child and the adult, the child and other children, as well as a deeper understanding of the self for both the child and the teacher. For the teacher there was a shift from the familiar to the unfamiliar because both the music and the dance were from a different culture than her own.

As the stories of both Sione and Sid show, the dances children offer will reveal things which may be unfamiliar or unknown to us, especially if they are from other places and nationalities. Nevertheless, it would be a travesty to deny or overlook the life stories or lived worlds conveyed through the child's dance just because they are unfamiliar. Children bring their lives with them in their bodies. They might have knowledge about being refugees, immigrants, living in poverty or homeless, belonging in extended, mixed or 'non-conventional' families, living with different abilities (Igoa, 1995; Matos, 2008; Nieto, 2002; Risner & Stinson, 2010). Teachers may find that the lived experiences revealed through dance are alien encounters, and they may have difficulty in relating to the child's offering. Yet, if adults fail to pay heed to the child's dancing body, the stories embedded in the body will never come to the fore and the relationship between the adult and child can lack real connection.

Dance Curriculum: The Role of the Teacher

Advocacy for dance can draw on a number of arguments. Young children spend many hours of their lives in early childhood centers and other schooling institutions. It is important, then, for their teachers to recognize that their work is not only the delivery of programs and curriculum, but of equal importance are the 'social functions that teachers perform' (Giroux, 1988, p. 126). Dance plays an important part in the wider culture and society beyond the early childhood setting. If teaching is morally and ethically grounded and responds to the rights of all children, then the teacher has a role to play in ensuring the presence of dance in the curriculum.

On the other hand, dance that occurs within an early childhood emergent curriculum (Bond & Deans, 1997) is not always dance that has been prearranged or planned for by the teacher. Dance, in this sense, is part of the child's culture and play (Anttila, 2007; Lindqvist, 2001; Stinson, 1997). Within the emergent or non-content driven curriculum, areas such as dance may be barely present if the teacher's preferences do not include dance. Although a non-content driven curriculum provides room for maneuver and the possibility of a range of learning experiences, spontaneous opportunities that could be found in dance may not materialize if dance is not the teacher's passion.

It may also be possible that in an area such as dance the child could know more than the adult (Bond, 2000). When a child becomes completely absorbed in her dance she can demonstrate a level of skill and abandonment that leaves the adult way behind. Developmental theory assumes the expertise lies with the adult, the insufficiency of the knowledge with the child. In moments when this is proven not to be the case, teachers can back away from the experience altogether, fearful of the loss of what it means to be 'the teacher', the one who always knows more or better. These uneasy moments can prompt teachers to adopt Foucault's (1967) example of heterotopia, 'the mirror', in order to interrogate their image not only of the child but also of the adult or teacher (Jones et al., 2010).

In a climate that has provoked some to decry the disappearance of childhood, the disappearance of play, add to this another loss—the disappearance of 'the body' (Tobin, 2004). Just as research has shown that children notice adults' lack of participation in the visual arts (see McArdle & Wong, 2009), the situation when it comes to dance could predictably be further compounded. Confronting personal attitudes about dance comes in a more bodily form for many teachers. Early childhood educators may find that joining in the dancing alongside the children can raise internalized and inscribed fears about their own bodies (Butler, 2006; Cannella, 2002). As a consequence, dancing with children may appear to be impossible for some teachers. Children gradually begin to observe that adults do not get overly involved in bodily or physical forms of expression. They see adults who act as bystanders, unwilling to engage or participate in the dance activities young children can so eagerly and spontaneously initiate. A lack of physical participation with others (including children) can convey that it is not right or proper for adults to dance, except perhaps in places where dance is expected such as clubs or discos.

The physical nature of dance may be a concern for adults, causing them to eschew anything that may be associated with a focus on the body. They may wish to avoid not only exposing their own bodies in teaching and learning experiences such as dance, but also any unwarranted concentration on children's mobile and expressive bodies (see Johnson, 2000). This 'societal fear of the body is manifest in curriculum' (Cannella, 2002, p. 160) and transfers into a construction of regulating children's bodies in a way that mimics the regulation of adult bodies in society. Thus, the procedures put into place in early childhood teaching and learning settings regulate not only what the children do, but also what adults do, especially from a corporeal perspective.

The fears and risks associated with dance in the curriculum then can see teachers avoiding or ignoring dance, whether because of their lack of confidence and/or expertise, their own body issues, or their aversion to acknowledging young children's corporeal ways of being. One response to risk is to 'take steps to guard against danger' (Grieshaber & McArdle, 2010, p. 29) and this can often mean circumventing problematic situations by keeping the child subjugated through an adherence to rules. When it comes to dance, this might mean that teachers confine dance to set times and set places. The teacher maintains control over what occurs. The repertoire is conventionally controlled as well, with children learning set dances, such as simple 'traditional' folk dances or actions songs where the adult demonstrates and the children echo back. Controlling the circumstances under which children dance can serve to diminish the focus on the teacher's body as well as minimize the unexpected or unwanted behaviors that might result if the dance experience was left open to the children's creative desires.

As a result of these various fears and potential 'risk factors', the presence of dance in the curriculum can be limited to a particular codified form of dance decided upon by the teacher—or, at the other end of the spectrum, simply left to happenstance, where dance is devoid of any adult attention. In some early childhood centers the children dance but the adults do not join in, preferring instead to sit at a nearby table or move to other areas to participate in alternative activities. The teachers may provide the music but once they leave the area where the children begin to dance, the children's dancing can eventually dissolve into what could be termed rough and tumble play, or dissipate altogether. This is especially so if the children have had little exposure to dance or, additionally, have had minimal attention paid to their dance. One consequence of this lack of attention is that children soon turn to other activities—activities that their teacher attends to, and where their teacher supports them in their development and growth. Dance becomes a lower priority, and other ways of knowing and being replace it.

While some areas become favored through prior constructions and a hierarchical value allocated to them, others become optional extras, or disappear almost entirely. Certain fields of learning and ways of knowing remain well within the accepted frames of reference, and experience, while others are outside, or absent (Jones et al., 2010). The final section of this chapter is a reflection on why dance, as a field of learning, tends to sit on the perimeter of our experiences, or is, at times, absent from our lives. And yet, dance is a powerful means through which we have come to know people and their cultures, across histories, and across geographies. The world recognizes New Zealand's haka, Hawaii's hula, Russia's Cossack dances, Spain's flamenco dance and the Viennese waltz.

Dance and the Body in Education—Fears, Challenges and Concerns

Canadian dance educator Kipling Brown (2008, p. 144) refers to her experiences teaching dance to students: 'They tell me they don't want to dance and describe it as "sissy" and "silly".' Despite the numerous renderings of the haka performed by the All Blacks, as well as many other cultural dances from the Pacific region which would be seen as far from 'sissy', there is still a pervasive fear of what others might say or think.

In a New Zealand university, students enrol after twelve years in the schooling system, and for many, their own dance education has been minimal. As they are preparing to be generalist early years teachers they bring with them their fear of dance and, thus, reluctance to take part in dancing experiences.

"I have no musical or dancing talent in my body."

"I can't dance!"

"I was mocked as a child because I couldn't dance very well and it put me off dancing for the rest of my life."

"I was forced to try to dance like everybody else and because I didn't I was laughed at. Now I am very self-conscious and shy about dancing in front of people."

"Just participating in dance is a huge challenge for me and right outside my comfort zone."

"I look silly when I dance."

"I feel embarrassed if people watch me dancing."

(EDCURRIC 110, 2012)

These fearful perceptions of dance can continue to perpetuate the already marginalized status dance has (Chappell et al., 2011), even in comparison to the other art forms. Fear can act as a deterrent preventing 'anything from happening' (Olsson, 2009, p. 128). Fear of 'losing face' or 'looking silly' concerns these student teachers. But the hierarchy of discipline areas goes further than this. Status or standing in the professional community might be acquired through careful nurturing, and a loss of this established self-perceived status might be high stakes. Fears of being ostracized or overlooked, or being disregarded and losing one's position (or job), are not easily overcome. Attitudes such as these devalue the discipline of dance and maintain the marginalization not only of dance, but of all the arts in education.

Taking into account all these factors that make dance a 'risky business' (McWilliam & Jones, 2005) it is understandable that adults in early childhood settings may find solace in disregarding the body. Unfortunately, because of societal constructs that surround the body and the messages that are conveyed about who is deemed able to dance and who is not (Shapiro, 2008) (e.g., the All Blacks), teachers may never venture further than sitting on the edge of the sand play area, or instructing from a safe place. There is a fine line between the didactic 'copy me' actions to songs, and the mirroring and invitation to dance alongside, inviting and inducing creative ways to move. For example, when singing groups such as The Wiggles are used by teachers as entry points into movement to music, it is important that the creative potential the child has to offer for the creation of dance is also realized. If opportunities to explore ideas beyond the directive instructions are never provided, then the message is that there is only one way to do things and that is the adult's way.

Yet, in the same way that each child brings their own 'cultural capital' into the teaching and learning space, so do teachers. Given that the body is essential to dance, recognizing how bodies are viewed and treated in education is crucial. The noticeable tendency in early childhood education to suppress the involvement of the body (and thus, the whole person) in the teaching and learning experience requires further examination. Educational institutions fail 'to recognize the bodies of the students we teach' (Sapon-Shevin, 2009, p. 168), and thereby create a form of disembodied learning. The all too prevalent separation of 'mind' and 'body' continues to perpetuate the belief that the mind or rationality is the only aspect worthy of educational attention, thus leaving the body virtually outside the classroom or teaching and learning space.

By association, many of the experiences young children engage in such as physical exploration and play also come under threat. The fear of bodily pursuits, especially in the interest of physical safety, denies children (as well as adults) the right to enjoy the pleasures of physicality. As Silin (2006, p. 235) reminds us, however, 'The body is always present at the scene of pleasure.' Unfortunately, it is also because the body is the site of our desires and pleasures that bodies become regulated by teacher management, especially to maintain order and control (Phelan, 1997).

A disembodied pedagogy dishonors bodily experiences or the personal lives of both children and teachers. The privileging of academic performance that concentrates on mental acuities believed to exist only in the mind equates to learning which is devoid of affective ways of knowing, kinesthetic intelligence, and the significance of social interaction. An exclusion of the body from education negates bodily approaches to learning. Subsequently, dance (together with other physicalized forms of pedagogy) can be viewed as superfluous to the educational process. In addition, a decreased visceral engagement with others could result in minimized empathy or diminished 'empathetic perspectives' (Risner & Stinson, 2010, p. 10) because one of the ciphers through which we develop the ability to understand or interact with one another is severely curtailed. Dance, nonetheless, is one of those ways of coming to know ourselves (including our bodies), others, and the world. Such knowing is achieved not just through the process of doing it, or through clinical analysis and disconnected rationality, but also through how we feel or sense the world in which we live. Dance, therefore, is essential in all our lives.

Conclusion

Reflecting on who we are as teachers can open up alternative ways to support children's excursions into the wonderful world of learning, imagination and expression, including dance (Jones et al., 2010; Stinson, 2002). Rather than assuming the mantle of the all-knowing expert and overtly instructing children what to do in dance, or alternatively, leaving children entirely to their own devices when showing an interest in dance, adults can consider being fully present with children.

It was a lovely autumnal morning at the kindergarten and all the children were gathered on the mat. Cara, the teacher, offered the children the opportunity to be involved in a dance experience about autumn leaves. The initial intention presented by Cara was to discuss and physically explore the various qualities the leaves exhibited when falling from the tree. For Cara this conjured up possible movements such as softly twirling down to the ground, floating or meandering as if the leaf had been caught on a soft breeze, or rising high and dipping low as if the leaf was buffeted by the wind. In order to assist developing these concepts with the children, Cara brought in an actual pile of autumn leaves that had fallen from the large trees that surrounded the kindergarten. She placed the pile of leaves in the center of the carpeted area where the children were gathered. Cara then picked up a handful of leaves and, holding them aloft, let them drop down toward the floor. While some of the children picked up on the idea of turning their bodies around, or twirling, or moving up and down to resemble a leaf floating on the breeze, a number of the children were far more fascinated by the pile of leaves placed in the center of the room. Gradually, some of them ventured forward and delved into the pile, picking up handfuls of leaves and tossing them into the air. Their intention was not to imitate the leaves falling from the tree as Cara had suggested, but to play and interact with the actual leaves. Rather than seeing this experience as a failure, Cara, who was an accomplished pianist, began playing the piano to accompany the movements the children exhibited, replicating the strong energies of leaps and jumps, together with the twirls and spins executed by the children. Not content to let this experience lapse, Cara extended the experience by finding recorded music that continued to support the energies and movements created by the children and joined the children in their dancing. Additional props were offered, such as scarves or pieces of fabric, to elicit other possible movements, but the children's reactions to the actual pile of leaves became the catalyst for much of the dance that evolved.

Here is an example of a teacher being fully present with the children and their desires to create dance in multiple ways. As a consequence, a creative dance experience was produced from children with the opportunity to explore and experiment, to share and develop ideas in the company of a receptive and attentive adult. When one is fully present and devoted to what children are doing, as well as modeling active engagement in the events in which children participate, there is a clear illustration of valuing dance as something that is important not only in the child's life, but also in the adult's life.

Conversely, if teachers continue to remain on the outside of the child's world as an observer, an interloper, a voyeur—rather than as an inter-actor or actor in the event—what occurs might not really matter. Under these circumstances adults may abandon responsibility for the unknown—those things they do not have control of in the child's world or child's culture.

As a result, adults can get caught up in seeing only themselves and not the overall situation, thereby reverting to judging the self rather than focusing on the event of children dancing. This judgement of the 'self' becomes entangled in the 'discursive shadows' (Jones et al., 2010, p. 298) of the constructs of dance and the body. Just as the classical dancer may become controlled by the image she sees in the mirror and thus the prescribed images she is instructed to imitate in order to present an agreeable aesthetic, teachers are also constrained by the social constructs that circumscribe both dance and the body. The teacher can choose to imitate or shadow these prescribed images or, alternatively, break free from the constructs and re-discover her dancing self. When we come out of the shadows and into the light there can be a sense of liberation from the shackles that held us down. Teachers', as well as children's, bodies can feel and release the tacit knowledge stored within, born from culture and lived experience. The stories of the All Blacks' rendition of the pre-match haka, Sione's spontaneous performance of the haka and Sid's dancing to an Indian song all attest to the knowledge that we *all* have in our bodies, derived from culture and life. Knowing what we want and feel for young children as well as for ourselves as teachers can move us one step closer to taking that leap of faith and daring to dance.

○   Dance deserves to be accessible and evident in a young child's life. Dance also deserves to be explored, experimented with, and created by the child. But how can this be a reality if the adults in young children's lives do not pay heed to dance as an area that is worthy of attention? In what ways can adults risk their own sensitivities in order to engage in dance with young children? What are the obstacles that prevent changing from the known to the unknown? What do we dare do to create change in our own lives as well as in the lives of children?

References

Anttila, E. (2007). Children as agents in dance: Implications of the notion of child culture for research and practice in dance education. In L. Bresler (Ed.), *International handbook of research in arts education* (pp. 865–879). Dordrecht, The Netherlands: Springer.

Bond, K. (2000). Revisioning purpose: Children, dance and the culture of caring. In J. E. LeDrew & H. Ritenburg (Eds.), *Conference Proceedings, 8th Dance and the Child International Conference 2000, Extensions and Extremities* (pp. 3–14). Regina, Saskatchewan, Canada: University of Regina.

Bond, K., & Deans, J. (1997). Eagles, reptiles and beyond: A co-creative journey in dance. *Childhood Education, 73*(6), 366–371.

Butler, J. (2006). *Gender trouble.* New York: Routledge.

Cannella, G. (2002). *Deconstructing early childhood education: Social justice and revolution.* New York: Peter Lang.

Chappell, K., Rolfe, L., Craft, A., & Jobbins, V. (2011). *Close encounters: Dance partners for creativity.* Stoke on Trent, UK: Trentham Books.

Edwards, C., Gandini, L., & Forman, G. (1993). *The hundred languages of children.* Norwood, NJ: Ablex.

Foucault, M. (1967). *Of other spaces: Heterotopias* (J. Miskowiec, Trans.). Retrieved from http://foucault.info/documents/heterotopia/foucault.heterotopia.en.html.

Foucault, M. (1998). Different spaces. In J. Faubion (Ed.), *Aesthetics: The essential works of Foucault 1954–1984, Volume 2* (pp. 175–185). New York: The New Press.

Giroux, H. (1988). *Teachers as intellectuals: Toward a critical pedagogy of learning.* Westport, CT: Bergin & Garvey.

Grieshaber, S., & McArdle, F. (2010). *The trouble with play.* New York: McGraw-Hill Open University Press.

Igoa, C. (1995). *The inner world of the immigrant child.* Mahwah, NJ: Lawrence Erlbaum.

Johnson, R. (2000). *Hands off! The disappearance of touch in the care of children.* New York: Peter Lang.

Jones, L., Holmes, R., MacRae, C., & MacLure, M. (2010). Critical politics of play. In G. S. Cannella & L. D. Soto (Eds.), *Childhoods: A handbook* (pp. 291–305). New York: Peter Lang.

Kipling Brown, A. (2008). Common experience creates magnitudes of meaning. In S. B. Shapiro (Ed.), *Dance in a world of change: Reflections on globalization and cultural difference* (pp. 141–157). Champaign, IL: Human Kinetics.

Koff, S. (2000). Toward a definition of dance education. *Childhood Education, 77*(1), 27–31.

Lindqvist, G. (2001). The relationship between dance and play. *Research in Dance Education, 2*(1), 41–52.

Matos, L. (2008). Writing in the flesh: Body, identity, disability, and difference. In S. B. Shapiro (Ed.), *Dance in a world of change: Reflections on globalization and cultural difference* (pp. 71–91). Champaign, IL: Human Kinetics.

McArdle, F., & Wong, B. (2009, June). *Asking young children about art: A comparative study.* Paper presented at 3rd International Art(s) in Early Childhood Conference, Singapore.

McWilliam, E., & Jones, A. (2005). An unprotected species? On teachers as risky subjects. *British Educational Research Journal, 31*(1), 109–120.

Ministry of Education. (1996). *Te whāriki: He whāriki mātauranga mō ngā mokopuna o Aotearoa: Early childhood curriculum.* Wellington, New Zealand: Learning Media.

Nieto, S. (2002). *Language, culture, and teaching: Critical perspectives for a new century.* Mahwah, NJ: Lawrence Erlbaum.

Olsson, L. M. (2009). *Movement and experimentation in young children's learning: Deleuze and Guattari in early childhood education.* New York: Routledge.

Pere, R. (1994). *Ako: Concepts and learning in the Māori tradition.* Wellington, New Zealand: Te Kohanga Reo National Trust Board.

Phelan, A. (1997). Classroom management and the erasure of teacher desire. In J. Tobin (Ed.), *Making a place for pleasure in early childhood education* (pp. 76–100). New Haven, CT: Yale University Press.

Pinar, W. (1975). Currere: Toward reconceptualization. In W. Pinar (Ed.), *Curriculum theorizing: The reconceptualists* (pp. 396–414). Berkeley, CA: McCutchan.

Pinar, W. (1994). *Autobiography, politics, and sexuality: Essays in curriculum theory, 1972–1992.* New York: Peter Lang.

Pinar, W. (2004). *What is curriculum theory?* Mahwah, NJ: Lawrence Erlbaum.

Risner, D., & Stinson, S. (2010). Moving social justice: Challenges, fears and possibilities in dance education. *International Journal of Education & the Arts, 11*(6). Retrieved November 5, 2010, from http://www.ijea/v11n6/.

Ritchie, J. (2008). Honouring Māori subjectivities within early childhood education in Aotearoa. *Contemporary Issues in Early Childhood, 9*(3), 202–210.

Sapon-Shevin, M. (2009). To touch and be touched: The missing discourse of bodies in education. In H. S. Shapiro (Ed.), *Education and hope in troubled times: Visions of change for our children's world* (pp. 168–183). New York: Routledge.

Schiller, W., & Meiners, J. (2012). Dance: Moving beyond steps to ideas. In S. Wright (Ed.), *Children, meaning-making and the arts* (2nd edition) (pp. 85–114). Frenchs Forest, NSW: Pearson.

Shapiro, S. B. (2008). Dance in a world of change: A vision for global aesthetics and universal ethics. In S. B. Shapiro (Ed.), *Dance in a world of change: Reflections on globalization and cultural difference* (pp. 253–274). Champaign, IL: Human Kinetics.

Silin, J. (2006). Reading, writing, and the wrath of my father. In G. M. Boldt & P. M. Salvio (Eds.), *Love's return: Psychoanalytic essays on childhood, teaching, and learning* (pp. 227–241). New York: Routledge.

Stinson, S. (1988). *Dance for young children: Finding the magic in movement.* Reston, VA: American Alliance of Physical Education, Health, Recreation, and Dance.

Stinson, S. (1997). A question of fun: Adolescent engagement in dance education. *Dance Research Journal, 29*(2), 49–69.

Stinson, S. (2002). What we teach is who we are: The stories of our lives. In L. Bresler & C. M. Thompson (Eds.), *The arts in children's lives: Context, culture, and curriculum* (pp. 157–168). Dordrecht, The Netherlands: Kluwer Academic.

Tobin, J. (2004). The disappearance of the body in early childhood education. In L. Bresler (Ed.), *Knowing bodies, moving minds: Towards embodied teaching and learning* (pp. 111–125). Dordrecht, The Netherlands: Kluwer Academic.

White, J., Ellis, F., O'Malley, A., Rockel, J., Stover, S., & Toso, M. (2009). Play and learning in Aotearoa New Zealand early childhood education. In I. Pramling-Samuelson, & M. Fleer (Eds.), *Play and learning in early childhood settings: International perspectives* (pp. 19–49). London, England: Springer.

4

TEACHER, RESEARCHER AND ARTIST

Thinking About Documentary Practices

Christina MacRae

Introduction

I began my career in the 1980s as an early years teacher, working in a variety of inner city nursery schools in London and Bristol. Over 15 years later, I applied to become a doctoral researcher. At the same time I enrolled in a degree in fine arts. As a teacher with early years experience, this was exciting— the opportunity to conduct research into young children's art practices, and do this at the same time as I was undertaking art education myself, as a learner.

This chapter is about these three identities—teacher, researcher and artist—and the constructing of new knowledges that became possible through both intellectual and imaginative work. But this is not a simple matter of my seeing these three identities as separate, and me oscillating between them. I use this chapter as a means of thinking through ways in which these roles might work together, creating a space for reflecting on practice. I suggest there is potential for artist productions (sketchbooks, works of art, textual reflections) as a means of developing and thinking about documentary practices in early years settings. At times, I was acutely aware of these different identities pulling me in different directions. This became obvious most strongly and specifically in my observations of children. Firstly, my teacher/researcher/artist identities produced shifts in the formal observations that I was expected to keep as part of children's ongoing assessment. Secondly, the effects of this teacher/researcher/ artist practice produced shifts in *what* I observed, *how* I saw the children, and *what I made of* what I saw and learned. In this chapter, I map the changes in my ways of being with young children, and how art provides me with new methods —for observing, for teaching, for researching, and for theorizing.

The chapter draws on a/r/tography (Irwin & Springgay, 2008) to blur the roles of artist, researcher and teacher, rather than seeing them as oppositional identities. I use an a/r/tographic approach to produce this chapter. I draw from the personal, but my reflections are grounded in writing. I trace my own professional identities as they emerge, re-emerge and, also, merge. Firstly, I begin with my teacher education and how it played a large part in making me the teacher that I am. I then map my shift into research, and my practices as an artist. I recently took up an artist residency in an early years setting, and my documentation of this project involved some blurring of my professional roles of artist/researcher/teacher. This partial account draws on a/r/tography as a way to think about the potential of bringing these roles together and allowing some blurring between them to take place. Finally, this chapter does not finish with easy answers. Rather, I finish by reflecting on some of the tensions and questions that arise when habitual roles and positions are disrupted.

The Teacher

My teacher education was over 15 years ago, and I was taught to observe through the grid-lines of what was called the Target Child Observation Schedule (Sylva, Roy, & Painter, 1980). The creators of this observation system compare the person observing the child with the animal behaviorist. They devised a procedure that was marked by detailed, formal and minute-by-minute note-taking. These 'field notes' were then analyzed and then finally coded and quantified. The child-watcher was advised to 'crouch sideways on to the child, but not directly facing him [sic]' and to try to 'avoid meeting his gaze' (Sylva et al., 1980, p. 230). The claim was that static scientific discourses were out-moded and fixed the child, and instead, their challenge was to appeal to the methods of natural history as an experimental approach to observing children.

At the same time, this 'naturalistic' knowledge produced through observation was then subjected to classification through the application of procedure. The purpose of this process of coding and quantifying was to deliberately create a distance between the observer and the observed, in order to construct objective knowledge. Because procedure separated out the observed behavior from its analysis, it claimed to 'make explicit its ways of filtering and interpreting' (Sylva et al., 1980, p. 230). As this ordering process was founded on the 'nomination of the visible', it had an 'air of naivete' about it (Foucault, 1994, p. 132). This simplicity meant the order and neatness was produced by the procedure, and yet appeared to be 'obviously imposed by the things themselves' (Foucault, 1994, p. 132). The procedure acted, as do more developmentally oriented observations, to demarcate the facts of what occurred from the subsequent interpretation of these facts.

As a trainee teacher, my writing was literally confined by the grid-lines of the observation framework—I had to stay inside the lines of the observation schedule. To achieve this, I would 'tidy' up my observations before I submitted them. I recall how I would take my original notes as the unpredictable life of the classroom unfolded. These initial scribbled notes would overrun the schedule lines. Later I would alter them. I inserted the text into the boxes named 'time' and 'category', even though I was not quite sure where I should put them. There was no room for uncertainty, every observation had its specific time and place. And yet, in practice, I was dogged by failure in my attempts to conform to this method.

In the thick of an actual observation I didn't have time to write everything that I saw; my seeing was always interrupted by my frantic scribbling as I made notes; I was distracted by the world that was unfolding out of the field and it often seemed impossible to isolate my child observation from this wider field of activity. My finished sheets might have looked orderly, but they glossed over my ongoing failure to observe accurately and systematically. And there, on the other side of the observation framework, was the child, the object of my gaze — who did not always fit into the designated space of observation. When I observed children at play, I couldn't decide in which categories the data belonged, or when themes of activity began or ended. The very complexity of lived experience defied such order and categories: it was these failures that were so easily overlooked in my efforts to be a good teacher.

The Researcher

My doctoral thesis was designed as an inquiry into children's art-making. My knowledge of children's art-making had its foundations in those research practices such as classifying and categorizing. My training had oriented me to focus on what Dahlberg, Moss and Pence have termed 'a discourse of quality' (1999, p. 92). As my research studies had me read Dahlberg et al. (1999), I was alerted to an individualistic orientation that focuses on 'individual outcomes and relationships' (p. 100), as well as to the reproduction of normative conceptions of child development (p. 146). It was important to attend to the effects that this organization had on the way knowledge about the child had been created.

My thinking shifted from a focus on the children and moved towards a focus on the way we *see* children through particular framing devices. And these devices, in turn, produce particular discourses around the child. Rather than looking harder or more closely, Patti Lather (1993, p. 675) urges us to look at 'what frames our seeing'. This enables us to see 'spaces of constructed visibility' that produce relations of power and knowledge (Lather, 1993, p. 675). For instance, when the curriculum is organized into age/stage developmental norms, with 'knowledge' narrowly defined, then this dictates the teacher's judgment, and how the teacher 'knows' the child.

Turning away from these normatively oriented observations, I began to write messier impressions that included my own thoughts as I was observing, and sometimes I even captured what I saw with line sketches instead of in

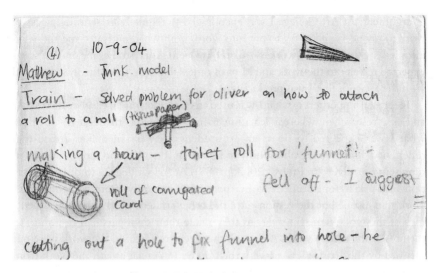

FIGURE 4.1 Fragment of doctoral fieldwork, 2006.

words (see Figure 4.1). This was a more self-reflective approach borrowed from ethnography, but I continued to be wary of the effects that turning an event into text might have. I was aware that an early years *avant-garde* who had been to Reggio was beginning to use the term 'documentation'. But I hesitated to use the term myself, for fear that while it signaled something different from the earlier approaches to observation, it might still continue to have similar effects—even at the same time as marking itself as something different. Just as the ethnographer colonizes its subjects with cohesive intention, the teacher/researcher observer transforms the 'ambiguities and diversities of meaning' of any recorded event into an 'integrated portrait' (Clifford, 1988, p. 40). Thus, with observation still at the heart of the process, children might continue to be colonized because 'we have created them as psychological beings whose worlds we (as adults) can define, explain, and know' (Cannella & Viruru, 2004, p. 79).

As my eyes moved away from the child and towards the frameworks that define the ways we look at them, I became aware of the dialogic process. Not only is the child produced as an object within an apparatus of normalization (Walkerdine, 1984, p. 170), but the teacher and researcher are also simultaneously constructed. Adherence to procedure produces knowledge that keeps the observer within a disciplinary frame, organizing knowledge in particular ways. My doubts about the effects of adhering to procedure led me to seek ways to inject vigor, rather than rigor, into my data collection.

It was here that my newly emerging artist identity started to take me in new directions. Up until then I was used to studying in the academic context of the Social Sciences, where seminars focused on disciplinary knowledge and soundness of argument. At Art College I was encouraged to regularly present my pieces of work to my peers and to try to put into words both what motivated me and what ideas led me to make the work. Similarly, my contextual studies meant that I was expected to refer to the work and ideas of others, but still, to be firmly connected with the artwork that I was producing.

Representing others is what I was used to doing both as an early years teacher and as a researcher, whereas learning to present myself through my work is what I was expected to do as an art student. Viswesaran makes a case that reflexivity should be less about how to represent the other and more 'to learn to represent ourselves' (in Pillow, 2003, p. 188). At Art College, a studio presentation of work by one student to her peers was not only about presenting her work, but also about the responses of the other students. Other students' readings of the work came into play as they made their own personal responses to the presenting artist's work. Although the intentions behind the work were put forward by the artist, viewers were then invited to engage with the work from their subjective positions, and often new interpretations of the work would emerge through this process. The artist, who spoke on behalf of their work, sometimes welcomed and sometimes rejected these views and interpretations; but the process of critique brought differences of interpretation to the fore, undermining any over-arching meaning residing in the work. It also opened the possibility for the artist to further develop their work in unexpected directions and see their own work differently.

I made artworks that explored and experimented with ways of looking. In particular I investigated systems for drawing from observation. I began to explore the history of perspective. I researched Renaissance theories and methods of perspective and how systems, such as Euclidean geometry, worked to frame what we look at, and how we see (MacRae, 2008). This in turn led me to experiment with various different looking devices, and I also created a series of light boxes (Figures 4.2 and 4.3). This 'mobilising' of subjectivity (Schratz & Walker, 1995, p. 139), this following my nose, was invigorating. The materialities of medium became important, so that connecting a practical and a theoretical understanding of materials and processes was now seen in relation to personal ideas and themes. In the inter-play of personal ideas, themes, theories and materials, new thinking was gradually generated.

As a research student who was simultaneously an art student, I began to revel in passages of connection-making which made me feel like a detective moving crazily from clue to clue accidentally, happening on series of fragments of text from the web, from media, and from books noticed by chance at flea markets. I found that the history and theories of art became directly implicated with ethnographic research practices, while the process of life drawing shed light on research methods. This nomadic strategy that I began to consciously adopt was 'decidedly unmethodological' (Van Manen, 1990, p. 3), but allowed me a new kind of thinking space. It was a place where knowledge produced often

FIGURE 4.2   "Alberti's Veil", 2008.

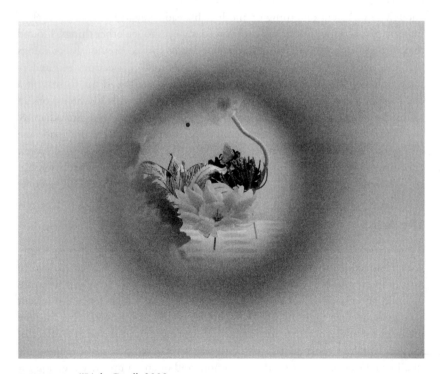

FIGURE 4.3   "Light Box", 2008.

undermined intention and plan and, although it was marked by instability, it felt more exciting than the more habitual analysis to which I had become accustomed.

My research inquiry into children's art-making was influenced by the art practice I was developing at the same time. My field notes and observations shifted to become more than simply the translation of what is seen into text, or represented as photographic evidence. I began to see my field notes, conversations I had with children, images and models produced by the children in my presence, photographs—all as artefacts of documentation produced in a continually expanding and unfolding field. I began to wonder about how these artefacts could be harnessed as catalysts for disrupting settled ways of seeing. I was drawn to use Latour's idea of a more 'symmetrical anthropology' (1993), where the observed is allowed to exert a power that can match that of the observer.

Moving on from my attention to the frames through which we view children, I was now interested in the artefactual documentation generated through encounters. Field notes, photographs and film whose original function was to represent the field, became objects to be looked at—not to confirm what was already there, but to bring to the surface un-thought connections. Focusing on the way that the material qualities of these artefacts contained a complex inter-layering of traces of observer/observed, the objects never stayed still long enough to represent one thing or another. Instead, they distributed themselves into my past and my future, and they forced my eyes to see other things. I found that through them I could attend to small details missed previously, or things that now became visible and important because of new connections and understandings. For instance, the field notes in Figure 4.1 allowed me to re-visit a child in the process of making, and make connections with his later work in terms of themes, ones that I had not recognized at the time (see Frankham & MacRae, 2011). The documentation generated from my fieldwork made me aware of the depth and complex assembling that was going on as children encountered materials. It demonstrated what close attention to this relationship could tell me as an artist about process, playfulness and a materially-led practice.

The Artist

As an artist, I found that my initial interest in early models of perspective, which had led me to flea markets and objects found by chance, began to evolve into an interest in the potential of found objects themselves as catalysts. I started to build an eclectic collection of found objects from which I made transient arrangements (see Figure 4.4). The growing collection of objects became the medium for my work that investigated collecting practices and the effect of the accidental. I experimented with different ways of temporarily arranging the small groups of objects from the collection, and opening up the collection for other people to respond to and to arrange.

FIGURE 4.4   Untitled arrangement, 2009.

I completed my doctoral thesis, and I continued to undertake educational research projects. However, I felt increasingly constrained because I had not found a way to combine my art practice with my research practice. While I had been involved in evaluations of collaborations between schools and artists and museums, these were very much focused on the educational benefits for the children, rather than what the artist might learn about their own practice. I wondered how an artist and their practice might be developed through working with children in a schooled setting. I began a practice-led artist residency where I could explore ways of engaging my artist's practice in an early years setting. My residency, the 'Secret Life of Objects', was funded by a practice-led small grant from the Arts and Humanities Research Council in 2009–2010. It set out to explore how my artistic practice could be developed by working alongside young children in the workshop environment of a Foundation Stage Unit.

While artists have often been employed in early years settings for short-term and product oriented projects to bring creativity into the classroom, my intent was different. I wanted to explore how my art practice might develop as a result of visually engaging with children's collected objects. The benefit for the children was that they would have my collection in their classroom, and they could play and interact with all the objects in my collection. I was interested in the potency of objects, and I was inspired by Walter Benjamin who saw potential in the collected objects kept by children because of the way that the object has been removed from the 'original functions of its use' (Buck-Morss, 1993, p. 352). During the residency, my intention was to approach the child as both artist and collector in their own right by closely observing how they interacted with and reassembled objects from my collection. I would also observe how they attended to their own collections of objects (those that they became attached to in school and also those objects at home).

'Secret Life of Objects': An Artist Residency in School

At the outset, my plan for my arts practice was to document what happened to my collection of objects when I brought them into the classroom. During the research project, I used the medium of digital film, both still and moving, to draw attention to children's making. This was a central way of producing material that I could use to reflect on the relationships between my collection and the desires and actions of children. In this process, the observed guides the observer. Short pieces of film documented children's hands as they played with and arranged the collection. This sometimes appeared partly to be an aesthetic process; sometimes the process was based on collaborative decisions between two or three children. And sometimes a process unfolded according to shifting narrative threads. My sketchbooks mainly consisted of photographs accompanied by my reflections and theorizing on what I saw (see Figure 4.5). Rather than seeing myself as the creative expert, I hoped I could develop my practice and thinking by drawing from the different practices I encountered while working alongside young children. The original plan was to have an exhibition at the end of the residency, jointly organized and curated by the children and myself.

As well as creating space for me as an artist to reflect on everyday practices of collection and curation, I also encouraged children to document their own objects and assemblages (see Figure 4.6). The idea behind this was to enable both objects in school and from home to be shared and reflected on with others. The photographs were then posted on a project blog-site. Here children could show their parents their work at home, and I could also share my reflections with staff and children. During the residency, the importance of the project computer as a site of collected photographs taken by children became increasingly apparent. It became a site of engagement between children, as well as between children and adults.

As I documented the project, extra, unanticipated issues appeared and reappeared in my documentation. A dominant theme became the tensions arising

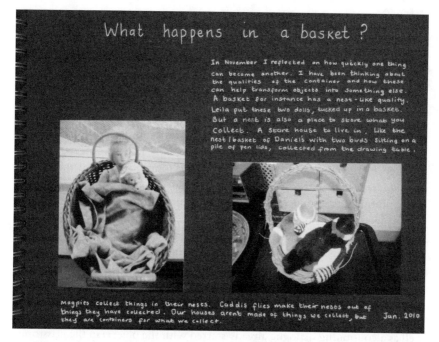

FIGURE 4.5   Artist sketchbook: "Secret Life of Objects", 2010.

FIGURE 4.6   Photograph taken by child of their temporary arrangement: "Secret Life of Objects".

from the presence of an artist working in a school setting. Elsewhere in the literature, similar issues are raised in varying contexts (see Burnaford, Appril, & Weiss, 2001; Kaomea, 2003; McArdle, 2008). In this instance, as an artist I was not accountable in relation to the curriculum or in terms of supervision tasks. In this sense I did not fulfill a direct function in the classroom. Sometimes support staff would ask me to supervise children as I wasn't apparently 'doing' anything. While I was usually willing to help out, the teacher in charge often felt that they were taking advantage of me and that this was not my role. For my part, I often was surprised how little the staff actually listened to what children had to say, so busy were they in the routine aspects of their work. When I reflected with the teacher at the end of the project she expressed disappointment that some of the more confident and physically active boys had not engaged as much as other children. However, I did not feel that my role was one of inclusivity and ensuring that all children participated equally.

Added to these tensions were those raised at the end of the residency when the exhibition was presented. This had originally been envisaged as jointly organized and curated by myself and children, but this proved too difficult to actualize. Finally it was artist-led and took the form of a participatory installation where I tried to create an object-led environment for the viewer, as well as a continuing dialogue already started with the objects in the classroom. These tensions around art practice in the context of a schooled environment have become the basis of a continuing dialogue in terms of my research (both arts and education oriented). They also contributed to a group of local artists creating a community of practice that supported and reflected on our work in early years settings.

The residency was very productive in terms of the opportunities it gave me to develop my thinking around my collections. It allowed me to explore my practice of collecting and the relationships that we make with objects during our daily life. It also afforded me enriched relationships with children where I was deeply engaged in their practices and in what Carla Rinaldi calls a 'pedagogy of listening' (2001, p. 80). This deep level of listening was something that I struggled to achieve as either a researcher or a teacher. However, I felt that my relationships with many of the staff in the setting, while positive, did not reverberate through their professional practice. Historically, this is one of the stated aims of artist-in-residence schemes—the opportunities for exchange of professional expertise and knowledge (Pringle, 2002).

While the staff were eager to share their personal collections with me, I did not feel that my residency affected their own pedagogies of listening to the children. Although at the outset I had disavowed any aims to impact on the practice of staff, in retrospect I felt disappointed that I had not engaged with staff in terms of their pedagogical practice. I did at a later stage find out that one of the practitioners had continued the practice of sending the camera home with the children. After I left, she continued to develop the archive of photographs taken by the children that had been initiated during the residency. In this way a new pedagogy of listening to children had begun to become part of practice as a direct result of the residency. Opportunities to explore how this might have affected practice and relationships were lost through my stance during the project of not engaging with teaching practice in the setting.

At the time of the residency, I had made a point of marking out my role as someone who engaged specifically with children's practice in order to reflect on my own practice. While I was interested in developing a participatory practice, I was extremely aware of the tensions that had to be negotiated by an artist in a schooled setting. While artists interviewed by Emily Pringle spoke of tensions about expectations about teaching which they felt uncomfortable with, they also spoke of a wish to 'give participants "a voice" and to encourage their broader critical and reflective thinking' (Pringle, 2008, p. 45). I was, however, suspicious of the idea of 'giving' voice to others, let alone having something to 'say' myself. Anish Kapoor repeatedly has stated that it is important for the artist to have nothing to say, 'because it's the not knowing that leads to the work' (Marks, 2009), and it allows you to 'stumble on things that might feel as though they're relevant' (Kapoor, quoted in Byrnes, 2005). I saw my role as an artist as necessarily ambiguous and open. I wanted to see what would happen if I set myself up in a complementary rather than partnership role in relation to the teaching staff. My focus was always on the objects themselves; the power they might exert, and what they might show me about the part they play in our lives.

This 'not knowing' how things would unfold did indeed lead to a very productive relationship with the children, and for me personally as an artist. It also allowed me to openly and explicitly explore tensions thrown up when trying to maintain a valid art practice in the context of school, which became an area of very productive dialogue with the teacher when reflecting on the project. So while I was surprised at the sense of failure I felt at not engaging with pedagogy and practitioners, at the same time I was not sure how to do so in a way that would have allowed me to maintain validity in my work as an artist.

The potential that I felt I was able to harness in terms of building a rich pedagogy of listening was in part generated through my interest in the everyday, and in the relationships between objects and people. But in part it was possible because of my marginal position as an artist who could operate outside the tightly organized and planned structure of school. At times I felt a failure because, in comparison to the staff, I seemed to be doing nothing, just listening to children. And yet these moments of disappointment, sometimes tinged with a sense of failure, arose from adopting a role that I deliberately chose. So when I felt 'guilty' because I was not as busy as the staff who were concerned with maintaining classroom routines, this is because I made a conscious choice to try to do 'nothing' as a direct provocation to their sense of direction, purpose and business. In one sense I was acutely aware of my 'useless-ness' in the classroom, and yet on the other it was precisely this lack of obvious purpose and ambiguity that allowed me to listen to children, and my genuine interest in their objects meant they had an interested other person to enter into dialogue with. My redundancy was productive in terms of my relationships with the children, but I did not seem to be able to harness it in order to create a space of dialogue with the practitioners.

A/r/tography: A Hybrid Role?

> Drawing attention to a/r/t (artist/researcher/teacher) is not intended to single one identity out, rather it is an encounter between bodies that releases something from each.
>
> *(Springgay, 2008, p. 159)*

In my work life with young children I have moved from teacher, to researcher, to artist, and yet, while the multiple identities have to some extent merged into each other, I am now looking for ways to try and bring these identities together so that I no longer speak from one position or the other. I am currently working on a Creative Partnerships funded project working with two Sure Start Centres. While I feel the short-term nature of the project is problematic (only 16 half days in each center), I am seeing it as an opportunity to try to integrate my researcher self with my teacher self and my artist self. I bring to the project both the successes and the failures of my previous project, as well as a reflective space created by a small community of practice consisting of local artists and early years practitioners. The key difference in this project is that I share my documentation of each session with the staff, but staff also document the sessions, and our project sketchbooks consist of both sets of documentation. I am also trying to use the practice/theory from an arts based movement that comes from Canada called a/r/tography. What I would like to do here is to pick out some of the main ideas that I find useful in this conception, in order that I can use them to try to think how these ideas might resonate and become generative with the work I am undertaking at the moment.

Theory as Practice

> Practice is created through the negotiation and sharing of aesthetic and educational stories and understandings.
>
> *(Irwin, 2008, p. 74)*

One of the first things that drew me to a/r/tography was its insistence that theory is not separate from practice, but rather that they are mutually entangled. It is described as a living space of inquiry that 'radically transforms the idea of theory as an abstract system distinct from practice' (Irwin & Springgay,

2008, p. xx). It is through process that knowledge is built, but this knowledge is always local, particular and always on the move. It is to be discovered in the in-between spaces that lie between people, culture and things, but it emanates from one's own experience of these. For instance, in my current project where practitioners share the documentation, I noticed that one practitioner used a heading called 'my thoughts from the session'. I loved this way of being clear about personal responses, and so I started to include a sub-heading entitled 'my thoughts and feelings' on the documentation that I shared with practitioners for each session. By theorizing your own experience you must engage in your 'reflective capacities in order to become an author of that experience' (Britzman, 2003, p. 64), or as Rinaldi says, 'our theories represent us' (2001, p. 80). But this kind of subjective theorizing is always provisional. We think about our responses, we draw on other people's theories, but we are never sure of ourselves. It is this uncertainty that leads us to share our theories with others. And what we produce from this are matters of shared concern rather than matters of fact. What practitioners choose to focus on emerges from their own interests, as well as the questions they have about how to respond to the particular group of children they are working with.

Conflicts around snatching are an event that occurs so often that we barely think about it any more, and an event that is often dealt with in stock ways using terms like sharing and taking turns. By introducing novel and desirable objects from my collection, conflicts over particular toys were often documented. In my current project I am once again bringing objects into the setting and responding as children interact with them. The shared documentation of the sessions has the effect of drawing our attention to the small things, often the things that happen all the time. It is an approach that insists on what Irwin and Springgay call 'the openness of everyday phenomena' (2008, p. xxxi) and the collecting of everyday stories. It has also drawn our attention to how certain objects seem to hold a singular desire for certain children, and to start to tune ourselves more finely into these interests. For example, a child whose narratives often returned to pirate themes, turned out to have expert knowledge about particular shells and knew their names in Spanish, a language that staff didn't realize was being used at home.

After one session, having watched the children using my collected objects to create clay sculptures, a practitioner and I both noticed the way that certain objects suddenly became more desirable and sources of conflict. This led to us reflecting on the nature of desire: whether it is purely the object that is desired, or how much you want an object because it is desired by others? This was not a question that we could settle, but perhaps it made us pay a little more attention to conflicts over desirable objects.

Returning to these moments in shared discussions allowed us to think about how we could encourage children to find ways of resolving these conflicts themselves. So, by exploring tacit and implicit knowledge around these moments, a 'repertoire of stories is created, one that can be used to negotiate interpersonal, theoretical and practical aspects of our lives and work' (Irwin, 2008, p. 72). We could also refer children back to the collection of stories involving conflicts they had had in the past and remind them of the solutions that they had come up with before. Through revisiting this repertoire of stories, certain children gained reputations for being good at 'sorting things out'. They would sometimes step forward in order to help other children to work out ways of taking turns.

Relationality

Documentation becomes a means of making our experiences and understandings, provisional as they are, visible. For Rinaldi, documentation is a way of 'listening', and a close listening that has the effect of overturning the teaching–learning relationship, towards a focus on children's self-learning and the learning achieved by a group of children and adults together (2001, p. 82). This close listening both forges and deepens group relationships.

Through documentation we can map this relationality at the heart of both our, and children's, learning paths and processes. While fragments of documentation are imbued with the subjectivity of the documenter, 'it is offered to the interpretive subjectivity of others in order to be known or reknown, created and recreated, also as a collective knowledge building event' (Rinaldi, 2001, p. 84). Thus education itself is seen as a 'relational place' (Rinaldi, 2001, p. 85). Meanings that we give to events do not prescribe, but they orient us towards possible directions. Thus true didactic freedom lies 'in the space between the predictable and the unexpected, where the communicative relationship between the children's and the teachers' learning processes is constructed' (Rinaldi, 2001, p. 85).

In my current project, observing the children closely while they encounter and construct with materials is drawing our attention to the relations between the children. Harry[1] and Ollie are both boys who like to lead and be in control of play; Ollie wants to participate in Harry's play, but Harry does not want him to as he wants to remain in control. This leads to an impasse of anger expressed both by the boys in question and with staff who end up directing the boys in order to maintain order. However, close observation does reveal that the two boys do build on each other's ideas and unfolding narratives, and that this may be an area in which they may be able to begin to work collaboratively. It is also drawing our attention to the ongoing tension between singular motivation and its relationship to the group. It has made us think more about what kind of activities foster a singular as well as a group identity.

---

1 Children's names have been changed to pseudonyms.

Stopping to linger and reflect on such moments may open up spaces for us to talk about things that usually are left unsaid. It also has the potential to start to attempt to articulate feelings we find difficult to express. We are continually confronted by tensions and seemingly intractable situations, and because these are difficult and often unresolvable they may become things we feel scared to speak about: they are uncomfortable and make us feel as if we have failed. Rather than avoiding difficult subjects as potentially dangerous and products of failure, it might be that it is possible to learn more by complicating our thinking. It can give us the confidence to proceed as Rinaldi urges us to through a process of trial and error (2001).

Documentation (or 'graphy')

> Documentation not only lends itself to interpretation but it is itself interpretation.
>
> *(Rinaldi, 2001, p. 86)*

Recording is the 'graphy' of a/r/tography, and in relation to early years practice it has overlaps with the Reggio-inflected concept of documentation that is increasingly gaining currency. It gives almost a material (an *artefactual*) form to the idea of theory and practice dissolving into each other (see Figure 4.7).

As an artefact it has a material and physical presence, one that can therefore continually be returned to for re-reading, at the same time as bearing the trace of both the event that it records and of the person who recorded it. It does not give us a representation of the event, as it is both constructed and at the same time is itself of the event. It is in the documenting that a space is opened up that has the potential to be contemplative and creative.

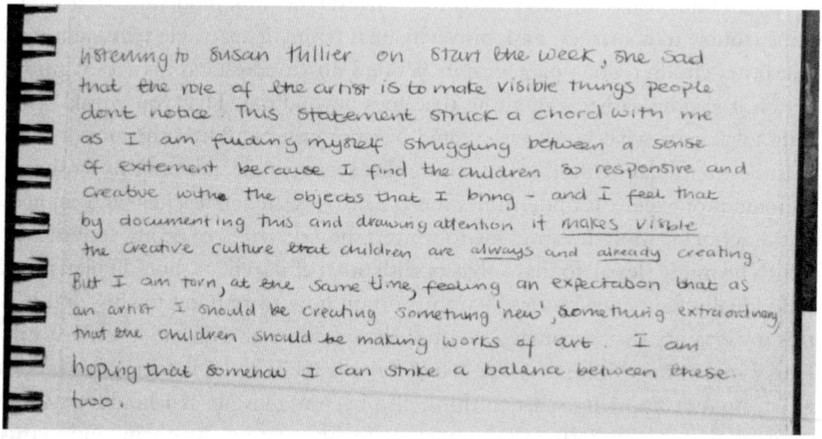

listening to Susan Tullier on Start the Week, she said that the role of the artist is to make visible things people don't notice. This statement struck a chord with me as I am finding myself struggling between a sense of excitement because I find the children so responsive and creative with the objects that I bring – and I feel that by documenting this and drawing attention it makes visible the creative culture that children are always and already creating. But I am torn, at the same time, feeling an expectation that as an artist I should be creating something 'new', something extraordinary that the children should be making works of art. I am hoping that somehow I can strike a balance between these two.

FIGURE 4.7   Sketchbook fragment, 2011.

> While many forms of arts-based educational research focus on the creation of artistic products as representations of research, a/r/tographical inquiry is constituted through visual and textual *understandings*, and *experiences*, rather than visual and textual *representations*.
>
> *(Springgay, 2008, p. 159)*

The important distinction here is between display, evidence, and recording as accountability, versus interpretation, theory-building, and provocation. Documentation is slow work, but it should not be solitary; it is about living together even if this takes more time. Documentation can also be a way of heightening awareness of everyday moments; to see the 'extraordinary in the ordinary' (Strozzi, 2001, p. 58). When I carried out my artist residency, in my sketchbooks I used photographs as memory traces in order to provoke my thinking around objects and our relationships with them. They helped me to see differently but I was not using them as a space of dialogue with other practitioners; they were in general part of an internal dialogue, occupying a space between myself, the objects, and the children. However, I am beginning to see the potential of documentation as a focus for a wider dialogue. Instead of the artist acting alone to create work that makes us see things anew, in a/r/tography this should be conceived of more as a joint enterprise arising through dialogue created by opening a space for documentation. As text, documentation 'is like having an interface with yourself and with whoever enters into this sort of hypertext' (Rinaldi, 2001, p. 87). Using Bakhtin's ideas about inter-textuality, documentation might be seen as a text between people that is now 'internally persuasive', rather than 'authoritative' (Haynes, 1994, p. 14). The performance of documentation and the gathering of observational fragments relate both to the context of the subjectivity of the documenter and to the context of the inter-subjective exchange of ideas, so it can become a 'collective knowledge building event' (Rinaldi, 2001, p. 84).

When four-year-old Harry starts to dismantle the junk model he has gone to some trouble to construct, I ask him why he is taking it apart. He tells me it is so that other children don't play with it. While I now understand his action a little better, it also unleashes something that goes beyond me. That you would willfully take apart what you have created because other children threaten it with their desire to play with it, is something that seems intolerable; in this sense it is a moment of excess. It undermines me as artist/researcher/teacher who rejoices in the act of creation. It causes me to stutter: should I think of group activities in which he might 'learn' to share objects with other children, or should I plan more individually focused activities? I am uncertain how to respond to this, and it is this uncertainty that becomes a point of shared concern with other staff. While Harry makes his thinking visible when he tells me why he is taking his model apart, my not knowing what to think also becomes visible as I hold on to this moment through rendering these events as documentation. By documenting this event it becomes one to share with other practitioners, not in order to provide a solution, so much as to inquire and explore further the balance between keeping control and allowing others to have control. Documenting this event also has the effect of encouraging me to continue to 'listen' when Harry interacts with materials and with other children, and to continue to ask myself how I should respond.

Conclusion

Given the short-term nature of most art-funded projects, I think generating this kind of shared thinking is unlikely to become part of a sustainable and ongoing form of practice. And it certainly cannot become this unless time is given to practitioners to jointly reflect on documentation. If we believe that reflective practice can strengthen relationships and generate local knowledge in early years settings, we need time devoted to this.

When Carla Rinaldi was asked what the recipe was for the vibrant and creative environments in Reggio Emilia, she replied that:

> There is no secret, no key, if not that of constantly examining our understandings, knowledge, and intuitions, and sharing and comparing them to those of our colleagues.
>
> *(2001, p. 88)*

These are words that I try to hold on to as I struggle to negotiate my way through some of the difficulties that I am encountering along the way of trying to bring my role as artist/researcher/teacher together. I remind myself that any promise of a recipe, while often tempting, is illusory; that it is only through a process of trial and error, by negotiating relations and ideas using documentation in a specific site, that I can come closer to creating a hybrid role. I think that seeing error as generative and an important marker as something other than inadequacy—in confronting error—we can allow ourselves to begin to bring to the surface what is difficult, messy, and in the language of a/r/tography, excessive.

In my current position, employed for a short-term engagement with an early years setting, I am very conscious of the tensions of exploring this role. I am not part of the staff group, I come in from the outside and do not work from inside the organizational culture of that staff group. This means that I have a space from which to act slightly differently and I hope through shared documentation that this attention to the everyday but significant aspects of daily practice may become more visible and more consciously thought about. At the same time, it is a 'messy' and marginal position to work from (McArdle, 2008). As a way to support me through this mess and uncertainty, I have joined up with other artists locally on similar projects to both meet face to face, as well as to form a website through which we can blog and hopefully begin to reach a wider community of practice in which to share and think about practice, as we build up networks.

I would like to finish, not by answering questions, but by raising a series of questions that keep returning to puzzle me and my immediate community of practice. Some of them may have tentative answers, others may perhaps indicate tensions that will always exist, and may be ones we must continually negotiate.

o **How do we as outsiders create reflective and open relationships with practitioners?**

o We are all struggling with tensions raised by working within institutions that are run strongly on organizational principles and where the relations engendered by this run deeply in the culture of the institutions. To further complicate this, artists are often employed by arts organizations and have therefore an added organizational layer (who we are contracted to) that we are outside of and marginal to.

o **How do we balance the needs of the individual and those of a group with a common purpose?**

o In the process of documenting I keep encountering difficulties where the interests and desires of the individual child conflict with collaborating with another. Whether it is a question of children wanting a toy that someone else has, or whether it is about joining each other's play, the problem is always about accommodating your singular motivation with that of an-other. As adults trying to resolve these tensions, we often resort to phrases such as taking turns or sharing, forgetting how difficult these tensions are to resolve. Also, as adults trying to build our own communities of practice, this 'sharing' can be hard, time consuming and complicated to negotiate. In both cases we need time to balance our needs as individuals and as a group with shared points of connection.

o **How do we negotiate documenting our own thoughts, feelings, and responses in a way that stays true to ourselves, but that does not pass judgment on other people and is something we can openly share with them?**

o The process of documenting seems to be very closely tied up with ethics and how we build generous and careful relations with other people, people who may not be part of our immediate community of practice, people with very different views from ours. The dilemmas about how and what to document are ones in which at the moment I need a lot of support from my artists group, they are ones that we return to again and again. But making documentation the site of our relationship and an open space means we have to think in ethical terms as we write.

○ **How do we make sure that our practice of documentation is sustained as part of our process and that it does not slip into a more evidential and representative mode?**

○ I struggle with my wish to keep my documentation as a product of my ongoing curiosity, and not let it become hijacked and used as evidence of learning, of creativity, and of expertise. This can become complicated as early years settings and schools need to use knowledge generated by documentation to provide evidence of assessment. As artists (or whatever we are) we must be allowed to put process, enquiry and engagement with materials before learning outcomes during our work. We should also be careful about how we use documentation as a way to promote and evaluate our practice/projects, as once we do this the documentation is fulfilling a different function.

References

Britzman, D. (2003). *Practice makes practice: A critical study of learning to teach* (revised ed.). New York: SUNY Press.

Buck-Morss, S. (1993). *The dialectics of seeing: Walter Benjamin and the Arcades Project.* Cambridge, MA: MIT Press.

Burnaford, G., Aprill, A., & Weiss, C. (2001). *Renaissance in the classroom: Arts integration and meaningful learning.* Mahwah, NJ: Lawrence Erlbaum.

Byrnes, S. (2005). Anish Kapoor: The Prince and the artist. *Independent,* 20 November.

Cannella, G., & Viruru, R. (2004). *Childhood and postcolonisation: Power, education, and contemporary practice.* London: RoutledgeFalmer.

Clifford, J. (1988). *The predicament of culture.* London: Harvard University Press.

Dahlberg, G., Moss, P., & Pence, A. (1999). *Beyond quality in early childhood education and care.* London: Falmer Press.

Foucault, M. (1994). *The order of things: An archaeology of the human sciences.* London: Routledge.

Frankham, J., & MacRae, C. (2011). Ethnography. In B. Somekh & C. Lewin (Eds.), *Theory and methods in social research* (2nd ed.) (pp. 34–42). London: SAGE.

Haynes, D. (1994). *Bakhtin and the visual arts.* Cambridge: Cambridge University Press.

Irwin, R. (2008). Communities of a/r/tographic practice. In S. Springgay, R. Irwin, C. Leggo & P. Gouzouasis (Eds.), *Being with a/r/tography* (pp. 71–80). Rotterdam, The Netherlands: Sense Publishers.

Irwin, R., & Springgay, S. (2008). A/r/tography as practice-based research. In S. Springgay, R. Irwin, C. Leggo & P. Gouzouasis (Eds.), *Being with a/r/tography* (pp. xix–xxxii). Rotterdam, The Netherlands: Sense Publishers.

Kaomea, J. (2003). Reading erasures and making the familiar strange: Defamiliarizing methods for research in formerly colonized and historically oppressed communities. *Educational Researcher, 32*(2), 14–25.

Lather, P. (1993). Fertile obsession: Validity after poststructuralism. *The Sociological Quarterly, 34*(4), 673–693.

Latour, B. (1993). *We have never been modern*. Cambridge, MA: Harvard University Press.

MacRae, C. (2008). Representing space: Katie's horse and the recalcitrant object. *Contemporary Issues in Early Childhood (Special Issue), 9*(4), 275–286.

Marks, L. (2009). *Anish Kapoor*. Retrieved August 20, 2009, from http://www.openmagazine.co.uk/pictures/article/anish-kapoor.

McArdle, F. (2008). The arts and staying cool. *Contemporary Issues in Early Childhood (Special Issue), 9*(4), 365–374.

Pillow, W. S. (2003). Confession, catharsis, or cure? Rethinking the uses of reflexivity as methodological power in qualitative research. *Qualitative Studies in Education, 16*(2), 175–196.

Pringle, E. (2002). *We did stir things up: The role of artists in sites for learning*. London: Arts Council of England.

Pringle, E. (2008). Artists' perspectives on art practice and pedagogy. In J. Sefton-Green (Ed.), *Creative Learning* (pp. 41–50). London: Creative Partnerships.

Rinaldi, C. (2001). Documentation and assessment: What is the relationship? In C. Guidici, C. Rinaldi & M. Krechevsky (Eds.), *Making learning visible: Children as individual and group learners* (pp. 78–93). Municipality of Reggio Emilia, Italy: Reggio Children.

Schratz, M., & Walker, R. (1995). *Research and social change*. London: Routledge.

Springgay, S. (2008). An ethics of embodiment. In S. Springgay, R. Irwin, C. Leggo & P. Gouzouasis (Eds.), *Being with a/r/tography* (pp. 153–165). Rotterdam, The Netherlands: Sense Publishers.

Strozzi, P. (2001). Daily life at school: Seeing the extraordinary in the ordinary. In C. Guidici, C. Rinaldi & M. Krechevsky (Eds.), *Making learning visible: Children as individual and group learners* (pp. 58–77). Municipality of Reggio Emilia, Italy: Reggio Children.

Sylva, K., Roy, C., & Painter, M. (1980). *Childwatching at playgroup and nursery school*. London: Grant McIntyre.

Van Manen, M. (1990). *Researching lived experience: Human science for an action sensitive pedagogy*. London, ON, Canada: The University of Western Ontario.

Walkerdine, V. (1984). Developmental psychology and the child-centred pedagogy: The insertion of Piaget into early education. In J. Henriques, W. Holloway, C. Urwin, C. Venn & V. Walkerdine (Eds.), *Changing the subject: Psychology, social regulation and subjectivity* (pp. 153–202). London: Methuen.

PART II

Ways of Seeing—Children

5

BECOMING INTENSE

Kortney Sherbine and Gail Boldt

It is writing time in Kortney Sherbine's second grade class. In one corner of the room, eight children are tightly huddled around one small computer, staring intently at the action on the screen. They are engrossed in an online site called *Poptropica*, a role-playing game written by Jeff Kinney of *Diary of a Wimpy Kid* fame, geared for children from 6 to 15 years old. *Poptropica* allows children to personalize an avatar and control its movements using the arrows on the computer keyboard or the computer's mouse. Each avatar explores variously themed islands (e.g., Vampire Curse Island, Shrink Ray Island, Red Dragon Island, Wimpy Wonderland) in an effort to solve problems by collecting hidden objects and eventually saving the world, or at least the island (Retrieved from http://www.Poptropica.com/about, April 13, 2012).

One child, Charlotte,[1] is seated directly in front of the computer. She is allegedly the one playing the game. And yet to imagine that there is a central player and an audience is to entirely miss what is taking place. Rather, the children are wiggling between one another to get to the mouse. They place their hands one over the other, creating a hand pile that attempts to control the movement of the mouse and so the avatar. The children talk all at once, guiding and urging the avatar's progress. They feel each action of the avatar as theirs, collectively laughing and shouting when something exciting happens or yelping, groaning, and sighing when disaster strikes. They bounce and sway, embodying their attempts to influence the avatar to turn a corner or run faster.

---

1 Children's names have been changed to pseudonyms.

Their bodies meld into, shifting with and against one another, the floor, the furniture and equipment as they unconsciously seek leverage or support or extension to lean around or through, to surge forward, to stroke the keyboard, mouse or screen, to jump or spin with excitement.

In other parts of the classroom, children who do not have access to the two computers are nevertheless improvising to engage with *Poptropica*. Near the center of the room, Ben and Desmond have shoved their desks together. Ben's head is down; his concentration is intense. Occasionally, a gasp escapes his lips and he moves his body even closer to the surface of his notebook, as if trying to crawl into the page, to fall into the adventures of Speedy Raptor, Cave Man, Fire Serpent, a lizard named Rock, Meteor Turtle and the others, Ben's creations, the products of his improvisational desire. Desmond looks on. His admiration for Ben's drawing prowess is clear in the comments he offers and the look on his face. Ben draws Speedy Raptor in full color; the others are mostly rendered in pencil. To look in his notebook—a space originally designated for recording written stories but long since given over to drawing—is to see something of a collage, portraits of characters crowded together, filling the white space. Some are carefully detailed and identified by name—Fat Chicken, the one-month-old pterodactyl, described as 'dreadful' and 'hideous,' flesh-colored, hairless, with bulging eyes and incredibly sharp claws that could rip an enemy to shreds; Robotic Bob, an absent-minded professor of sorts, who has the power to control meteors and is also called 'The Meteor King.' Other drawings are seemingly incomplete, the characters unnamed. Then there are the drawings of places— Science Island, where they all live, and important sites on Science Island, an underwater headquarters, a secret passage, and two circles simply labeled 'past.'

The intensity of these scenes repeats throughout the classroom, as the seven- and eight-year-olds fill up their writing time with *Poptropica*. The fervor for *Poptropica* began in Kortney's classroom in the unofficial times and spaces. As a growing number of students engaged with the computer game outside of school, drawings of *Poptropica*-looking avatars began to make an appearance in school. At the beginning of each day, students huddled together near their book bags to share drawings they started or finished at home the evening before. In transitions from one activity to the next, students hurriedly sketched avatars and symbols, as if were they not put on paper, they might be lost forever. Simultaneously, conversations emerged about *Poptropica*. On the playground at recess, children discussed news of new *Poptropica* islands that would become available to play in the coming weeks. As students waited in line for lunch, they exchanged gaming tips:

Anna: *I just don't get how you figure all the stuff out. What about the guy in the subway train thing? With the robbers?*

Alex: *I don't know. I mean, you sort of have to jump and wait in the air for a minute or something and then you can bounce on them. Once you bounce on them you're good.*

This incessant talk, play, and drawing captured Kortney's attention and when she realized the breadth of the students' interests, she set aside daily time for drawing, discussion, and play with the online game. This was time that normally encompassed their writing workshop activities. For two months, the students were engrossed in creating their own islands, describing the problems to be overcome on their island and designing the island's residents. The excitement of immersing themselves in the world of *Poptropica* filled the classroom, overflowing their notebooks as the children covered scraps of paper and corners of desks with *Poptropica* drawings and writings; as they sang and danced, played the game online and incorporated *Poptropica* fantasies and worked out its logistics in their physical and verbal play; and as they talked and talked and talked about problems to be solved, their latest ideas for characters, islands and problems, and the newest adventures that were unfolding in what became known as The *Poptropica* Project.

In this chapter, we[2] use stories from The *Poptropica* Project to argue for the value of recognizing, respecting, and, when possible, following children's collective, embodied, spontaneous intensities in contemporary classrooms. In the United States and elsewhere, we are in an era when the arts, children's play, and all other uses of time that cannot be quantified and measured through standardized tests are being quickly marginalized or eliminated. In this climate, we believe that it is worthwhile to provide teachers with a language for recognizing and valuing those events in the classroom that are, above all else, alive and enlivening. To do this, we look to what the French philosophers Gilles Deleuze and Felix Guattari (1972) described as receptivity to a given moment, to powers of transformation that are present in any moment, the becoming of something unexpected, of the power of intensity itself (Blake, 2010).

We begin by describing challenges facing early years teachers in the contemporary era of curricular standardization and describe ways that both art teachers and general education teachers have turned to a broad definition of literacy as a way to defend classroom spaces for student interest, the arts, and playfulness. While this is an important strategy, in this chapter our goal is to highlight what else is happening, things that may make use of things we would call 'art' or 'literacy' but are not about art or literacy. To do this, we turn to the work of Deleuze and Guattari because their theories have given us new language and new perspectives from which we can think about teaching and learning. The terms from their work that are important to our thinking about The *Poptropica* Project are 'assemblage', 'becoming', and 'nomadic.' Each term will

---

2 When we refer to 'we', 'our' or 'us' in this chapter, we are referring to the two co-authors of the chapter. When referring to Kortney and her students, we shift to the third person. The stories or 'data' in the chapter are Kortney's; we collaborated on analyzing and theorizing the material and on the writing.

be explained and used to provide a different way to think about curriculum and what children and teachers are doing together in classrooms. We use these terms to describe and analyze how for over two months in Kortney's classroom, *Poptropica* proved to be an enormously rich field that allowed for the production of constant flows of intensity moving between the expected codes and conventions of daily classroom life and the new and unexpected. We demonstrate how Kortney and her students embraced curriculum as improvisation in a way that kept their engagement with the *Poptropica* curriculum, with their own physical and emotional energies, and with one another, constantly fresh and alive. We believe that the relationships the children and Kortney had to themselves, one another, and the materials produced realities that entailed something in addition to the overly regulated elementary school discourses that subjected children to a standardized and often deadening curriculum.

Literacy and Art Education in an Era of Standardization

The *Poptropica* Project took place during a time when many of the teachers in the mixed income, urban elementary school where Kortney taught were preparing their students and themselves for yearly statewide standardized testing. Students in 'tested grades' (third and above) were in the throes of practicing specific test-taking strategies as the teachers covered standards–driven content. Kortney's awareness that this was the last spring during which her students would be sheltered from the anxious frenzy of test-based writing prompts and practice exams gave a particular poignancy to her determination that they use their classroom time together to explore the things that excited and engaged them. Indeed, she recognized her classroom as its own kind of island, a unique and passing moment in the lives of her students.

Kortney's efforts to support a curriculum that honored and engaged students' interests were often not in easy alignment with the pressures she felt as a primary grades American public school teacher. As a result of the passage of the *No Child Left Behind* federal legislation in 2001, expectations about what needs to happen in these early years have changed dramatically. Under the provisions of *No Child Left Behind*, all American school children are expected to perform as 'proficient' in standardized tests of reading and mathematics by the end of third grade (8- to 9-years old). Early childhood settings in preschools through second grade classrooms have experienced a significant push-down of standardized reading and mathematics curriculum from upper grades, and enormous pressure to eliminate the traditional mainstays of early childhood classrooms, including play and free and structured explorations of the arts (Genishi & Dyson, 2012; Paley, 2004).

Although many administrators and teachers have found the promise of better test scores through administration of a standardized, commercial curriculum of early literacy and mathematics skills to be alluring, there continue to be competing visions of primary grades teaching that make space for play, the arts and exploration (e.g., Genishi & Dyson, 2012; Salvio & Boldt, 2009; Wohlwend, 2011). Many argue, in fact, that the best approach for supporting children in achieving the desired levels of proficiency in literacy involves play, talk, drawing and painting, drama, music, digital production, and other multimodal engagements drawn from the students' existing and developing interests. As literacy educators and researchers working in early years classrooms, we look to the seminal work of the New London Group's (1996) powerful redefinition of texts and practices that helped to shift the field from 'literacy' to 'literacies' through recognizing multiple ways of communicating and making meaning, including such modes as visual, audio, spatial, behavioral, and gestural.

The New Literacies movement draws from the work of the New London Group. In the New Literacies movement, the integration of the arts into the daily literacy classroom is understood as an important move toward supporting the multiple ways that children can make and express meaning in the world. The New Literacies movement draws from the arts to attend to the ways that children become powerful users of multiple kinds of literacies as they design their own literacy experiences from the materials around them. The New Literacies movement also draws from Dyson's (2003) work, wherein she argues for a 'permeable curriculum,' one in which teachers deliberately create space for children to use reading and writings skills in service of pursuing their playful and social interests in popular culture. Integrating children's culture into classroom literacy practices both allows children to use literacies and the arts in ways they find to be meaningful and also provides opportunities for teachers to scaffold children into being able to employ an ever-wider array of literacy and arts skills, including skills more usually recognized as important in and beyond school.

In other words, it helped Kortney as a teacher to be able to describe the deeply engaged pursuits of her students as literacy, since literacy development (along with mathematics) is what is most valued in American elementary schools. To teachers and administrators who looked in, it appeared that the students were engaged in literacy activities. But to name The *Poptropica* Project as literacy, to give over writing time to it, was not a cynical ploy. To be sure, the children were reading, writing, and sharing texts. They composed narratives that accompanied the avatars, settings, and collectible artifacts they drew in their notebooks and on pieces of scrap paper. Kelly, who created the components of 'Weather Island,' wrote the following in her notebook, on a sheet of paper separate from her drawings of tornado suits, snowboards, and thunderstorms:

> *The problem on Weather Island is that you always think of a weatherperson as a good person, but on Weather Island, she is the most powerful, evil woman. She now controls the whole island's weather. To stop her, you must get weather power and put her own power against her. THINK YOU CAN TAKE HER?!?!*

Kelly's narrative emerged as she explained her drawings to her classmates and as she elaborated on her stories. She demonstrated her understanding of the *Poptropica* genre, appropriating the discourse of challenging potential players from the narratives of *Poptropica* itself. She wrote with her audience in mind, as she used a direct form of address to engage her audience and persuade those interacting with her drawings and writings to want to enter the world of Weather Island and to want more. Kelly understood that the words she used alongside her drawings positioned her as the one calling the shots, the one who ultimately knew the secrets of Weather Island, when no one else did. Much as Dyson (1997) described, Kelly found great satisfaction in being able to create and articulate in her drawings, writing, and speech, the negotiation between the fantasy world of an omnipotent meteorologist who could be overthrown at the hands and mind of a second grader, and the reality of being able to share stories with her peers and to animate the shenanigans of Weather Island on the playground during recess and in the hallway waiting for a sip of water. Clearly Kelly was learning to use the power of literacy and in so doing, her literacy skills were developing and improving.

At the same time, however, there are pitfalls and limitations with naming what was happening here as primarily or only literacy. In fact, drawing dominated the children's written work. In response to the demand that children produce recognizable 'literacy' products at an early age, some teachers make allowance for children to use modalities more usually associated with art production such as drawing and painting, creating music, photography or film, by naming these as forms of literacy or as being in service of supporting children's production of literacy. While we applaud the tenacity of teachers in continuing to make room for the arts in their classrooms, we share the concerns of art educators that rarely is there space left in elementary grades curriculum for art production to exist as its own value. When children's art is viewed primarily as a form of literacy, this can diminish attention to other real benefits of art making, and can ignore the unique contributions of visual languages to children's repertoires of meaning making possibilities (Mirzoeff, 2011).

While this is an important caution, it is not the focus of this analysis. Rather, in this chapter, we are interested in what is frequently missed in discussions of curriculum in both literacy and the arts. That is, we are interested in exploring what emerges for us as researchers and early childhood/primary teachers if we attend to the idea that what first appeared as sketches on the corners of desks and chatter in the cafeteria developed into an all-consuming immersion for the children, not because of the power of what literacy or art practices produce, but because of how the children and Kortney combined and recombined their energies, passions, and experiences with the materials to produce intensity, a continual flow of the excitement of the new.

The Assemblage and the Excitement of the New

Deleuze and Guattari argue that newness and intensity are possible, indeed inevitable, because human beings are not the same from moment to moment. This is because the human exists in an ever-changing field as just one object among the many that happen to comprise that landscape at a given moment. They called this coming together in a given field the 'assemblage' (Deleuze & Guattari, 1987). At this moment, the assemblage that you, the reader, are a part of includes (in part) you, everything that is in the room you are in, things you might notice that are going on outside the window, sounds that float in, people, animals, insects, and plants that you might perceive through sight or smell, and the thoughts, feelings, and emotions that are preoccupying the background of your thinking or that pop into your consciousness, breaking your attempts to concentrate on your reading. This assemblage changes constantly—a fly lands on your book; it begins to rain; someone calls you from another room; a dog barks; you get a whiff of something cooking nearby; the song playing in the background changes; you read a new sentence in this chapter. Each of these changes, perceived consciously or even unconsciously, at the level of unconscious physical or affective perception, has the potential to send you off in a new trajectory with new thoughts, concerns, and desires or a different activity. In other words, humans come into ever-changing assemblages with one another and with the materials and ideas present in their ever-changing surroundings and because of that, the human is different from moment to moment, is never the same person s/he just was. These connections occurring within the assemblages might be thought of as forces that change in speed and intensity, leaving the assemblage always precarious, capable of producing, of affecting and being affected. While most connections or changes in the assemblage are too small to even register as significant, each and every change—each and every new element in the assemblage—has the potential to cause a change in direction or attention, to produce a greater or lesser level of intensity and a new engagement. It is not a matter of what an assemblage means or is, but what it does or can give rise to.

Curriculum in the era of standardization strives for sameness. In Deleuze and Guattari's theory, change and newness are the norm; it is sameness we have to work toward producing, maintaining, and perhaps enforcing (Massumi, 2002). At some level, many of us know this as teachers, as we struggle to keep children 'on task.' This becomes even more of an issue as standardization drives teachers away from curriculum developed from child-centered content, art and play. Whether deliberately or spontaneously, many children push back, seeking novelty and excitement as part of what is often an otherwise dull, overly-routinized and repetitious school curriculum.

In Kortney's classroom, she and the children experienced heightened intensities created through the constant emergence of new possibilities. It wasn't simply that *Poptropica* was an exciting basis for curriculum. It was that Kortney was able to tolerate the uncertainty of a curriculum that she mostly allowed just to emerge or unfold, that she simply went with.

It was also that while she did not have language for it at the time, Kortney recognized the incredible power of what was happening as a result of the children's collaborations, their relationships. One of the many lessons of Deleuze and Guattari's assemblage is that the limit of the body is not at the skin. Rather, the body is always 'the-body-and-.' The body is . . . and . . . and . . . and . . . and . . . in its ability to join and transform in relation to potential that is present in the assemblage at any moment. Deleuze and Guattari point to the open potentiality of the body, its constant ability to vary, which dismantles whatever stagnancy or attempts to close down or standardize that may exist in a given system. The power and energy of the opening scenario, the children at the computer, is just one of many possible examples of 'the-body-and-.' Each child was part of something that exceeded her/himself, was part of an assemblage that included the other children; the game; the computer equipment, chairs and floor; the classroom and all that was in it; and also the collection of experiences, ideas, emotions, and desires that the children expressed verbally and through their bodies. The excitement, desire, and knowledge was greater than and different than any one thing in the assemblage.

Standardized curriculum is geared toward individual assessment, yet the explosion of energy in Kortney's classroom was never about individuals laboring at tasks that were predefined by others. Rather, the children were in enlivening, constantly changing assemblages with one another, with the materials and the environment, and with their own desires and imaginations. Deleuze and Guattari describe these ever-changing assemblages as working always within the present, the known, what already exists, but because they are combined and recombined, with new things entering the equation and other things exiting, the assemblage works 'to dis-organize and free itself from instincts and habits so as to experiment with new modes of perception and action, new modes of existence' (Holland, 2011, p. 63). In other words, it was precisely the excitation of the unknown, the anticipation of what could happen, and the potentiality of the constantly changing assemblages—a new child, a new drawing, a new idea, a new adventure—that generated intensities and kept the curriculum alive.

---

o   If we think of learning as taking place as part of an assemblage rather than as individual undertaking, how might this impact our planning and thinking as teachers? What things would we need to take into consideration in our planning?

Becoming-*Poptropica*, Becoming Intense

What emerged in Kortney's classroom as an intense time of drawing, playing, talking, listening, and relating was not primarily about playing the computer game, nor was it primarily about what the children drew and wrote on paper. Rather, the engagement of the children and Kortney with these ideas and activities was more about the generation of intensities moving through and among them, as they related with one another and with the materials in ways that opened spaces to create the excitement of newness, to feel alive. The project became what Deleuze and Guattari (1972) describe as a 'becoming,' a 'becoming-*Poptropica*' that involved relationships emerging in temporary or liminal spaces, among drawings, bodies, games, words, and classroom and playground environments; becomings which created new realities, new intensities, and unexpected possibilities. From a Deleuzo-Guattarian perspective, it is the emergence of the unexpected that generates momentum and excitement. That powerful new possibilities for learning occurred in the midst of the unexpected is something we have to attend to as teachers and researchers.

Deleuze and Guattari conceptualize the human as in a state of constantly becoming other. Becomings involve the 'processes of desire' (Sotirin, 2011, p. 120) in which materials (e.g., bodies, drawings, words, computers, writing utensils, conference tables, playgrounds) are related to one another as they flow into and out of assemblages, and as the coming together in a new assemblage creates, much like a chemical reaction, new flows and intensities which create and recreate new realities. They create constant change and along with that 'modes of passionate attachment to reality' (Holland, 2011, p. 63; see also Deleuze & Guattari, 1987; Malins, 2004; Roy, 2003).

Consider again Ben as he combined with the realities and materials in his field. He was, in the parlance of Deleuze and Guattari, variously notebook paper-becoming, Speedy Raptor-becoming, pencil-becoming, computer mouse-becoming, Desmond-becoming and on and on. In other words, his relationship with each of these things had the potential to transform Ben into something more and different than Ben was without these things. Each of these combinations afforded their own possibilities for Ben to be different than he was before; each was a precarious, momentary relationship that provided an opportunity for him to experiment, create, and transform.

Ben mostly came across in the classroom as shy and introverted, yet when he drew the adventures of Speedy Raptor and his compatriots, Ben was to his classmates and teacher every bit the hero that Speedy was. Like Speedy, he was tenacious, intelligent, and creative. Ben was the student his classmates sought out when they needed help drawing dinosaurs or other reptilian creatures. Usually, he offered a quick sketch and handed it to his classmate, before returning to his own drawings. 'For Deleuze,' writes Blake, 'we need reasons to believe in this world, and the key factor is not one of action but of receptivity: receptivity to the event and to its powers of becoming and transformation, to its intensity and to the effacement of identity it implicates' (2010, para 27). Like Speedy, who was known to the townspeople of Science Island as a trickster and as the one brave enough to save them from the mad scientist and his explosive time machine, in his receptivity to Speedy-becoming, Ben's identity could dance; he became known as an important if quiet member of the classroom, a kid who kept his own counsel but would respond when needed.

Just as the children's identities could be understood as emergent, as 'becomings,' so too play and work with *Poptropica* was emergent and rapidly changing. Watching Ben at work, he appeared to be pure momentum. He flipped rapidly from page to page in his notebook, skipping pages as he added characters and scenes. At times he ignored his notebook altogether, grabbing any scrap of paper to draw collectible cards with pictures of objects labeled 'the sorcerer's dagger: use' and 'the feather of light: use.' Many of these products were misplaced or fell on the floor under his desk. When a piece was finished, it may have become central to a conversation with a classmate or else it may have been forgotten altogether. For Ben, it was about what the drawing did for him as he was producing it, not about what it was.

Becomings were, as well, collective. Each afternoon, a crowd gathered at the computer table; students stood on their tiptoes and used one another's shoulders for leverage as they tried to get a look at the computer screens.

Ben: *You have to make him jump up on the roof and then over to the tree. Then you can crawl up on the thing and get the card.*
Angela: *Wait, this roof? How do you get . . . oh, I see. Wait, I got it.*
Brian: *Now you have to . . . yeah, you. See the card? Click that thing. You can click the guy, but you don't need to. If you do, you have to read that stuff.*

There are only vague directions on the *Poptropica* website for how to maneuver the avatars. There was little indication of where to go, what exactly needs to be collected and the means by which to do it. To get some help, players can click images of residents of the islands and receive clues, but not every resident is equally helpful and there are never exact instructions. As a result, there are many possibilities for directions to take, items to collect and how to get to them, and the timeframe in which the players get to an end result is open-ended. The children built their intelligence about how to proceed collectively (Jenkins, 2006), from conversations with siblings or peers who also played the game and from cheat videos posted to *YouTube* (www.youtube.com) that some were able to watch at home or at the public library. Yet this image of building suggests a linearity or a building toward a kind of single mastery that overwrites the improvisational, accidental, and temporary nature of many of the students' maneuvers, investments, and solutions as they talked over one another, debating and encouraging each other as they tried out moves.

It would be a mistake, however, to imagine that the excitement of the new exists in isolation from what was stable, what was already known. Becomings start with something and then become something new. The children's abilities to relate to one another unfolded within a classroom where much was already known, where a respectful and supportive community had already been built. Their intense engagements with one another took place against the background of a game with established rules and recognized modes of interaction, factors that allowed them to talk and think and strategize meaningfully. The fact of what was known was in constant interplay with the improvisational, the temporary, and the new. This kind of moving back and forth between the known and the new is what Deleuze and Guattari (1987) called the 'nomadic'.

> ○ When we consider children and teachers to be in constant processes of becoming, what might that mean for classroom relationships?

Teaching and Learning as Nomads

Within the assemblages of Kortney's classroom, there were multiple forces that worked to stabilize or define their activities—for example, the demands of a standardized curriculum or of testing; the expectations of the administration or of parents; Kortney's beliefs about teacher professionalism and practices of good teaching; the existing experiences, expectations, and desires of the children— and there were unpredictable forces that moved The *Poptropica* Project away from definition, predictability, and controlled outcomes. It was a curriculum that was powerful and invigorating precisely because it was charged with potential against a background that was known. What might happen next? What else could they make happen, deliberately or inadvertently? Which of the things they tried ignited a new conflagration and which fizzled out? The destabilizing forces manifested themselves in moments of the experimental but drew on the known to accomplish the new.

This back and forth was evident in a conversation between Desmond and Ben. The boys collected their notebooks and folders full of drawings and narratives and sat shoulder-to-shoulder as they considered one another's work. Desmond updated Ben on the problem that he had created for his island:

Desmond: *They [sea dragons] have to find the missing piece of the tomb. And it's missing from the underwater sanctum, where they live.*
Ben: *That sounds cool!*

As Desmond said this, he did not refer to the stack of drawings and narratives that he clutched in his hand. Instead, he looked over Ben's shoulder, seemingly fixated on the drawings of dinosaurs, meteorites, and mad scientists that covered the pages of his notebook. In fact, the paper on which Desmond had jotted ideas about the problem for his island was tucked on the bottom of his stack of papers. What it said bore no relationship to the problem Desmond presented to Ben:

> *The problem on Razor Blade Island is there is a new place to eat. Everyone likes it so much, but one day the secret ingredient goes missing and everyone goes nuts.*

Within a classroom project that provided a valued space for talk, relationships, and experimentation, Desmond was able to play with the possibilities of composing stories off the page. He did not feel bound to what he had written; rather, his words and ideas entered into the present assemblage and then (re) emerged with each retelling. Perhaps Desmond's sea dragons were concerned about the inner sanctum only when Ben was nearby; perhaps adventurous and daring sea dragons seemed more compatible with Ben's dinosaurs than the retrieval of a missing secret ingredient. The meanings of the drawings that the children composed were contingent upon who and what materials were available for the productive relationships that emerged and in that sense, even their own creations were not their own, but really creations of the assemblage. But what we most wish to point out now is that this kind of freedom to wander, to make use of the known while pursuing the new, the heterogeneous, the unexpected intensities, was what Deleuze and Guattari (1987) called becoming nomadic.

The nomadic in Deleuze and Guattari's writing is characterized by movement and change. It is not bound by loyalty to a set of rules, but rather by improvisation, and the use of what is known along with what emerges in the present field to negotiate the travel. 'Deleuze's nomad thinkers are like sudden, bewildering eruptions of "joyful wisdom" in an apparent continuum of stable meanings, standard commentaries, settled thought' (Tally, 2010, p. 15). Like a true nomad, Kortney went with the flow of the children's activities, but always had in mind the landscape through which they were traveling. Practically speaking, this meant understanding the expectations for student learning that framed discourses of 'second grade.' However, rather than trying to create a set of lessons whose fidelity was to a set of standardized, predetermined outcomes, she began with what the children were doing and then described how they were achieving the expected learning outcomes. This is nomadic thinking—that within a setting where the meanings of 'good teaching,' 'acceptable curriculum' or 'worthwhile learning' were already considered as known, Kortney was able to navigate among these settled knowledges to chart a course that was local, contingent, unique to that assemblage—that group of children in that time and space—and was, most importantly, alive.

For the children, appropriations of images and language already known from *Poptropica* fostered the basis for dialogic relationships in the classroom and these relationships in turn afforded space for children to improvise a multitude of selves as they negotiated play, and created new possibilities (Bakhtin, 1981; Holland, Skinner, Lachicotte, & Cain, 1998). While they could use the rules and conventions both of *Poptropica* and of their classroom writing time, they did not feel bound to the rules but were able to wander, to experiment and push the boundaries in pursuit of their desires. The computer game, the bodies engaged with the game, and the materials the children used to draw their own *Poptropica* islands allowed for exploration, as Dyson (1997) suggests, of 'the complexities—the ambiguities—of goodness and power and also, of their relationships' (p. 139) with one another but also with the materials that Kortney chose to name as 'curriculum.'

Why might it help to name this as 'nomadic teaching and learning'? It is precisely because the very uncertainty and instability that gave life to this project is what we as teachers have learned to fear, what standardized curriculum attempts to eliminate. In Deleuze and Guattari's thought, the nomad stands in contrast to the State. In writing, the idea of the State is used to represent that which is the static, the rigid, the homogenized; it is adherence to rules out of habit or fear. The nomad is responsive to the terrain in which s/he finds her/himself, an 'assemblage with no intrinsic properties, only situational ones' (Deleuze & Guattari, 1987, p. 353). The nomad is, in other words, loyal not to the rules but to her/his own receptivity to the possibilities that emerge in the present assemblage.

Through The *Poptropica* Project, the children used literacy and art with a level of enthusiasm, camaraderie, confidence, and daring that Kortney had not previously experienced as a teacher. And yet, faced with the pressures of a standardized curriculum, throughout the project, Kortney felt tensions about the validity of how they were spending their time. In spite of her anxiety and uncertainty, Kortney was nomadic in her receptivity to the situational realities and her ability to use the known to make space for the unknown. She persisted because the children were so engaged and enthusiastic, but it might have helped her to have some way to conceptualize the value of what was happening.

How might we think of curriculum differently if we imagine nomadic teaching and learning as at the heart of enlivening classroom lives? As teachers, we can't escape the fact that we have to account for structure-bound and overly determining curriculum. We have to be resourceful, strategic, and clever about the language we use. It may be the best decision at times to represent what we are doing through recognized discourses. And in fact, these things are going on. But in the midst of all of this, it is critically important that teachers do not miss or mistake what it is that drives impassioned classroom life. The children in Kortney's class, and indeed in every class, entered into relationships that were spontaneous, ephemeral, dynamic and that were never isolated, but flowed among people, materials, and the environment, among things that were already present and things that were just possible. The children's productions were not limited to what was produced on the page but rather involved their embodiment of the movements, characteristics, and vocalizations of the characters they created as well as the production of endless talk, singing and dancing, fantasy play and the presence of constant high energy. This all entailed the unpredictable, contingent construction of subjectivities that allowed for the unexpected to emerge in the spaces between the children, their drawings, and their play. It happened because the children and their teacher were receptive to the possibilities of the moment, the joys of the unexpected, and the intensities of the assemblage.

○ Reflecting on your past classroom experiences and considering your own tendencies, what efforts might you be willing to make to engage with your students in nomadic classroom practices? What risks and rewards might this entail?

References

Bakhtin, M. (1981). *The dialogic imagination: Four essays.* Austin: University of Texas Press.

Blake, T. (2010). Brain falls: The power of the falls. *Cycnos, 26*(1). Retrieved from http://revel.unice.fr/cycnos/index.html?id=6361.

Deleuze, G., & Guattari, F. (1972). *Anti-Oedipus: Capitalism and schizophrenia* (R. Hurley, M. Seem, & H. R. Lane, Trans.). New York: Penguin.

Deleuze, G., & Guattari, F. (1987). *A thousand plateaus: Capitalism and schizophrenia.* St. Paul: The University of Minnesota Press.

Dyson, A. H. (1997). *Writing superheroes: Contemporary childhood, popular culture, and classroom literacy.* New York: Teachers College Press.

Dyson, A. H. (2003). *The brothers and sisters learn to write: Popular literacies in childhood and school cultures.* New York: Teachers College Press.

Genishi, C., & Dyson, A. (2012). Racing to the top: Who's accounting for the children? In G. Boldt & W. Ayers (Eds.), *Occasional Papers 27: Challenging the Politics of the Teacher Accountability Movement: Toward a More Hopeful Educational Future.* Retrieved from http://bankstreet.edu/occasional-papers/op27/part-ii/whos-accounting-children/.

Holland, D., Skinner, D., Lachicotte, W., & Cain, C. (1998). *Identity and agency in cultural worlds.* Cambridge, MA: Harvard University Press.

Holland, E. W. (2011). Desire. In C. Stilvale (Ed.), *Gilles Deleuze: Key concepts* (pp. 55–66). Montreal: McGill-Queen's University Press.

Jenkins, H. (2006). *Convergence culture: Where old and new media collide.* New York: New York University Press.

Malins, P. (2004). Machinic assemblages: Deleuze, Guattari, and an ethico-aesthetics of drug use. *Janus Head, 7*(1), 84–104.

Massumi, B. (2002). *Parables for the virtual: Movement, affect, sensation.* Durham, NC: Duke University Press.

Mirzoeff, N. (2011). *The right to look: A counterhistory of visuality.* Durham, NC: Duke University Press.

New London Group. (1996). A pedagogy of multiliteracies: Designing social futures. *Harvard Educational Review, 66*(1), 60–92.

Paley, V. (2004). *A child's work: The importance of fantasy play.* Chicago: University of Chicago Press.

Roy, K. (2003). *Teachers in nomadic spaces.* New York: Peter Lang.

Salvio, P., & Boldt, G. (2009). 'A democracy tempered by the rate of exchange': Audit culture and the sell-out of progressive writing curriculum. *English in Education, 43*(2), 113–128.

Sotirin, P. (2011). Becoming-woman. In C. Stilvale (Ed.), *Gilles Deleuze: Key concepts* (pp. 116–130). Montreal: McGill-Queen's University Press.

Tally, R. (2010). Nomadography: The 'early' Deleuze and the history of philosophy. *Journal of Philosophy: A Cross-Disciplinary Inquiry, 5*(11), 15–24.

Wohlwend, K. E. (2011). *Playing their way into literacies: Reading, writing, and belonging in the early childhood classroom.* New York: Teachers College Press.

6

INCREASING THE ABUNDANCE OF THE WORLD

Young Children and their Drawings

Christine Marmé Thompson

Introduction

Andrew[1] was one of those children who immediately distinguished himself, as David Hawkins (1974/2002) tells us that children will do, 'when they're working at different tasks in different ways' (p. 90). The first time I visited his classroom, in the fall of 2008, he drew a small pumpkin and presented it to another boy in his class, cheerfully proclaiming, 'Happy Hallowe'en, Gabriel!' Andrew's teacher confided to me that Andrew's family does not recognize Hallowe'en as an event. Yet that morning, Andrew spent much of his time at school drawing pumpkins, turning one into a picture of his father carrying a prize specimen, boasting arms, legs, and hair. Andrew's mother, visiting the classroom that morning, questioned (disapprovingly) where his interest in Hallowe'en had originated. The center did not officially acknowledge Hallowe'en, but the excitement and fun of the event reverberated long before and well after the day itself, among preschool children who may have celebrated it consciously for the first time. It was not at all surprising that a child might be fascinated by the trappings of such an event with traditions that were associated with pleasure and excitement when they were being enjoyed by all the children in his group.

Later that morning, on the playground, Andrew again sought Gabriel's attention and participation in play: 'We'll play Power Rangers,' he proposed. 'I'll take this (smock) off so we can fly.' This time, it was Andrew's teacher who disapproved, reminding Andrew, and his mother, of their agreement about 'not bringing Power Rangers to school.' The teacher later explained that this prohibition was suggested

---

1 Children's names have been changed to pseudonyms.

the year before by a cognitive therapist who believed that children tend to run faster and play more aggressively when superheroes are involved.

As a researcher becoming familiar with this urban preschool program, and someone intrigued by the things that children choose to represent in their drawings and pursue in their play, I wondered about the extent and the effect of these restrictions on children's explorations, even as I respected the concerns that motivated them. I wondered if there were other regulations on the infusion of popular culture or other sources of fantasy, and how the children accepted or subverted such prohibitions. In the months ahead, Andrew became my best source of information on these issues.

More than once, by the time I arrived in Andrew's classroom at 9 a.m. to begin drawing with his class, I found Andrew sitting in his cubby, in self-imposed exile, thwarted yet again from some compelling pursuit, pouting. There were very few things that Andrew actually wanted to do. Drawing was foremost among them. In a matter of two months, drawing an hour each week, he filled all 80 pages of his sketchbook with images of Superman, Spiderman, Batman, and Iron Man. He drew like a child possessed, rapidly and with assurance, rarely raising his eyes from the page, all but unaware of the activity and conversation going on around him. When he spoke, it was usually to an adult and usually in response to a question posed or an observation inaccurately

FIGURE 6.1

offered. I asked Andrew, early in our acquaintance, if he drew all the time at home too. He answered, head bent to his drawing, 'Yes, but I don't like to tell people that I am an artist.'

His drawings were found on every surface of the room. And yet, you would not have known that anything special was going on with Andrew, if you saw his pictures in the hallway, posted along with those drawn by the other children in his class, in response to a group assignment. His drawings of family events, or field trips, or traffic lights were unremarkable, even careless. When he did not care about the subject matter, when the drawing was not his idea, he was often indifferent to the outcome. Drawing became a task like many others that Andrew encountered in preschool, something to be disposed of as quickly as possible so that he could return to the self-initiated drawing projects that he truly loved.

When he drew the things he wanted to draw, he was inspired, plunging in without hesitation, always with a new project at the ready. Andrew had chosen drawing (or perhaps, drawing had chosen Andrew) as his signature pursuit. In Vygotsky's (1978) terms, it was his 'leading activity,' his passion, his play, and his work, his hobby, and his preferred means of expression.

Andrew seemed to live in a world where the most exciting things happened on the page. His sketches were unique creations, though always inspired by movies he had seen and books he had read. He was the acknowledged expert-in-residence on the exploits of spacemen and superheroes; he craved the adventure of flying, leaping, transforming, battling, prevailing. Otherwise a quiet child, Andrew came alive when he drew. He became compulsive, practically humming with energy.

Andrew's drawings were beautiful and adept, composed with tremendous skill, astonishing in the sophistication of character and poses he noticed and captured with such economy. I continue to wonder at the mind that can so quickly analyze images of bodies in motion and invent visual equivalents that are so perfectly suited to the task at hand. There seems to be no developmental theory to explain what four-year-old Andrew could do.

---

o   Why are children attracted to drawing images that adults find unacceptable?
o   What are the arguments for and against excluding certain subject matter from the classroom, from children's play and their drawings?
o   How do children's drawings of controversial subjects contribute to their processes of meaning making?

Research Context

I met Andrew when I moved to Chicago to undertake a year-long study of preschool children drawing in sketchbooks while in the company of teachers and peers. The overarching purpose of the study was to gain greater insights into the processes by which young children, enrolled in an urban Head Start program, documented their lives and learning through drawings and the talk that surrounds their making and sharing. Head Start programs were instituted in 1964 by the US Department of Health and Human Services, to provide early learning experiences for children whose families subsist below the federally-designated poverty level and are thus considered 'at risk' of school failure. The children enrolled at this center were almost all of Mexican American origin, primarily second- or third-generation immigrants to the United States. The center they attended is internationally known for the excellence of its approach to bilingual and bicultural education. I was interested in the things that children chose to draw, the stories they told about them, and the extent to which these choices reflected their immediate life experience or the mediated worlds they share with children beyond the relatively homogeneous and insular neighborhood they inhabit.

This study was an extension of research on children's voluntary art practices that I have been conducting for more than 20 years, primarily in university-sponsored art programs for children and youth in the communities surrounding the universities where I have taught (Thompson, 1996, 1999, 2002, 2005, 2006, 2009; Thompson & Bales, 1991). In this particular study, I was eager to see whether observations made in those earlier contexts would hold true in a very different setting with children whose life experiences differ fairly radically from the more cosmopolitan children I have studied in smaller university communities. I was unwilling to make recommendations for practice based on my more rarefied sample of privileged children who were, after all, coming voluntarily to art classes on the weekends, at some inconvenience to their parents and themselves. I wanted to know how sketchbooks would work in a different cultural context.

Why Sketchbooks?

I first began to work with children and sketchbooks many years ago, when Sandy Bales invited me to introduce them in Saturday art classes at the University of Illinois at Urbana-Champaign. Our method was extremely simple: To the young children enrolled we presented spiral bound volumes of blank pages, markers, and the invitation to draw whatever they wanted in the first 15–20 minutes of each week's class. I was inspired to explore this possibility by my interest in the writing process approach and particularly the writings of Anne Dyson (1989). As a language arts educator, Dyson's interest in children's drawings focused on 'drawing events,' on the evolution and content of drawings, and the talk and gestures that surrounded them. This was a welcome shift of perspective from the formalist emphasis on the analysis of finished drawings that continued to prevail in art education research at that time. While much of the research in art education continued to focus exclusively on drawings as texts, Dyson acknowledged their importance as pretexts for dialogue and interaction, embedded in the context of classrooms, communities, and culture. From the beginning, the combination of sketchbooks and young children seemed no less than magical, as if this were something they had waited for throughout their entire lives. This is a response that has been duplicated in every setting in which my students or I have presented the opportunity to children.

Often, especially when young children are involved, we tend to speak of drawing as if it were a generic activity, as if all forms of drawing were alike and undertaken for a similar purpose. But people draw for many different purposes and in many different ways: The map I might draw to show you the shortest route to my house would be very different from the detailed observational drawing I would do to show you what it looks like. The type of drawing that sketchbooks encourage is 'voluntary' in the sense defined long ago by Lark-Horovitz, Lewis, and Luca (1973): produced in response to an occasion provided by an adult, but with the essential choices of subject matter and execution (and sometimes drawing medium) determined by the child. This is similar to other

FIGURE 6.2

exploratory activities in early childhood classrooms, in which children are encouraged to undertake self-initiated projects with materials and during time periods set aside by their teachers. It is also a relatively familiar way for children to experience drawing in their lives outside of school when they are invited to busy themselves with paper and markers or digital graphic programs at those interminable moments spent in cars and waiting rooms. It is the kind of drawing to which many young children are most accustomed and at which they are often most adept.

Visual art professor Howard Ikemoto recounts a conversation with his daughter that highlights the manner in which children approach drawing, and the all-but-universal loss of that capacity as we mature:

> When my daughter was about seven years old, she asked me one day what I did at work. I told her I worked at the college—that my job was to teach people how to draw. She stared at me, incredulous, and said, "You mean they forget?"
>
> (Ikemoto, n.d.)

It is possible to read this quotation as an endorsement of the view that children's drawing bubbles forth unimpeded from deep biological sources. However, the situation is more complex, and more deeply embedded in cultural provisions that channel the flow of that resource. Loris Malaguzzi (1995) and his followers in the preschools of Reggio Emilia recognize this forfeiture of the languages of the hand and eye, the graphic languages, as a significant loss of the potential represented by every human being. The exclusivity of cultural and educational focus on words and numbers, beginning in infancy, diminishes the ways in which we are able to represent, share, and refine our understandings of the world. As George Forman (1994) explains, the affordances of each specific medium—paint versus clay, for example, or drawing versus photography—provide specific ways of understanding a phenomenon. Since the 1970s, Brent Wilson and Marjorie Wilson (1977, 2009) have acknowledged the existence of multiple graphic languages, or drawing programs, which even professional artists may use with varying degrees of skill and assurance. This concept of 'multiple drawing repertoires,' subsequently discussed by Wolf and Perry (1988) and Kindler and Darras (1997), among others, was instrumental in debunking the myth that children's drawings follow a well-worn, one-way path toward a single destination of ever greater visual accuracy. Recognizing that there are innumerable styles of drawing, just as there are countless reasons for engaging in the activity of drawing (Leeds, 1989), allows us to recognize and appreciate the differences of engagement and intention that each approach entails (see, for example, Knight, 2008).

The drawings that happen in the spaces of the sketchbooks as we conceive them, especially for very young children, are what Wilson and Wilson (2009) describe as ways of worldmaking; they tend to be drawn from imagination and memory and that amalgam of experience and invention that is often favored by young children. Some children may choose to draw from direct observation of images or objects in their environment. Some use their sketchbooks for the purposes of planning play scenarios or constructions. Most often the drawings appear to be like mash ups of things that children have seen and remembered, and contexts and relationships they invent on the spot. They are fragments of children's lived worlds, appropriated for the purposes of inquiry and play.

Valuing Children's Choices

Like drawing itself, sketchbooks are used in many different ways. The approach I describe here differs in critical respects from the ways that sketchbooks are used in the United Kingdom's Sketchbooks in the Schools initiative (Access Art, 2012), for example, or in Korean schools, where topics for drawing are assigned and teacher direction plays a central role (Park, 2004). Here, the children are calling the shots; their interests are the subjects of their drawings. Traditionally art education (like so much of schooling) tends to avoid those topics in which children tend to be most interested. As Donna Grace and Joseph Tobin (1998) observed years ago:

> Although child-centered curricula emphasize connecting the world of school to the lives of children, many of their everyday pleasures and interests lie untouched and untapped in the classroom. Movies, television, videos, popular magazines, fiction and video games contribute to the shaping of student experiences and subjectivities. However, these interests must typically be left on the doorstep when arriving at school each day.
>
> *(pp. 45–46)*

This remains the case today, as Andrew could readily attest.

In part, this is due to our resistance to children's culture, a fear of introducing controversial topics or opening the gates to the carnivalesque (Bakhtin, 1984), those things we might dismiss as offensive or silly or off-color or simply a waste of good time and paper. In part, it is due to our conviction that our role as educators is to help children to learn what they don't know, to accomplish things that they could not do without our assistance (Hawkins, 1974/2002), to elevate the state of childhood to something that approximates our own standards of good taste. Adult authority may be threatened by that which we do not understand about children's culture and have no desire or no ready or palatable means of learning.

When we focus on children's self-initiated visual projects, the balance of power and authority that typically exists in American classrooms shifts dramatically, allowing teachers to learn from children and to engage in dialogue with them about the ideas, issues, and images that matter most to children as individuals and as members of cultures that are uniquely their own. In doing so, both children and adults temporarily suspend their customary classroom roles. For some adults, this feels like a precarious space.

Marjorie Wilson and Brent Wilson (2009) describe this difference:

> Contrast the conditions and motives when the child decides to make a drawing for her own satisfactions with the situation in which a teacher asks a classroom of students to make drawings of an assigned topic. One drawing episode is initiated by a child to please herself or himself; the second is initiated by an adult to meet an educational objective deemed important by the adult—but not necessarily by the students. When children initiate their own drawing activity for their own purposes, we call it the *first drawing site*. When adults assign children to draw, in schools or museums, we term it the *second drawing site*. When a child and an adult, for a period of time, set aside the status and authority that generally separate the realms of adulthood and childhood, when they become near equals and colleagues, and make joint contributions to a drawing we call it the *third drawing site*.
>
> *(p. vii)*

Brent Wilson, in particular, advocates the technique of graphic dialogue in which child and adult draw together on the same page, each contributing ideas and images to an evolving graphic narrative. While this literally creates a third drawing site in the classroom, sketchbooks, properly conceived, do much the same.

The choices children make in the images they draw and the ideas they explore present the foundation of a 'pedagogy of listening' (Rinaldi, 2006). At the same time that this drawing practice increases children's communicative capacity, it enables teachers and researchers to understand children with greater clarity and specificity, as individuals, as members of multiple social groups within the classroom, and as participants in and producers of cultures beyond the classroom. In a preschool committed to dialogical approaches to education, sketchbook sessions provided an opportunity to expand the languages available to children and to establish greater reciprocity between children and adults.

What Children Draw

Most of the drawings made by the three- and four-year-old children I came to know in Chicago explored issues and ideas that are very much on the minds of preschool children everywhere. Families provided endless material for drawings; often families lined up and labeled, but sometimes families at the park or flying to Mexico. Houses were often featured. Dwellings tended to be closely packed brownstones, complete with stairs and many windows, seldom surrounded by expansive lawns or play structures. Playgrounds had an urban feel. Monsters and ghosts were frequent and exciting subjects for drawing. Once they were introduced in conversation, these fascinating and scary creatures were sure to replicate themselves around the drawing tables. Superheroes and media creations appeared frequently in children's drawings, as they did in the T-shirts, jackets, backpacks, and shoes they wore and proudly displayed each day when I came to their classrooms. While Batman was officially *persona non grata* in the classrooms, it was difficult to keep him from cropping up in children's drawings, and often impossible to explain the difference between a depiction of *lucha libre*, the Mexican wrestlers who the children admired and emulated, and a drawing of The Incredible Hulk.

The children's teachers worried about the drawings of superheroes and monsters. These seemed incompatible with their efforts to define the school as a 'safe space' in a neighborhood that was often dangerous. Some teachers outlawed violence of any kind, from rough-housing on the classroom rug to pushing on the playground to drawing confrontations between Batman and The Joker. Others took pains to remind children that the monsters they drew were imaginary; that there were no 'real' monsters, and that the school itself was a safe place, where nothing could hurt them.

Still other teachers saw no contradiction in allowing children to draw what they wished without censorship, while maintaining a ban on active superhero play in the block corner or the playground. These teachers had a different understanding of children and their drawing, and what children are doing when they draw. They recognized the drawing table as a safe space in itself, a place where children could explore their questions about life as it is lived and as it is imagined, embracing fictional characters and their actions as ways of thinking about persistent questions of power and conflict, good and evil, comfort and contingency (Edmiston, 2008; Holland, 2003; Jones, 2002; Katch, 2001).

As Henry Jenkins (1998) remarks:

> Our grown up fantasies of childhood as a simple space crumble when we recognize the complexity of forces shaping children's lives and defining who they will be, how they will behave, and how they will understand their place in the world.
>
> *(p. 4)*

All of the teachers at the center were fully aware of how challenging the process of making meaning could be for children living in poverty and cultural isolation within sight of the towering skyscrapers of a booming city.

Intriguingly, the more dramatic incidents in children's lives were seldom invoked as subjects for drawing, challenging the notion that children's drawings can be read diagnostically. Disclosures such as 'My Mommy saw a *ratito*, and she screamed,' or 'My Daddy hit my Mommy in the stomach,' were inter-jected into conversation, matter-of-fact statements addressed to me or to another adult at the table where we gathered to draw. These were incidents reported without context or elaboration. They were clearly things that struck the children as distressing, but not things to be dwelt upon or belabored or even addressed in drawings. They were things that happened, part of the complex lives that they shared, as young children growing up in a community where large families, crowded apartments, and financial constraints were common. These experiences were certainly not taken-for-granted, but part of the life that children live, part of the experiences that they bring with them to the classroom.

It seemed that the complexities of the children's personal lives were revealed more often, surely more directly, in words than in pictures. Yet it may be that children's choices of media-inspired themes were influenced by the circum-stances of their daily lives: might these stories stand in for some of the puzzling aspects of being a child? Because so much of what children draw carries 'media traces' (Gotz, Lemish, Aidman, & Moon, 2005), I have followed children into the realm of kinderculture and what Allison James (1998) terms the 'ket aesthetic,' the kinds of cultural productions that only a child could truly love. Henry Jenkins (2007) points out that commercial culture provides contemporary children with robust sources of play:

> For children of the television age, the most readily available play materials are those that the media bring into their homes. Children draw upon the prefabricated characters and situations of popular culture to make sense of their own social experience, reworking them to satisfy their own needs and desires. The children's manipulation of these televisual materials rarely stops when the broadcast does.
>
> *(pp. 182–183)*

For children whose afternoons and evenings were often spent confined to quarters, in deference to the daily escalation of gang activity in their neighbor-hood as the day progressed, these materials were at least as influential as their experiences in the 'real' world (Wright, 2010).

Andrew, the Gabriels, and The Incredible Hulk

Like many young children who draw with great intensity of purpose, Andrew's love of drawing was entangled with a fascination for a particular category of subject matter. In Andrew's case, it was superheroes—Batman, Spiderman, Iron Man and The Incredible Hulk in particular—who captured his imagina-tion and constituted his repertoire. Unlike the other children in this setting, Andrew depicted his superheroes in a range of styles, constantly exercising and stretching their capabilities, and his own, by putting them in situations that involved crossovers from one story to the next. Andrew's comprehensive knowledge of the mythologies represented by each of his characters allowed him to create scenarios that both followed and deviated from their original stories. His drawings were a form of mythic play (Edmiston, 2008). Since his preschool prohibited the kinds of active superhero play he might otherwise have enjoyed on the playground or in the classroom, drawing became Andrew's primary way to play.

Like many young children who are so intensely devoted to drawing, Andrew's absorption in the activity was absolute. Howard Gardner (1980) observed this style of symbolic play in his description of children he called 'patterners,' children who are fascinated by the visual qualities of the things they explore in their constructive and symbolic play. Gardner described these children as content to work alone in a crowd, preferring to talk with adults about their drawings and constructions. Although this description fits Andrew to a degree, he was by no means an isolated child. Andrew was more than willing to talk with other children who shared his interests, despite the fact that his own expertise far exceeded theirs, both in terms of his knowledge of the superheroes and their exploits, and in his ability to capture their characteristics in drawing. The acknowledged expert in currently popular superheroes, Andrew's drawings were admired by many and emulated by a few of his closest friends.

Late in the year that I spent in Andrew's preschool, the children in his class had filled their sketchbooks to bursting, and so we made do with large sheets of paper when I came to visit their class. The small tables where the children gathered to draw were crowded with paper and markers, and Andrew protested when the vigorous sweeps of three-year-old Angelica's marks violated his own pristine page. Relocating Andrew to a table where he could work by himself, I took advantage of the opportunity to sit with him in a relatively quiet spot and to document his drawing. His plan was to draw The Incredible Hulk. As I sat and filmed Andrew drawing, he noted, 'I need to make his face green.' As he finished this last detail, Angelica arrived at the table, took one look at Andrew's drawing, and proclaimed in an apprehensive tone, 'OOOH, monster!' Andrew assured her, 'He's a good guy. He's a good guy.' I explained to Angelica that the Hulk gets mad when he sees people doing bad things, and intervened when she sat in Andrew's chair, prompting Andrew to declare, 'I need my space!' When Angelica was called away by her teacher, I told Andrew that I was filming his Hulk drawing. He moved his markers off the page and watched through the viewfinder as I filmed his drawing, beginning to rock the camera gently back and forth to give the impression that the drawing was in motion.

This was enough to attract the attention of Andrew's two best friends in the class, Gabriel D. and Gabriel R. The Gabriels were seated at the second drawing table, but they both kept an eye on what Andrew was up to, occasionally

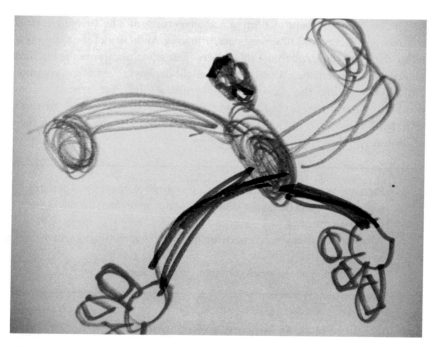

FIGURE 6.3

wandering over to watch him draw or to seek his advice on some fine point of superhero expression, anatomy or regalia needed for their own drawings. The Gabriels' superheroes each had their own distinctive styles, more generic than Andrew's and far less apt to be engaged in moments of high drama, much more likely to simply stand, alone or in company, on the page. Both Gabriel D. and Gabriel R. were eager to share their drawings with their teachers and to wait patiently as the captions the boys dictated were added to the page.

Accustomed as they were to my obsessive photography of their work, the boys were fascinated by the possibility of using the camera's video function to put their drawings in motion. The Gabriels returned to their places at the table and began to draw their own versions of The Incredible Hulk. Always enthusiastic about drawing, Gabriel D. began the year inscribing a few marks on paper, just enough to support the elaborate stories he loved to tell in conversation with a teacher whose attention was his and his alone for the time it took to write down his thoughts. His first drawing of the Hulk preserved the rotund quality of many of his early drawings, but as he continued to produce drawings for the Hulk project, his version of the character slimmed down and accrued detail. Gabriel R's Hulk, alone among the images he had drawn that year, had a scowling face, a feature of Andrew's drawing that Gabriel apparently decided was critical to depiction of the fearsome visage of the Hulk transformed.

The impromptu event of filming the adventures of The Incredible Hulk continued over a period of several days, allowing Andrew and the Gabriels to refine their drawings and to use the camera themselves to capture the lurching movement of a fascinating superhero. It brought the boys together in a common project, cementing the more sporadic collaboration that existed among them throughout the year. This spontaneous project allowed me to think differently about each of the three children involved and the nature of their relationship.

---

o For many young children, drawing is a performance, made up of gestures, sound effects, and narrations as much as (if not more than) the marks that end up on the page.

o What can teachers learn about children by watching and listening to them as they draw?

o How can these observations contribute to curriculum planning?

The Incredible Hulk as Responsive Pedagogy

When he worked in his sketchbook, Andrew was constantly constructing new problems for himself. Other children in his classroom did the same, as they posed problems related to their experiences and interests, as they drew their families and neighborhoods, ghosts and monsters, pumpkins and fruit trucks. Given the opportunity to gather together each week to draw in their sketchbooks, each child created projects that, to a greater or lesser degree, reflected his or her experiences and interests. Alongside these personal inclinations, it was possible to observe the unique drawing strategies each child was in the process of mastering. Each was actively engaged in the construction of problems. Olsson (2009) points out how critical this is: 'It seems that the important thing for children is to *construct* the problem that they are working upon. They rarely seem to be interested in already defined problems that have predetermined solutions' (p. 17).

It is tempting to consider Andrew as a special case, a remarkable child whose intelligence is clearly manifested in his drawings. But, if we look at children only, or even primarily, as individuals, we miss the important social dimensions of these drawing sessions, and the fact that the most potent learning opportunities emerge in the spaces between children and teachers and researchers. As Olsson (2009) suggests in her study of a long-term project in a Swedish preschool, a shift in adults' thinking is required in order to allow for the kinds of collaborative play with ideas and media that Andrew and the Gabriels enacted. This shift requires a fundamental rethinking of our image of the child, as well as of the source of the curriculum:

> . . . children are no longer looked upon as identified and already repre-
> sented individuals with a predetermined development or as flexible,
> autonomous learners . . . [T]he problem to be worked upon is not clear
> from the beginning; children and teachers work on its construction . . .
> Teachers no longer solely define children as individuals according to rigid
> lines created by theories of children's predetermined development and
> children's interests or desires and beliefs are in these moments no longer
> tamed and controlled. Teachers rather look for what took place in between
> children, their interests are treated like contagious trends and they do not
> reside in each individual. This is exactly where lines of flight are born.
>
> *(Olsson, 2009, p. 71)*

Lines of flight, Deleuze and Guattari's (2004; see also MacRae, 2011) term for sudden eruptions of creative divergence and inspiration, locate the sources of curriculum in the spaces between those who live within the classroom, the spaces shared by children and adults. Introducing a very rudimentary technological elaboration into the boys' superhero play, I opened a line of flight that allowed them to pursue an interest that they shared. Seeing each boy as a member of a collaborative partnership, with his own style and pace of learning, and his own path of becoming, allowed me to see beyond the ways that Andrew, in particular, was regarded in his school. Seen in a developmental perspective, Andrew was considered artistically gifted (even though he stubbornly withheld that giftedness when topics were assigned and the drawing did not present its own intriguing problems). Viewed from the perspective of classroom discipline and *esprit de corps*, Andrew was seen as stubborn, a bit on the moody side, all but impervious to instruction, as apt to choose self-imposed exile as to participate in classroom routines that failed to capture his imagination.

But what if we choose to see Andrew as neither exceptional nor challenging, or as both exceptional and challenging and a great deal more? What if we see him more simply, as a child who is constantly becoming? A child whose identity is by no means fixed? A child whose learning, against all evidence to the contrary, is occurring within a field of relations that includes the world within school, as well as the world of popular media culture that so profoundly feeds his imagination? From that angle, we see a very different child, socially situated, constantly changing, and very much open to the influence of teachers and peers and the worlds of experience they share.

- ○ Frisch (2012) describes the 'wildfire effect' that happens as children draw together and share ideas and images around the drawing table.
- ○ How does this process support children who are learning to draw?
- ○ How might it help children to find and solidify friendships based upon mutual interests?

CODA: 'So you will remember me as an artist'

One morning in May, Andrew took his cue, with uncharacteristic enthusiasm, from his teacher's suggestion that the children draw something related to their field trip the week before to the Shedd Aquarium. He began by drawing a diver, tethered to a diving bell at the top left corner of the page and holding onto a cage to capture whatever might come his way. He then added water. At this point, he became intrigued by colors mixing and performed a few experiments just to see what would happen, for example, if he colored red over yellow. He added a shark, a whale, and several small fish jumping out of the water.

At the end of class, Andrew, who was typically very stingy with his drawings, told me that he wanted me to keep this one, 'so that you will remember me as an artist.'

Of course, I was honored to do so. I shared this story with several teachers and administrators during the morning. Everyone I spoke to recognized the story as very touching, but those who saw the drawing itself seemed to be less impressed with Andrew's quick, splashy style. Perhaps they did not see the difference between the way that Andrew draws and thinks through his drawing and the rapidly scribbled lines favored by other children learning to draw. Perhaps they did not recognize the sophistication of his use of occlusion and the ingenuity of the ways in which he depicts figures in motion. And, as a result, I wondered, how is it that we develop an appreciation for child art that encompasses a variety of styles and a range of graphic strategies? How can we recognize drawings such as these as important, as significant representations of what children know and what they want to know?

The choices that Andrew makes may tell us something quite significant about the ways that adults might help children to continue to find drawing a way to express their ideas and explore their experiences. Henry Jenkins (2007) suggests that preschool children may be more interested in spectacle than in narrative in their choice of media fare. This could certainly apply to their drawings as well. Andrew's interest in moments of high drama or extremity is evident in his work; it is almost as if he is conscious of the need to select visually compelling moments to capture a compelling story within the constraints of a single frame. This is, quite probably, a convention that he has picked up from comics (along with the motion lines that trail a leaping superhero) or illustrations in children's books or paintings, though its origins, in Andrew's case, seem to be cinematic. Many children begin to construct scenes in drawings made during their preschool years, but these drawings tend to be more static, enumerations of objects or people and props. But I suspect that the motive to depict dramatic moments is shared and may be one of those things, several years from now, that will stymie many of the children whose intentions bound far ahead of their abilities to depict the things that intrigue them.

Andrew and his two friends named Gabriel demonstrate Henry Jenkins' (2007) proposition that young children's viewing strategies may be intimately related to the ways in which they make sense of the world. Jenkins (2007) suggests that the meanings children derive from media sources:

> are localized and transitory, reflecting an immediate response both to the specific program content and to particular concerns of preschool life. But, the meaning-production process described here—the resistance to adult dominance over their cultural space, the process of textual fragmentation and the accruing of associated meanings around the bits of program material, the translation of narrative content into images for drawings and jokes, the forging of intertextual links between seemingly disparate texts, the manipulation of modal relations to create proximity or distance from represented materials, etc.—reflect children's characteristic ways of making sense of television texts.
>
> *(p. 168)*

Andrew and the Gabriels were fortunate in preschool to have two incredibly responsive educators who valued each of their students' interests, questions, ideas and cultural experiences, including popular culture. Andrew's teachers, Luz and Erin, told me late in the spring, as the drawing sessions we had shared with the children twice each week throughout the year came to an end, that they treasured this time, recognizing that it was an opportunity to learn about the children in ways that they could not at any other time, in any other way. The attention that is given to the children, the respect for their interests, their thoughts and their explorations, that occurs when we provide opportunities for children to construct knowledge in meaningful social contexts with teachers and peers is truly essential to early learning.

I wonder often how these children are faring in the public schools, and hope that they have found responsive educators who value their diverse abilities, their interests, their questions, their ideas and cultural experiences, including those that are best expressed for the moment through the fictional heroes of popular culture who allow children to contemplate together how they might act in the world. I hope that they have found teachers who are willing to watch and to listen, and to engage in dialogue with them about the worlds that emerge on the drawing page.

'Coming to know, as is the great and terrible task of schooling, can be imagined as *adding to* the abundance of the world, not diminishing it' (Jardine, Friesen, & Clifford, 2006, p.xxvi). Among the greatest challenges we face, as educators and researchers concerned with the art experience of very young children, is the unending task of convincing other adults of the capacity of children's drawings to increase the abundance of the world. In order to do so, we must recognize these drawings as texts that tell of children's experiences, as pretexts for dialogue with children, and as indicators of the contexts in which children struggle to make sense of a challenging world.

References

Access Art. (2012). *Sketchbooks in the schools*. Retrieved May 25, 2012, from http://www.accessart.org.uk/.

Bakhtin, M. M. (1984). *Rabelais and his world*. Bloomington: Indiana University Press.

Deleuze, G., & Guattari, F. (2004). *A thousand plateaus: Capitalism and schizophrenia*. New York: Continuum.

Dyson, A. H. (1989). *The multiple worlds of child writers: Friends learning to write*. New York: Teachers College Press.

Edmiston, B. (2008). *Forming ethical identities in early childhood play*. New York: Routledge.

Forman, G. (1994). Different media, different languages. In L. G. Katz & B. Cesarone (Eds.), *Reflections on the Reggio Emilia approach* (pp. 41–54). Urbana, IL: ERIC.

Frisch, N. S. (2012, March). The wildfire effect: Learning to draw as a social process. Paper presented at the National Art Education Association conference, New York.

Gardner, H. (1980). *Artful scribbles: The significance of children's drawings*. New York: Basic Books.

Gotz, M., Lemish, D., Aidman, A., & Moon, H. (2005). *Media and the make-believe worlds of children: When Harry Potter meets Pokémon in Disneyland*. Mahwah, NJ: Lawrence Erlbaum.

Grace, D., & Tobin, J. (1998). Butt jokes and mean-teacher parodies: Video production in the elementary classroom. In D. Buckingham (Ed.), *Teaching popular culture: Beyond radical pedagogy* (pp. 42–62). London: University College London Press.

Hawkins, D. (1974/2002). *The informed vision: Essays on learning and human nature* (reissue edition). New York: Algora.

Holland, P. (2003). *We don't play with guns here: War, weapon, and superhero play in the early years*. Philadelphia: Open University Press.

Ikemoto, H. (n.d.). In *ThinkExist.com*. Retrieved August 27, 2012, from http://thinkexist.com/quotation/when_my_daughter_was_about_seven_years_old-she/208131.html.

James, A. (1998). Confection, concoctions, and conceptions. In H. Jenkins (Ed.), *The children's culture reader* (pp. 394–405). New York: New York University Press.

Jardine, D., Friesen, S., & Clifford, P. (2006). *Curriculum in abundance*. Mahwah, NJ: Lawrence Erlbaum Associates.

Jenkins, H. (Ed.). (1998). *The children's culture reader*. New York: New York University Press.

Jenkins, H. (2007). *The wow climax: Tracing the emotional impact of popular culture*. New York: New York University Press.

Jones, G. (2002). *Killing monsters: Why children need fantasy, super heroes, and make-believe violence*. New York: Basic Books.

Katch, J. (2001). *Under deadman's skin: Discovering the meaning of children's violent play*. Boston: Beacon Press.

Kindler, A., & Darras, B. (1997). Map of artistic development. In A. M. Kindler (Ed.), *Child development in art* (pp. 17–44). Reston, VA: National Art Education Association.

Knight, L. (2008). Communication and transformation through collaboration: Rethinking drawing activities in early childhood. *Contemporary Issues in Early Childhood, 9*(4), 306–316.

Lark-Horovitz, B., Lewis, H., & Luca, M. (1973). *Understanding children's art for better teaching*. Columbus, OH: C. E. Merrill Books.

Leeds, J. A. (1989). The history of attitudes toward child art. *Studies in Art Education, 30*(2), 93–103.

MacRae, C. (2011). Making Payton's rocket: Heterotopia and lines of flight. *International Journal of Art & Design Education, 30,* 102–112.

Malaguzzi, L. (1995). Your image of the child: Where teaching begins. *Child Care Information Exchange,* no. 96, 52–61.

Olsson, L. M. (2009). *Movement and experimentation in young children's learning: Deleuze and Guattari in early childhood learning.* New York: Routledge.

Park, S. (2004). How four- and five-year-old children learn to draw. Unpublished doctoral dissertation. Urbana: University of Illinois at Urbana-Champaign.

Rinaldi, C. (2006). *In dialogue with Reggio Emilia: Listening, researching and learning.* New York: Routledge.

Thompson, C. M. (1996). 'What should I draw today?' Sketchbooks in early childhood. *Art Education, 48*(5), 6–11.

Thompson, C. M. (1999). Action, autobiography, and aesthetics in young children's self-initiated drawings. *Journal of Art & Design Education, 18*(2), 155–161.

Thompson, C. M. (2002). Drawing together: Peer influence in preschool-kindergarten art classes. In L. Bresler & C. M. Thompson (Eds.), *The arts in children's lives: Context, culture, and curriculum* (pp. 129–138). Boston: Kluwer Academic Press.

Thompson, C. M. (2005). Under construction: Images of the child in art education. *Art Education, 58*(2), 18–23.

Thompson, C. M. (2006). The 'ket aesthetic': Visual culture in childhood. In J. Fineberg (Ed.), *When we were young: New perspectives on the art of the child* (pp. 31–43). Berkeley: University of California Press.

Thompson, C. M. (2009). Mira! Looking, listening, and lingering in research with children. *Visual Arts Research, 35*(1), 24–34.

Thompson, C. M., & Bales, S. (1991). 'Michael doesn't like my dinosaurs': Conversations in a preschool art class. *Studies in Art Education, 33*(1), 43–55.

Vygotsky, L. S. (1978). *Mind in society.* Cambridge, MA: Harvard University Press.

Wilson, M., & Wilson, B. (1977). An iconoclastic view of the imagery sources in the drawings of young people. *Art Education, 30*(1), 5–11.

Wilson, M., & Wilson, B. (2009). *Teaching children to draw: A guide for parents and teachers* (2nd ed.). Worcester, MA: Davis.

Wolf, D., & Perry, M. (1988). From endpoint to repertoires: Some new conclusions about drawing development. *Journal of Aesthetic Education, 22*(1), 17–34.

Wright, S. (2010). *Understanding creativity in early childhood: Meaning-making and children's drawing.* London: SAGE.

7

CHOREOGRAPHED CHILDHOODS

Patterns of Embodiment in the Lives of Contemporary Children

Eeva Anttila

Introduction

This chapter is a critical discussion aimed at unravelling various patterns of embodiment that govern children's lives. More specifically, the focus is on patterns of embodied interaction and expressive movement. For a long time I have been fascinated about the beauty and vitality of children's movement. I have keenly observed how they move in space in relation to each other and to adults, and what kinds of dynamics are present in their everyday actions and interactions within their social and physical environments. Recently, I have become increasingly concerned about the range of expressive dynamics that seems to become more limited for children. Instead of education building human capacities, it seems that with education comes the reduction of bodily expressivity.

Children's embodied interactions and movements are without doubt relevant in understanding them. The connection between embodiment and lived experiences is complex and contingent, and consequently difficult to verify by research. I approach this challenging question with the support of practice-based and theoretical literature, some recent findings in empirical research, as well as with accounts by experienced dance and movement educators. This includes my own reflections that stem from practice as a dance educator. However complex the connections between inner life and embodiment are, the questions that follow are thought-provoking. Who is in charge when it comes to creating and molding the patterns of embodiment? How do educators re-enact them? What models of interaction does a 'western' educational system subscribe to—a flock of flying birds, or an army? What other metaphors for patterns of embodied interaction can be detected, and, once recognized, how might they be modified? In this chapter, the concept of choreography serves as a frame for analysis and critical reflection. Different analogies are drawn between dance choreography and a wider application—the choreography of life, or social choreography.

In the field of contemporary dance, the meaning of the term choreography is shifting. Its field has expanded to the field of human relations, and to 'the everyday governance of relations and dynamics, expressed in physical movements or ideas' (Klien & Valk, 2008a, p. 22). According to Michael Klien and Steve Valk, choreography has become a metaphor for dynamic constellations of any kind, as well as intrinsically embodied or superimposed order:

> If the world is approached as a reality constructed of interactions, relationships, constellations and proportionalities, then choreography is seen as the aesthetic practice of setting those relations or setting the conditions for those relations to emerge.
>
> *(Klien & Valk, 2008a, p. 20)*

In this chapter, a number of questions related to choreography are probed from multiple points of view. Who is the choreographer? What is being choreographed and why? What kinds of methods and approaches are being used in connection to the choreography of childhood? The aim of this discussion is to highlight children's capacities to be co-choreographers of their own lives. In order to ground this discussion, in the first part of this chapter I use the analogy of the 'solo dance', to think about children and their ways of being. To a certain extent, the solo dance can be considered as autopoietic, that is, created within the living organism. The focus here is on internal connections and fundamental movement patterns that lay the foundation for all external movements, interactions and choreographies that become shaped in relationship with the world and other human beings. The self-organizing nature of the solo dance does not mean that it becomes created or performed in isolation (see Thompson, 2007).[1]

This chapter is devoted to embodied interaction between human beings in a range of contexts: between the child and the caretaker, in the context of play and peer relationships, and finally, within arts education, dance education and formal education. The sequence of this discussion suggests that children become increasingly ordered and constrained by predetermined patterns as they grow and develop. In conclusion, I propose that this progression could be altered if educators became aware about their role as co-choreographers in children's lives. Becoming a collaborative choreographer entails, first, understanding the significance of internal patterning that lays the groundwork for all embodied actions.

---

1 Autopoiesis is a concept introduced in the 1970s by Chilean biologists Humberto Maturana and Francesco Varela. Since then, this notion has been widely used and developed in, for example, cognitive sciences and systems theories. According to Evan Thompson (2007, p. 127), autopoiesis entails cognition 'if autopoiesis is taken more widely to mean internal self-production sufficient for constructive and interactive processes in relation to the environment'.

Solo Dance: Internal Choreography as Basis for Relating

The solo dance, while always performed in relation to others and the outer world, commences before birth. The neuro–physiologist Sally Goddard Blythe describes the origin of this dance eloquently:

> From the very beginning of life there is movement. Just a few days after conception, inside a tiny ocean, an acrobat starts to perform. Beginning with gentle rocking movements in response to the inner ocean's tide, small primitive movements gather in strength until spontaneous movements and reflex responses gradually unfold. These early movements will eventually become part of the dance of development, the stages of which have been choreographed over the course of many millennia through the evolution of humankind.
>
> *(Goddard Blythe, 2004, p. 4)*

As a dance and movement educator, my intuitive understanding calls for more attention towards these early movements. The solo dance, that is, internal neuro–muscular patterning, provides a deep structure for increasingly complex actions and interactions. This sophisticated system of internal connections develops in the early years through active exploration and reciprocal interaction between the embodied human being and their surrounding social and physical world. It becomes manifest in fundamental movement patterns that make chained, integrated movement sequences possible. According to the renowned movement analyst and educator Peggy Hackney, fundamental patterns are movement sequences that are supported by habitual neuromuscular pathways, or neuromuscular models (Hackney, 2000). For example, rolling over from the back to the tummy is a complex movement sequence where the infant uses total body connectivity, especially cross-lateral connectivity.[2]

In Klien and Valk's terms, these patterns are to a large extent intrinsically embodied by self-organizing systems (2008a, p. 20). Fundamental patterns can be conceived as an internal structure that allows the infant's movements and actions to become organized into fluent flowing movement chains. This structure, when resilient, provides safety and facilitates the quest to explore further, learn more, and to build relationships. For this structure to develop, the infant needs ample opportunities for physically active and self-initiated exploration in a rich and varied environment (Goddard Blythe, 2004; Hackney, 2000; Thelen, 2008).

When restrained from active exploration, this internal structure may not develop favorably (Goddard Blythe, 2009; Hackney, 2000). In this case, the

---

2 There are six different patterns of body connectivity: breath, core–distal, head–tail, upper–lower, body-half and cross-lateral connectivity (Hackney, 2000).

children may be more likely to encounter frightening or intimidating incidents, like falling, tripping, bumping into others and into objects, dropping and
breaking objects and hurting themselves. While falling, mistakes, frustrations
and disappointments are necessary and inevitable for every child, a balance
between challenging moments and satisfactory experiences is important for
nurturing the quest to explore the world further. If the world appears chaotic
and dangerous, the child may lose the will to interact with it voluntarily. This
can be the beginning of a vicious cycle that includes social pressure and negative feedback from peers, parents and teachers who expect certain patterns of
social interaction.

Fundamental movement patterns are, thus, functional, but they also have
expressive and experiential meaning, connected with security, safety, comfort,
trust and confidence. The development of these fundamental movement patterns
is of great importance for the children's wellbeing, development and learning,
including the development of conceptual thought and language. Recent
findings in cognitive science substantiate the view that the sensory-motor system
is intertwined with the cognitive, information processing system (Johnson,
2008; Pfeifer & Bongard, 2007). A growing number of scholars agree that
cognition is embodied (Damasio, 1999, 2010; Lakoff & Johnson, 1999; Thelen,
2008). According to Esther Thelen (2008) this means that cognition arises from
bodily interactions with the world and is continually meshed with them:

> . . . cognition depends on the kinds of experiences that come from having
> a body with particular perceptual and motor capabilities that are insepa-
> rably linked and that together form the matrix within which reasoning,
> memory, emotion, language, and all other aspects of mental life are
> embedded.
>
> *(p. 101)*

The philosopher Mark Johnson claims that meaning emerges in our sensory-
motor experiences, and that 'our bodily experience thus provides a prereflective
fund of meaning that makes it possible for us to think abstractly and to carry
out all forms of meaningful human symbolic interaction, expression, and
communication' (2008, p. 20). Recognizing the embodied origin of concepts
and thoughts elucidates the mobile and flexible nature of thinking. Contrary to
the more commonly held position that separates the body from the mind, dance
can be considered as a form of thought:

> Dance is the forming of certain configurations of thought, expressed in
> manifold ways by the birth of ideas or the shivering body . . . Hence
> dance is a matter of thought pointing towards the possibility of change as
> inscribed in the body.
>
> *(Klien & Valk, 2008b, p. 87)*

The ability to express one's views, opinions, feelings and ideas through embodiment is a vital element of choreography, whether on theatre stage or on the stage of life. From a perspective of movement and dance practice,[3] it seems that the nature and functioning of the sensory-motor system deserve more articulation within early childhood education. The brief introduction of internal connectivity and fundamental movement patterns presented here to begin this chapter is meant to illuminate the significance of this highly sophisticated dance that allows the child to move expressively and creatively in relationship to others, and to generate meaning based on embodied experiences.

Another set of patterns comes into play for the dancer on the stage of life, the shared world. The question is, how do children manage to keep strengthening and developing those internal patterns further, and what kind of external patterns will they adopt? How do these different internal and external patterns match and become merged into a coherent choreography? What happens if the child's internal patterning and creative use of embodiment becomes undermined? In the following section, the focus turns to recent research into the first dyadic relationships that the infant encounters.

The Duet: The Aesthetics of Reciprocity

It is now well established that newborns come into the world with innate capacities that predispose them to solicit physical care and elicit social and emotional interaction with others (Dissanayake, 2009, p. 150). An alert infant can show innate intersubjective sympathy shortly after birth:

> . . . it seems quite absurd to suggest that a newborn infant has intersubjective mental capacities. But detailed research on how neonatal selves coordinate the rhythms of their movements and senses, and how they engage in intimate and seductive precision with other persons' movements, sensing their purposes and feelings, gives evidence that it is so.
>
> *(Trevarthen, 2010, p. 1)*

This view challenges the developmental notion that, apart from innate reflex behaviors, newborns are 'pretty much wax tablets for their elders to inscribe' (Dissanayake, 2009, p. 150). These findings compel us to reconsider developmental theories that have the initial state of human mind lacking intentions, feelings and consciousness. Instead, this recent research suggests that the newborn can show a coherent rhythmic purposeful consciousness through

---

3   See, for example, Green (2007) for a discussion of the recent developments of scholarship in dance, including somatic dance research that draws from somatic practices, somatic theory, dance practice and theory. Somatic dance research focuses on studying embodiment from the first-person perspective, as well as from sociopolitical and cultural viewpoints (Green, 2007).

well-formed movements, selective awareness and affective appraisals (Trevarthen, 2010). These actions and movements sustain human intersubjectivity and motivate imaginative cultural learning (Trevarthen, 2010). These perceptual and cognitive abilities permit infants to engage with their caretakers in complex communicative interchanges, in playful behavior such as that often referred to as 'baby talk' (Dissanayake, 2009, p. 151).

Baby talk consists of rhythmic, repetitive utterances that have poetic features. The phrases have the temporal length of a poetic line and a musical phrase. Rhythmically regular sounds, physical movements and exaggerated facial expressions are also part of baby talk. The vocal behavior is accompanied by rhythmic body movements and babies respond with their own playful actions, like wriggles, giggles, kicks and smiles (Dissanayake, 2009). Dissanayake writes that 'the behaviour is dyadic, since infants actively elicit, shape, and otherwise influence the pace, intensity, and variety of signals that adults present to them' (2009, p. 152).

This duet is highly coordinated in time. It is also cross-modal. This means that the actions are not only copied and imitated as such by the dancing partners, but they are cross-modally matched and coordinated according to intensity, contour, duration and rhythm—qualities that apply to any sense modality. The duet develops and unfolds over time:

> Over much of the first year of the infant's life, the pair engage and disengage, synchronize and alternate, practicing their physical, physiological, and emotional "attunement" by means of these multimodal expressive signals.
>
> *(Dissanayake, 2009, p. 152)*

There is much more about the details and qualities of this delicate choreography, and about its significance for the developing child and for human communal life. However, the most notable feature for developing the thesis in this chapter is that this dance is *reciprocally choreographed*. It is not dictated by either of the partners, but a collaborative creation. Where the solo dance is created by, or within the infant with the support of a rich and varied environment, the duet is a reciprocal creation.

> A choreography of evolution, an intricate order of two people in relation to each other, an ether of mental fabrics being pulled into a dance not prescribed anywhere . . . These choreographies surpass the capacity of any choreographer, any conscious creator.
>
> *(Klien, Valk, & Gormly, 2008, p. 25)*

During the first year of life, the young child can act as the co-choreographer, provided that they have a safe, rich environment, possibilities to explore it, and an affectionate partner in this choreography, willing to share, play and create this dance collaboratively with them.

The notion of the infant as co-choreographer challenges the conception of a child as incomplete that has dominated developmental psychology and education for a long time. In most modern educational systems and in social institutions, the child has been thought of as a passive target of various measures with a minimal amount of active agency. The child is often seen as a problem, as a burden, as someone to be cultivated, developed and disciplined (Karlsson, 2000). The sociologist William Corsaro has presented an alternative view that reverses the notion of childhood as adaptation to society. Corsaro speaks about *interpretive reproduction* according to which 'children are active, creative social agents who produce their own unique children's cultures while simultaneously contributing to the production of adult societies' (1997, p. 4). Children can be seen as active subjects, multitalented and resourceful, and as competent experts about issues related to their own lives. Instead of childhood as preparation for adulthood, it could be conceived as a stable structure in society: although individual children become adults, children are always present and active participants in society (Corsaro, 1997).

At some point, children also enter the world of peer relationships. At the same time as caretakers are continuing as children's dancing partners, in the choreography of life, children's mutual play gains significance. In the next section, the discussion turns to children's play as 'instant' choreography, improvised and fluid interplay between equal partners.

Instant Choreography: The Improvised Dance of Children's Play

In the field of dance art, instant choreography refers to work that is created at the same time as it is performed (Stark Smith, 2011). The English dancer Julyen Hamilton, known for composing his dance works instantly, says that 'improvisation for me is the process . . . I never call a piece "improvisation". To me it is a piece' (Holzer, 2011).

From this perspective, children's play is not simply a 'rehearsal process' for real life. Play is significant in itself, as 'a piece', as an aesthetic, performative act created on the stage of life, for life. Play elucidates children's capacities for collaborative, instant choreography. In this view, play is:

> fundamentally dependent on the children's *participation* and *activity* and is predicated on their acquisition of *skills* in terms of expressive forms, aesthetic techniques, forms of organization, mises-en-scène and performance . . . the basic condition of play is the existence of a supra-individual cultural space.
>
> *(Mouritsen, 1998, pp. 13–14)*

Children practice these skills by taking part in play. Thus, play involves tradition, active participation, skills and techniques. Mouritsen claims that in play 'you have to be so good that you can improvise . . . the ability to improvise, and improvisation, capturing the moment, takes practice. It is not just divine inspiration but *practiced* spontaneity' (1998, pp. 14–15). Further, he claims that children's play is almost always organized and formed, and this happens through aesthetic techniques—that is, through creating form and patterns of their movements, language and voice, and the materials that they use (Mouritsen, 1998). Play culture includes expressive forms and genres actively created by children with limited adult control, such as games, tales, songs, rhymes, jingles, riddles and jokes that are based on orally transmitted tradition and influences from culture produced for children (Mouritsen, 1998).

Types of play can also be seen on a continuum from enjoyment, spontaneity and freedom to commitment to rules and aims (Kalliala, 1999).[4] According to Kalliala, rules and aims in themselves do not necessarily exclude the element of play. The Dutch philosopher Johan Huizinga (1938/1984) argues that play is meaningful action, it always has a purpose. Psychological and biological explanations of play do not tackle the question of the primary and intensive nature of play that is deeply anchored in aesthetics. Huizinga also connects play and art together. For him, art forms involving rhythm and harmony, that is poetry, music and dance, are closest to the inherent nature of play (Huizinga, 1938/1984).

The Swedish childhood researcher Gunilla Lindqvist (2001) asserts that dance and play should be linked together and that dance education for young children should originate in children's play. She has noticed that children love playing in their dance classes and that they thought that there was not much difference between dance and play. But, who choreographs children's creative dance?

Choreographing Creative Dance

Modern arts education can be considered as a continuation of the Romantic conception that considers art as separate from everyday life, and the artists as exceptional and gifted individuals. Adhering to a modernist framework, arts educators look for talent to further cultivate. In so doing, children are categorized early on and treated accordingly. Often, children who are considered talented get more attention and more encouragement. Modernist assumptions of human nature and child development posit human development as controllable and predictable; thus a goal of arts education is to cultivate children's

---

4 In her study on the development of play culture in Finnish society, Marjatta Kalliala (1999), following Roger Callois (1958), describes forms of play. Different types of play include games (agon) that involve competition, chance plays (alea) that involve an element of luck, e.g., lottery, games that involve 'dizziness' (ilinx: physical sensations, breaking taboos or order), and imaginary play (mimicry) (Kalliala, 1999, pp. 47–48).

talents by correct educational measures (see, for example, Anttila, 2007b; Dalton, 2001; Efland, 2007).

Arts education based on modernist ideals potentially reinforces dominant aesthetics and predetermined patterns of human interaction. In dance, this means that the aesthetic preferences of the teacher dominate the movement qualities and choreographical choices as well as the ways children are expected to interact among each other. Especially in diverse settings, this can have a homogenizing effect where cultural differences may become compromised. That is to say, in 'western' school settings, for instance, it is usually the western aesthetics that dominate in creative movement and dance education. This can be evident in movement dynamics, and the pathways that are used. For example, 'western' dance styles favor 'clear and smooth' pathways over other ways that are termed 'haphazard' or 'peculiar'.

According to Sherry Shapiro (2008), a global view of aesthetics involves the recognition of diversity and acknowledges that there are multiple meanings of what dance is or what good dance is. Despite growing awareness of diversity and multiculturalism in dance education, she points out that:

> . . . we must also examine the underlying assumptions and dispositions we continue to hold as part of our embodied ideology of the aesthetic. What I mean by this is the way we continue to see particular dance forms as superior while giving other forms less value.
>
> *(Shapiro, 2008, p. 255)*

Shapiro refers to 'western' forms of dance, and this includes historically established theatrical forms, like ballet, and contemporary, popular dance forms that are effectively distributed around the globe through mass media. It seems evident that respecting diversity has become ever more challenging and crucial in times of globalization, where 'children across the globe seek to imitate the fashion, music, and dance of the West' (Shapiro, 2008, p. 256).

Many dance educators have become aware of the homogenizing influence of western dance forms and modernist arts education. But few have raised critical voices concerning creative dance that for many dance educators represents a movement away from dominating aesthetics. Creative dance is generally considered a 'divergence from traditional training where dance students were treated as objects and their bodies material to be molded for artistic purposes' (Anttila, 2007a, p. 866). Usually taught through child-centered approaches, and loosely connected to humanistic ideas of creativity and self-expression, creative dance has largely evaded critical evaluation that much of traditional dance education and training has been subjected to. Among the few critical voices is dance scholar Sue Stinson, who writes that, 'the myth perpetuated by creative dance is populated by images of only bright and happy children, running and skipping joyfully, seemingly untouched by poverty, hunger, homelessness, or any of the other realities where so many children live' (1998, p. 37). She claims that creative dance may foster escapism and produce 'docile, well-disciplined individuals who will fit into the way things are rather than attempt to change them' (Stinson, 1998, p. 38).

Stinson's critical viewpoint seems fitting from my perspective as a long-time member and the current Chair of *dance and the Child international (daCi)*.[5] Based on children's dance performances in the context of the triannual conferences of daCi, dominating aesthetics seem to prevail. This may be due to the dominant status of western dance forms in the training of dance educators worldwide. Based on a number of conference presentations that I have witnessed in daCi and in other international arts education conferences, it is evident that dance is mostly taught by middle-class women, and that extra-curricular dance classes are populated by middle-class girls.[6]

According to Klien and Valk (2008b, p. 85) the development of western dance in the twentieth century is primarily about 'obedience and long legs'. They consider this development a kind of perversion, where the dancing body is subjected to choreography:

> Along the way, the map has been mistaken for the territory, the architecture for the experience. Maybe that's where it has all gone wrong. The structures are not the dance, they are perceptual orientations for getting there.
>
> *(2008b, p. 85)*

It concerns me greatly that children are put on stage, performing dances that are authored by their middle-class, western, female teachers. Through this practice the teachers, consciously or not, pass on to the next generation the aesthetic models that are inscribed within western dance training. These aesthetic models may overshadow fundamental movement patterns, patterns of dyadic interaction, and improvised, self-initiated expressive patterning and meaning-making. Alternately, as discussed earlier in this chapter, the 'solo dance', the 'duet', and the 'play' dancing could be supported and grow into creative dance choreographies initiated and co-crafted by children. During the homogenizing process of dance education, the child learns to limit their

---

5 Dance and the Child international (daCi) is a non profit association with the aim of promoting the growth and development of dance for children and young people on an international basis. daCi is a fully constituted branch of Le Conseil International de la Danse (CID), UNESCO (www.daci.org).

6 In Finland, dance is the second most popular after-school arts activity among children and youth. In 2007–2008, 36,000 pupils took part in basic education in dance (Koramo, 2009). This number represents only 5% of Finnish children and youth. About 90% of these dance students are girls. Out of all Finnish boys, less than 1% take part in dance.

expressive qualities and creative powers according to the aesthetic values present in the context of dance education. If choreography is understood in its wider meaning, as a way of seeing the world (Klien & Valk, 2008a, p. 22), then a predominant aesthetic will be significant also in the way children will perceive and understand the world.

Children certainly are capable of sustaining their own creative play culture, but they are also capable of making aesthetic judgments and creating aesthetic or artistic forms based on their judgments, views and experiences. In a project which involved young children at the Children's Centre in Melbourne, Australia, dance scholar Karen Bond argued for a renewed view of children's potential and expertise as creators, as choreographers. In this Melbourne project, young children's aesthetic and intellectual values were appreciated as the children who were four years old were co-creators of the curriculum. Evidence showed that the children perceived dance in multiple and mysterious ways. The project celebrated the 'capacity of young children to initiate, develop, and transform curriculum in areas of authentic interest' (Bond, 2001, p. 48). Despite this evidence of children's capacity for artistic expression, transformation and aesthetic growth, Bond considers that children's perceptions of dance, on the whole 'are not recognized as a basis of theory in education or the arts' (2001, p. 41). In my own research and practice, working with children in the context of elementary schools (Anttila, 2003, 2008), I have explored various ways of giving the students a greater role as agents of their creative work. For example, through the use of storytelling, drawing and improvisation for creating themes, ideas and material for dance, I have witnessed artistic content and style that originates from children's worlds and imagination, bearing little resemblance to western theatre dance. I believe that when given enough space and support, children can become artists, choreographers. This understanding of the process of choreography is explained as:

> The choreographer, at the center of his art, deals with patterns and structures within the context of an existing, larger, ongoing choreography of physical, mental and social structures, whereby he/she acts as a strategist negotiating intended change with his/her environment.
>
> *(Klien & Valk, 2008a, p. 20)*

Of course, there are different approaches to the choreographic process. Interestingly, they can be compared with various educational approaches. In the more traditional arts academy approach, the choreographer is the author who embodies their vision of the emerging art work and considers dancers as material to be molded for this purpose. In an interactive approach, the choreographer gathers ideas and material from and with dancers, and organizes this material into a coherent whole. In an open or collaborative approach the roles become blurred: the choreographer becomes a facilitator, and the dancers become co-choreographers. In this kind of approach there is no single author. The open approach differs critically from the Romantic notion of the artist as a sole creator (see, for example, Barthes, 1965/1988; Foucault, 1969/1988). In more recent times, the performing arts have moved towards a more collective approach to art-making. Increasingly, concepts of reality, knowledge and mind are considered as organizational systems, as networks of relations and contexts, and the focus on art is as socio-cultural activity (Bateson, 1972/2000; Klien & Valk, 2008a; Preston-Dunlop & Sanchez-Colberg, 2002). Whether or not this shift can be seen to have taken place in educational practices is another question, for later in this chapter.

In comparison to the dance studio setting, issues of diversity and gender become more pronounced in the context of formal education. Imposed patterns and conventions exist widely in culture and society, and children can hardly stay 'un-schooled' in relation to what is beautiful, what is ugly, what is appropriate—or, for example, how girls and boys are expected to behave. In dance, when the children are active creators and participants in the creative process, it is possible that predetermined aesthetic patterns and gender stereotypes are not distinctive. Patterns, models and stereotypes act on children's lives very early and in a multitude of ways. They govern children's expressive behavior in many ways and may gradually become internalized norms and embodied habits. Growing to be a girl or a boy, for example, is a complex process where implicit and explicit cultural expectations and patterns of behavior, language and thought become adopted as elements of children's identities.

Open identities mean giving up the struggle for fixed individual identity and leaving space for experiencing and accepting otherness (Szkudlarek, 1993). Fixed identities become shaped by linguistic, discursive practices and power relations that often are organized by oppositional and dualistic logic (Szkudlarek, 1993). Szkudlarek writes that this kind of identity construction can be challenged from below, that is, from the level of the body: from affects, desires and pretextual, imaginary experiences. Another challenge comes from above, from counterdiscourses within social practices (Szkudlarek, 1993). Identities that are flexible but coherent allow for a sense of subjectivity that is also the basis for feeling for others, understanding otherness and in taking on responsibility for others (Szkudlarek, 1993).

Dance researcher Kai Lehikoinen (2004) calls for more democratic approaches that appreciate students as subjects who identify in multiple ways. He has studied boys' dance classes and choreography created for boys and male dancers. The choreographies he analyzed depicted heteronormative masculinity in the form of heroism, physical prowess and combat scenes. Drawing from Judith Butler's (1990) notion of gender as performative, Lehikoinen points out that dance education participates in the process of performing, or embodying gender according to culturally constructed accounts of masculinity and femininity. He writes that, 'when bodies meditate culturally constructed meanings of gender they operate as "vehicles" of discursive power' (Lehikoinen, 2004, p. 139). Lehikoinen's call for more diverse practices in dance education seems to be closely connected to the notion of social choreography that has to do with 'how individuals can imaginatively order and reorder aspects of their personal, social, cultural and political lives' (Klien & Valk, 2008a, p. 21).

---

o   How does childhood become choreographed?
o   What kinds of dynamics are present in the choreography of childhood?
o   How does children's embodied interaction become organized in time and space?

Taming and Re-leasing the Choreographer

Once children enter formal education, a whole new set of patterns becomes imposed on them. They are inducted into different formations like circles, rows and lines. They are taught how to sit by a desk and how to hold a pen. They learn how not to interrupt an adult and how not to respond spontaneously. They learn various social norms and rules, rules of play and rules of social inter-action. Combined with decreasing time for play and self-directed exploration within the social and physical world, highly regulated body movement may begin to erode the foundation for integrated, connected embodiment. At the same time, the range of dynamics that children can use in their daily lives may become more limited.

In addition to visible limitations and rules, there are also obscure patterns that are imposed on children. There is social hierarchy and authority of knowledge. There is the hidden curriculum of power and submission, of the good student and the bad student, of the talented and the not-so-talented, the 'bold and the beautiful'.

School can be seen as a place, a micro-cosmos that is governed by special regulations. It consists of physical boundaries: a building, classrooms, hallways, equipment, materials and school yard as well as temporal boundaries. When school is over, the rules change. Even the physical building may become trans-formed when it becomes a location for after-school activities and special events. As an institution, school also includes the persons who inhabit the building, as well as their actions and interactions with each other. Each person has an assigned role and a power status that comes with the role: the principal, the teachers, other staff, the students, the parents. The encounters between persons in school are regulated by these roles. They create either formal or informal learning environments or situations that are governed by implicit or explicit rules and norms. The school can hardly be seen as a 'dancing system', because:

> Our civilization has been turning dance into a perversion of itself, applying to and onto it everything that will prohibit its existence in the form of predetermined rigid time, space and action.
>
> *(Klien & Valk, 2008b, p. 87)*

Michel Foucault's seminal work *Discipline and punish: The birth of the prison* (1975) sheds light on ways in which institutions in modern societies, including schools, utilize surveillance and discipline that becomes manifest in various ways of controlling the body and bodies in space. Disciplining the body in education is a phenomenon that deserves great attention even today. It is a topic of interest to dance education research. Dance scholar Jill Green has drawn from Foucault's notion of the docile body (Green, 1999, 2002–2003, 2004). According to her, mastering and shaping the body in dance education produces docile bodies that 'require a system of codification and methods that are, like Foucault's socialized bodies, under meticulous control and surveillance' (Green, 2002–2003, p. 111). The production of docile bodies certainly takes place in dance education, but it can be considered an integral element of all forms of modern education.

The Brazilian educator Paulo Freire has diligently questioned the justification of a patronizing attitude from one human being towards another. According to him this attitude is present in the teacher–student relationship that he named 'banking education'. For Freire, the following attitudes and practices of banking education are a mirror of oppressive society:

1. The teacher teaches and the students are taught.
2. The teacher knows everything and the students know nothing.
3. The teacher thinks and the students are thought about.
4. The teacher talks and the students listen—meekly.
5. The teacher disciplines and the students are disciplined.
6. The teacher chooses and enforces his choice, and the students comply.
7. The teacher acts and the students have the illusion of action through the action of the teacher.
8. The teacher chooses the programme content, and the students (who were not consulted) adapt to it.
9. The teacher confuses the authority of knowledge with his own professional authority, which he sets in opposition to the freedom of students.
10. The teacher is the subject of the learning process, while the pupils are mere objects.

(Freire, 1972, pp. 46–47)

He describes this kind of education as depositing, the teacher being the depositor and the students, depositories. The action left for the students is limited to receiving, filing and storing the deposits (Freire, 1972, p. 46). He insists on a resolution of this traditional teacher–student contradiction; instead of being 'the-one-who-teaches', the 'teacher-of-the-students' turns into a teacher-student, and 'the-students-of-the-teacher' become student-teachers. For Freire, the two are jointly responsible for a process in which all grow. He says that we 'teach each other, mediated by the world' (1972, p. 53).

Foucault's and Freire's critical observations are products of their time, the end of the modern era. Postmodern times and critical scrutiny of oppressive practices may have brought gradual changes towards more democratic educational practices in some societies or particular schools. In others, neo-liberal educational policies have created new forms of oppression. According to the feminist scholar Patti Lather, educators need to become aware of the 'power-saturated discourses that monitor and normalize our sense of who we are and what is possible' (1991, p. 164). What is at stake here is challenging dominant meaning systems, transforming the relations of dominance and generating less oppressive ways of knowing. The question is about a shift in thinking about what it means to know, about the politics of knowing and being known, about knowledge as contested and partial, shaped by the interplay of language, power and meaning (Lather, 1991, p. 153).

According to William Doll, postmodern pedagogy involves a reflective relationship between the teacher and the student, where the teacher does not ask the student to accept the teacher's authority, but '. . . to join with the teacher in inquiry, into that which the student is experiencing' (1993, p. 160). This kind of thinking turns the modernist idea of pedagogy around: the teacher is not the model, the master, or the expert. This postmodern perspective has enormous implications for education:

> I believe a new sense of educational order will emerge, as well as new relations between teachers and students, culminating in a new concept of curriculum. The linear, sequential, easily quantifiable ordering system dominating education today—one focusing on clear beginnings and definite endings—could give way to a more complex, pluralistic, unpredictable system or network.
>
> *(Doll, 1993, p. 3)*

As Doll advocates for playing with material in 'imaginative and quirky manners', this 'requires a curriculum rich in diversity, problematics, and heuristics, as well as classroom atmosphere that fosters exploration' (Doll, 1993, p. 164). When the environment is rich and open, it is possible that multiple interpretations and perspectives can come into play. Doll claims that anomalies, even mistakes, must be nurtured and this means dialoguing 'seriously with the students about *their* ideas as *their ideas*' (1993, p. 166).

Postmodern views on curriculum and education presented here are close to Klien and Valk's vision where:

. . . the constellations are loose enough to actually reach a state of excitement or play without falling apart, without losing identity. A system such
as society or a state can be dancing, unlike our present-day situation,
where the structures are too tightly constrained . . .

(Klien & Valk, 2008b, p. 84)

Tight structures have been evident in many areas of human life, including
the arts. In dance, the postmodern turn that started to take place during
the 1960s can be seen as a rebellion against the aesthetics that objectified
the body, movement and the dancer in its attempt to achieve symbolistic,
representational ideals. During this turn, individualism became replaced with
connectedness and presence. Somatic, contemplative practices replaced traditional dance training techniques. Improvisational, collaborative and experiential approaches to choreography emerged. Dance art escaped from proscenium
stages and inhabited unconventional spaces (Monni, 2004; see also Banes,
1980; Novack, 1990). The artistic approach of the choreographer Deborah Hay
reflects this new paradigm of dance justly. Her extensive experience in contemplative practices and her departure from objectifying the body generate dance
that does not represent truth or symbolize ideas. Instead, as the dance unfolds,
it opens and reveals something about reality (Monni, 2004; see also Hay, 2000).
In my understanding, while being painfully aware of the impossibility of
un-choreographing ourselves, at the same time, the quest is to unleash the
dancer.

Yet it is appropriate to ask: could this kind of turn take place in early
childhood education in any degree? What would happen if we unleashed the
children, or even further, if we refrained from leashing them in the first place?
Is it possible to envision childhood as a co-creative choreography?

Co-choreographing Childhood: A Vision,
or a Possibility?

In concluding this chapter, I consider how childhood could be choreographed
collectively—that is, through a reciprocal, interactive, creative, spontaneous
process, where each partner in dance is entitled to creative agency and input.
The starting point for such choreography is recognition of a living, moving
body, with its fundamental movement patterns and internal connectivity.
A moving, living body creates and transforms space. Movement involves
and activates multiple perceptual channels, and transforms the person's inner
space and state. Supported by this internal dance the young infant reaches
out to the world, relates to others and develops a sense of trust, security and
curiosity. Reciprocal dance happens with the closest caregivers. This intimate
mutual choreography lays the groundwork for learning, relating, feeling and
belonging.

The choreography acquires added complexity when children interact with each other, in play. During these various encounters, children take part in creative interaction with their social, physical and imagined worlds. The relationships between moving bodies become complex patterns of interaction, creating webs of ever-changing constellations. These encounters can be conceived as constantly evolving and transforming spaces between people. These spaces have physical, observable qualities—like the distances between persons, shapes or formations, and groupings that become created when people interact with each other. The interactions have directions, intensities and tones. They have different levels of energy, different dynamic qualities, as well as psychological and emotional attributes, like safety or fear. Within informal and formal educational contexts these patterns generate spaces for learning. In these spaces, different kinds of knowledge become constructed and transmitted through various perceptual channels and levels of reflection.

Knowledge is situated and created in a complex social reality. Partly, it is created within the overt curriculum, and partly within a hidden curriculum and beside it: among peers, within children's own culture of knowledge production. Adults may fail to understand the meaning of this obscure choreography, where power relations are negotiated, where judgments about what is worthy and valuable are made, where inclusions and exclusions are executed, and where learning beyond the official curriculum takes place.

Again it is appropriate to ask: how could we understand this choreography, and see how we can contribute to it, to co-choreograph education with children? Is it possible for us, adults and arts educators, to become more aware of our desires to choreograph our children's and students' lives and consciously widen the aesthetic perspectives and choices for them? All adults who interact with children are movement educators and co-choreographers of childhood. Thus, all adults who interact with children should become aware of the models and aesthetic preferences they pass on to future generations. Perhaps, by becoming aware of the great influence of these patterns, the patterns could gradually become more flexible and allow for greater agency for growing children to be in charge of their bodily actions and interactions.

> Patterns are everywhere . . . The fact is that patterns govern our lives . . . Patterns are flexible and fluid constellations, appearing and disappearing, crystallizing and dissolving, being born and dying. They are an ongoing dance of creation and de-creation . . . in this dance lies a world full of interaction, relationships, constellations, dependencies, arrangements and ecologies. To enquire into this reality of changing patterns and the forces at play, is to enquire into the choreography of life, examining what makes us dance and why.
>
> *(Klien, Valk, & Gormly, 2008, p. 11)*

- ○ Who is the choreographer of childhood?
- ○ What kinds of choreographers are we as educators?
- ○ What kinds of choreographic approaches are we using?
- ○ Are the choreographies of childhood flexible and open, or rigid and predetermined?

References

Anttila, E. (2003). A dream journey to the unknown: Searching for dialogue in dance education. Doctoral dissertation. Theatre Academy Helsinki: Acta Scenica 14. Retrieved from http://www.teak.fi/general/Uploads_files/Acta%20Scenica/a_dream_journey_to_the_unknown_AS14.pdf.

Anttila, E. (2007a). Children as agents in dance: Implications of the notion of child culture for research and practice in dance education. In L. Bresler (Ed.), *International handbook of research in arts education* (pp. 865–879). Dordrecht, The Netherlands: Springer.

Anttila, E. (2007b). Dance as a dialogical praxis: Challenging individualism in art and education. In S. Ravn, & C. Svendler Nielsen (Eds.), *Tidsskrift for dans i uddannelse 1* (pp. 57–74). Gylling, Denmark: Narayana Press.

Anttila, E. (2008). Dialogical pedagogy, embodied knowledge, and meaningful learning. In S. Shapiro (Ed.), *Dance in a world of change: Examining globalization and cultural differences* (pp. 159–179). Champaign, IL: Human Kinetics.

Banes, S. (1980). *Terpsichore in sneakers: Post-modern dance*. Boston: Houghton Mifflin Company.

Barthes, R. (1965/1988). The death of the author. In D. Lodge (Ed.), *Modern criticism and theory: A reader* (pp. 167–172). London: Longman.

Bateson, G. (1972/2000). *Steps to an ecology of mind: Collected essays in anthropology, psychiatry, evolution and epistemology*. Chicago, IL: University of Chicago Press.

Bond, K. E. (2001). 'I'm not an eagle, I'm a chicken!': Young children's experiences of creative dance. *Early Childhood Connections, 7*(4), 41–51.

Butler, J. (1990). *Gender trouble: Feminism and the subversion of identity*. New York: Routledge.

Callois, R. (1958). *Les jeux et les hommes: Le masque et vertige*. Paris: Gallimard.

Corsaro, W. A. (1997). *The sociology of childhood*. Thousand Oaks, CA: Pine Forge Press.

Dalton, P. (2001). *The gendering of art education: Modernism, identity and critical feminism*. Buckingham, England: Open University Press.

Damasio, A. (1999). *The feeling of what happens: Body and emotion in the making of consciousness*. New York: Harcourt Brace & Company.

Damasio, A. (2010). *Self comes to mind: Constructing the conscious mind*. New York: Pantheon Books.

Dissanayake, E. (2009). The artification hypothesis and its relevance to cognitive science, evolutionary aesthetics, and neuroaesthetics. *Cognitive Semiotics, 5*, 148–173.

Doll, W. E., Jr. (1993). *A post-modern perspective on curriculum*. New York: Teachers College Press.

Efland, A. (2007). Interlude: Arts education, the aesthetic and cultural studies. In L. Bresler (Ed.), *International handbook of research in arts education* (pp. 39–44). Dordrecht, The Netherlands: Springer.

Foucault, M. (1969/1988). What is an author? In D. Lodge (Ed.), *Modern criticism and theory: A reader* (pp. 197–210). London: Longman.

Foucault, M. (1975). *Discipline and punish: The birth of the prison.* New York: Vintage Books.

Freire, P. (1972). *Pedagogy of the oppressed* (Myra B. Ramos, Trans.). Harmondsworth, England: Penguin Education.

Goddard Blythe, S. (2004). *The well balanced child: Movement and early learning.* Gloucestershire, England: Hawthorne Press.

Goddard Blythe, S. (2009). *Attention, balance and coordination: The A.B.C. of learning success.* Chichester, England: John Wiley & Sons.

Green, J. (1999). Somatic authority and the myth of the ideal body in dance education. *Dance Research Journal, 31*(2), 80–100.

Green, J. (2002–2003). Foucault and the training of docile bodies in dance education. *Arts and Learning Research Journal, 19*(1), 99–124.

Green, J. (2004). The politics and ethics of health in dance education. In L. Rouhiainen, E. Anttila, S. Hämäläinen, & T. Löytönen (Eds.), *The same difference? Ethical and political perspectives in dance* (pp. 65–76). Theatre Academy Helsinki: Acta Scenica 17.

Green, J. (2007). Student bodies: Dance pedagogy and the soma. In L. Bresler (Ed.), *International handbook of research in arts education* (pp. 1119–1132). Dordrecht, The Netherlands: Springer.

Hackney, P. (2000). *Making connections: Total body integration through Bartenieff fundamentals.* Amsterdam, The Netherlands: Gordon and Breach.

Hay, D. (2000). *My body, the Buddhist.* Hanover, NH: Wesleyan University Press.

Holzer, S. (2011). Does it make you feel, think, imagine: A conversation with Julyen Hamilton about improvisation, dance, text, language, and performance. Retrieved October 19, 2011, from http://www.corpusweb.net/index.php?option=com_content&task=view&id =1546&Itemid=34.

Huizinga, J. (1938/1984). *Leikkivä ihminen: Yritys kulttuurin leikkiaineksen määrittelemiseksi* (Homo Ludens. Versuch einer Bestimmung des Spielelements der Kultur. S. Salomaa, Trans.). Juva, Finland: WSOY.

Johnson, M. (2008). The meaning of the body. In W. F. Overton, U. Müller & J. L. Newman (Eds.), *Developmental perspectives on embodiment and consciousness* (pp. 19–43). New York: Lawrence Erlbaum.

Kalliala, M. (1999). *Enkeliprinsessa ja itsari liukumäessä: Leikkikulttuuri ja yhteiskunnan muutos* [Angel princess and suicide in the slide. Play culture and the change in society]. Tampere, Finland: Gaudeamus.

Karlsson, L. (2000). *Lapsille puheenvuoro: Ammattikäytännön perinteet murroksessa* [Voice to the children. Breaking the traditions of professional practice]. Helsinki, Finland: Edita.

Klien, M., & Valk, S. (2008a). Choreography as an aesthetics of change. In J. Gormly (Ed.), *Framemakers: Choreography as an aesthetics of change* (pp. 20–25). Limerick, Ireland: Daghda Dance Company.

Klien, M., & Valk, S. (2008b). Dance as a metaphor for thought. In J. Gormly (Ed.), *Framemakers: Choreography as an aesthetics of change* (pp. 81–90). Limerick, Ireland: Daghda Dance Company.

Klien, M., Valk, S., & Gormly, J. (2008). *The book of recommendations: Choreography as an aesthetics of change.* Limerick, Ireland: Daghda Dance Company.

Koramo, M. (2009). *Taiteen perusopetus 2008: Selvitys taiteen perusopetuksen järjestämisestä lukuvuonna 2007–2008* [Basic education in the arts 2008: A survey on organizing basic education in the arts during academic year 2007–2008]. Retrieved January 30, 2012, from http://www.oph.fi/download/46516_taiteen_perusopetus_2008.pdf.

Lakoff, G., & Johnson, M. (1999). *Philosophy in the flesh: The embodied mind and its challenge to Western thought.* New York: Basic Books.

Lather, P. (1991). Deconstructing/deconstructive inquiry: The politics of knowing and being known. *Educational Theory, 41*(2), 153–173.

Lehikoinen, K. (2004). Choreographies for boys: Masculinism in Finnish dance education. In I. Björnsdóttir (Ed.), *Dance heritage: crossing academia and physicality. Proceedings of the 7th Nordic Forum for Dance Research conference* (pp. 138–145). Reykjavik, Iceland: NOFOD.

Lindqvist, G. (2001). The relationship between dance and play. *Research in Dance Education, 2*(1), 41–52.

Monni, K. (2004). Olemisen poeettinen liike. Tanssin uuden paradigman taidefilosofisia tulkintoja Martin Heideggerin ajattelun valossa sekä taiteellinen työ vuosilta 1996–1999 [The poetic movement of being: Philosophical interpretations of the new paradigm of dance in the light of Martin Heidegger's thinking and the artistic work of years 1996–1999]. Doctoral dissertation: Theatre Academy, Helsinki: Acta Scenica 15.

Mouritsen, F. (1998). Child culture—Play culture. In J. Guldberg, F. Mouritsen & T. K. Marker (Eds.), *Working Paper 2. Child and Youth Culture.* Odense, Denmark: Odense University Printing Office. Retrieved June 13, 2012, from http://static.sdu.dk/mediafiles/Files/Information_til/Studerende_ved_SDU/Din_uddannels e/Kultur_og_formidling/WorkingPapers/02_ChildCulture_PlayCulture%20pdf.pdf.

Novack, C. J. (1990). *Sharing the dance: Contact improvisation and the American culture.* Madison: The University of Wisconsin Press.

Pfeifer, R., & Bongard, J. (2007). *How the body shapes the way we think: A new view of intelligence.* Cambridge, MA: MIT Press.

Preston-Dunlop, V., & Sanchez-Colberg, A. (2002). *Dance and the performative: A choreological perspective—Laban and beyond.* London: Verve Publishing.

Shapiro, S. (2008). Dance in a world of change: A vision for global aesthetics and universal ethics. In S. Shapiro (Ed.), *Dance in a world of change: Examining globalization and cultural differences* (pp. 253–274). Champaign, IL: Human Kinetics.

Stark Smith, N. (2011). About performance and the making of improvised pieces. *Contact Quartely, 36*(1), 29–36.

Stinson, S. W. (1998). Seeking a feminist pedagogy for children's dance. In S. Shapiro (Ed.), *Dance, power and difference: Critical and feminist perspectives on dance education* (pp. 23–47). Champaign, IL: Human Kinetics.

Szkudlarek, T. (1993). *The problem of freedom in postmodern education.* Westport, CT: Bergin & Garvey.

Thelen, E. (2008). Grounded in the world: Developmental origins of the embodied mind. In W. F. Overton, U. Müller, & J. L. Newman (Eds.), *Developmental perspectives on embodiment and consciousness* (pp. 99–129). New York: Lawrence Erlbaum.

Thompson, E. (2007). *Mind in life: Biology, phenomenology and the sciences of mind.* Cambridge, MA: Belknap Press.

Trevarthen, C. (2010). What is it like to be a person who knows nothing? Defining the active intersubjective mind of a newborn human being. In E. Nagy (Ed.), The intersubjective newborn. Special issue of *Infant and Child Development.* Retrieved June 15, 2012, from http://www.psych.uw.edu.pl/lasc/Trevarthen2.pdf.

PART III

Ways of Seeing—Curriculum and Pedagogy

8

DESIGNING WITH PINK TECHNOLOGIES AND BARBIE TRANSMEDIA

Karen E. Wohlwend and Kylie Peppler

In this chapter, we take an expanded view of children's popular media to critically consider the design affordances, constraints, histories, and possibilities in Barbie *transmedia* (Jenkins, 2006; Kinder, 1991), the flows of licensed goods in popular media franchises that range from children's playthings to everyday consumer products. Although children are living in immersive flows of increasingly influential transmedia, in this era of high-stakes tests and narrowing curricula, they rarely have an opportunity at school to play, produce, or critically respond to popular media. Instead, we must look to out-of-school play spaces, like virtual worlds or children's museums, to find rich opportunities for children to play and design their favorite transmedia. These sites can inspire educators to redesign curricula to make them more relevant and vibrant, including increased recognition of child-directed design and play with popular media as crucial literacies for twenty-first century learning. However, it is just as important to be prepared to critically respond to and productively teach with transmedia's problematic texts.

In this chapter, we examine digital play and virtual dressmaking in a dress design game on the Barbie website and the hands-on experience of drawing and making dresses in a Barbie workshop at a children's museum. We compare the available designs in materials and practices across museum and virtual sites to understand how corporate branding practices (e.g., use of colors and image, simulation of high-end fashion and art; expansion of its brand/consumer relationship) shape the possibilities for children's *redesign*—remakings that resist, improvize or otherwise twist expected uses of the material (dolls and avatars, makeup and fashion in doll clothing) and the discursive (e.g., gendered and consumerist identities and practices).

The purpose of this chapter is to examine the nexus of media, play, and design, comparing fashion designs that are made available and child design opportunities that are made possible in *barbiegirls.com* virtual world and in a one-of-a-kind interactive Barbie Design a Dress exhibit at a children's museum. We examine available artifacts and practices in children's design opportunities, critically considering the 'pink technologies' (Marsh, 2010) and other connections across these sites that link Barbie transmedia to discourses of childhood, markets, and femininities. We use critical multimodal analysis (Norris, 2004; Wohlwend, 2011) to consider modes, the culturally-shaped meanings given to sensory aspects of material experience. For example, modes carry cultural meanings embedded in the curve of a vinyl doll's shape or the sheen of its dress fabric. We looked closely at modes to see how children might make and remake gendered stereotypes materially embedded with the pervasive force of glitter. Our critical analysis of Barbie artifacts reveals consumerist and post-feminist discourses (e.g., 'cool girl' and 'avid shopper') that traditionally position girls as susceptible fans who aspire to Barbie's beauty ideal and heterosexual norms (Seiter, 1993; Willett, 2008) or as consuming subjects who only seem to exercise 'choice' through shopping (Cook, 2007). But interestingly, there are also significant learning opportunities for designing and marketing that position girls as producers rather than consumers, rare in children's media. Finally, we consider our findings in the context of classroom practice to better understand how teachers might extend young children's learning through opportunities to design and redesign with children's popular media.

Barbie Transmedia and Design in Children's Cultures

Our work takes a sociocultural perspective on design and redesign that situates material designs in sociocultural contexts (New London Group, 1996). We consider how designs transform designer identities and power relations as well as the meanings, appearance, and uses of physical objects. Popular media pervade all aspects of everyday life through *transmedia* (Jenkins, 2004; Kinder, 1991). Popular transmedia are intertexts (Kinder, 1991) that must be read across products, as each Barbie doll or DVD, T-shirt or toothbrush links to every other product in the franchise and draws upon a semiotic gumbo of shared storylines from commercials, films, books, and video games. This means that an individual artifact cannot be analyzed in isolation but must be investigated for its connections to market histories and trends across diverse products in a global network (Orr, 2009). To complicate the ways particular identities and designs are made available or unavailable in the nexus of commercial branding practices and children's design practices, we situate the doll franchise in the critical literature on popular culture, consumerism, and childhood identified in feminist post-structuralist literature on Barbie, fashion, and post-feminist discourses (McRobbie, 2004; Willett, 2008).

Barbie and the Child Consumer: Gender, Post-Feminism, and Popular Culture

Barbie transmedia foreground consumption practices in two ways: as a franchise with products to be consumed and as a cultural model of a white female consumer to be emulated. Like many other mass-market toys, the Barbie franchise, with its signature hot pink packaging, foregrounds segregated gender categories. Part of Barbie's appeal in children's cultures lies in the exaggerated gender models that also circulate backgrounded whiteness beauty ideals and professional associations.

Early feminist deconstructions found much to critique in the popular doll: from the impossible proportions in the doll's features to an overwhelming emphasis on grooming and physical appearance in consumer products, Barbie transmedia uphold heteronormativity and hyperfeminine expectations for body, actions, and dress (Willett, 2008). Interestingly, these familiar concerns align with recent feminist poststructuralist critiques of post-feminism in media and popular culture. For example, the explosion of lifestyle television and fashion makeovers aligns with a post-feminist belief that women should consult fashion experts in order to buy better (newer and more expensive) clothing in the effort of improving their (body) image with the ostensible goal of pleasing themselves (McRobbie, 2004; Roberts, 2007; Wilk, 2000). McRobbie argues that a pervasive focus on designing and redesigning selves in post-feminist popular culture opens:

> a new, feminized, social space which is defined in terms of status, afflu-
> ence and body image. More generally by these means women are
> subjected to more subtle practices of power directed to winning their
> consent to and approval of a more competitive, consumer-oriented,
> modernized, neo-liberal, meritocracy.
>
> *(McRobbie, 2004, p. 105)*

Like makeovers and other technologies of the self (Foucault, 1988) that invite self-policing, Barbie fashions provide an introduction to post-feminist demands for continual self-improvement that urge women to keep up-to-date with the latest fashion trends by wearing the right clothes and buying the right goods that importantly create renewable cycles of demand and consumption for the fashion industry (McRobbie, 2004; Roberts, 2007; Wilk, 2000).

---

o   In what ways are Barbie brand texts passed down/transmitted?

o   What are the favorite toys in your school/classroom? What brand texts do these toys communicate? How are these texts read and circulated among children?

Barbie and the Child Producer: Design, Pleasure, and Peer Cultures

A Barbie doll is a child-oriented identity text (Carrington, 2003) that emphasizes particular identities over others, through the design of its materials and clothing as well as its marketing messages and film storylines (Wohlwend, 2009). The 'market child' (Sekeres, 2009) describes a fictional character and personality that grounds franchises such as Barbie. Such brand identities represent more than automatic association to a media narrative or product line; rather, marketers develop a brand persona to establish a personal relationship and connection to child consumers who affiliate and identify with a brand rather than merely purchase a product. The Barbie persona is a highly feminized and sexualized model of 'bubblegum, All-American' femininity (Grimes, 2008), but as a toy and an object of play, a doll is also a malleable text (Brougère, 2006) that enables multiple meanings.

Barbie is perhaps the preeminent example of the incorporation of design and redesign opportunities within a single brand—with Barbie's vast collection of interchangeable accessories and outfits, consumers are encouraged (and expected) to reimagine multiple 'looks' and identities for their Barbie dolls. In this regard, Barbie is not a monolithic, universal text for all youth, but is instead a pliable form upon which consumers design and construct their own texts. These multifarious opportunities for designing are therefore vehicles for youth to develop embodied and implicit understandings about design, arts and aesthetics—attributes not commonly fostered in toys intended for boys. For example, combining and recombining Barbie clothes and accessories attune youth to general distinctions in clothing (such as stylistic attributes that make formalwear distinct from casual dress) as well as more nuanced differentiations (such as attention to fabric manipulation, cuffs, zippers, sleeve style, skirt cut and length). Further, multiple varieties of dressing up Barbie dolls sensitize youth to how fashion contexts are forms of identity texts—how certain combinations of clothes create identities that are preppy or urban, etc. Matching what colors and shapes go together, furthermore, presents opportunities for learning about design grammars, such as color theory, shades, and tints. Most often, these sensibilities are not recognized and valued until they reach the professional level, indicated by the high cultural status adults give designers of clothes, furniture, and interiors (e.g., Vera Wang; Charles and Ray Eames; Frank Lloyd Wright).

Beyond these imaginable learning possibilities, widespread dismissing of the value of Barbie play comes at additional costs, given the complicated positioning and potential marginalization that comes with critiquing a toy so strongly associated with girlhood. Kuenz (2000) points out:

> To be frank, I find it strange that no one ever seems to think that repeatedly telling or intimating to kids, particularly girls, that their toys are stupid, or boring, or somehow just wrong, might actually do as much harm as we think the toys do. Has it not occurred to anyone that our

criticism of Barbie or My Little Pony or Strawberry Shortcake not only reproduces the criticism girls already hear all the time about their toys from boys, but repeats it in exactly the same terms: Girls' toys are dumb because they are so girly.

(p. 74)

Instead of positioning the child as a passive consumer of corporate messages, compounded by adult critique, we view children as actively co-constructing the meaning of Barbie, as active participants within peer cultures and global markets. In converged media cultures, Barbie fandom provides a way that children both transgress and reproduce middle-class tastes and adult expectations to establish peer cultures and find pleasure in spaces and things of their own. As a whole, Barbie transmedia offer considerably more options for Barbie in its video storylines and career narratives than, say, Disney Princesses, perhaps due to Mattel's attempts to tap into nostalgic memories of twenty-first century mothers who grew up with Barbie during second wave feminism (Orr, 2009). Further, a focus on innovative fashion design and play in Barbie products provides opportunities inherent in these semiotic practices that enable reconfiguring Barbie artifacts to suit the player/designer's purposes.

Comparing Sites of Design and Redesign

We visited a prominent children's museum to see the Barbie 'Fashion Experience,' a 10,000-square-foot exhibit dedicated to Barbie® and sanctioned by Mattel Corporation. The exhibit, the first of its kind, promoted an array of fashion design experiences, ranging from historical displays showcasing the history of professional and homemade designs for the doll, to dress fabrication and hair styling stations, to runway modeling. Original pieces from famous designers sat alongside stations as inspiration for museum participants as they created their own designs. Throughout our visit, we documented artifacts (i.e., fashions) designed by young participants at the exhibit and analyzed the play and design opportunities throughout the space. One area that was ripe for exploration was the Design a Dress workshop, which offered opportunities for young designers to design and construct 'no sew' Barbie outfits with fabric scraps, trim, buttons, ribbon, sequins, paper, and double-sided tape. The opportunities presented in the workshop offered multiple ways to redesign and personalize the Barbie brand.

We compared the dress designing in the museum space with young girls' digital play and virtual dressmaking in barbiegirls.com, focusing on the *Dazzling Designs* dress shop in barbiegirls.com.[1] Using video gathered once a

---

1 Although barbiegirls.com recently closed, the dress design shop game is still available on www. barbie.com

week for six weeks with girls (ages 5–8) in the computer room of an after-school program (referred to as the 'computer club' throughout this chapter), Karen documented girls' interactions with the computer and with each other, collecting video of barbiegirls.com screenshots from an over-the-shoulder angle and synchronizing these data with video from a second camera that recorded children sitting side-by-side at the computer desks. Dual video captured conversation and peer mediation as children chatted and consulted each other while they played on the popular virtual world website. From the launch of barbiegirls.com in April 2007 until Mattel closed it in June 2011, the virtual world accrued 22 million members (Chmielewski, 2010). Players who registered on the website could design a Barbiegirls online character, visit and decorate her bedroom, chat with other members, try on outfits, and shop at the mall. Some virtual products were freely available to all registered members but many items of clothing, jewelry, or furniture were only available to V.I.P. members who pay a monthly fee for deluxe design choices.

In the Barbie museum exhibit and in barbiegirls.com, we analyzed artifacts in terms of modes, those culturally meaningful, sensory aspects of the environment, including sound, proximity, texture, image and elements of color, shape, (visual) texture, and so on (Norris, 2004). Critical multimodal analysis (Wohlwend, 2011) examines the interaction among modes to see how aspects of activity are foregrounded or backgrounded, looking closely to see how modes support naturalized practices associated with particular situated identities (e.g., foregrounded modes of color in marketing and clothing design which make up a nexus of expected practices for Barbie fans who are expected to be exclusively girls). Foregrounded modes provide a way of tracking discourses through analysis of material artifacts and physical actions by creating a visible and/or tangible trace of prevailing discourses that legitimate (i.e., foreground) some modes, practices, and identities over others in a particular context.

Designing and Making Dresses in a Children's Museum

Within the Barbie 'Fashion Experience' museum exhibit there were many spaces for participants to engage in redesign, ranging from drawing and dress fabrication to runway modeling using life-size Barbie fashions. Of these activities, the most substantive opportunity for redesign came from the Design a Dress workshop, where participants were given materials and guidance toward the aim of designing their own three-dimensional Barbie fashions from scratch. The resulting artifacts from the workshop extended beyond basic wrapping and arranging of fabrics, ribboned belts and the like, to the more fine-grained elements of fashion design—paying attention to seams, cuts, placement of decorative elements (like buttons and trim), form-fitting shapes, and the details of operation. The one-hour workshop, offered twice each day, accommodated roughly 20 participants and occupied 6–8 tables in the exhibit, which were populated with miniature dress-forms, tools and design templates. At the front of the space were bins of one-square-foot fabric squares in a multitude of Barbie brand-approved colors and textiles. Notably, participants ranged across age groups and genders; parents, grandparents, sisters and brothers were all common participants in the workshop and it was not uncommon to find adults designing dresses even in the absence of children.

A facilitator opened the workshop with a brief overview of the design process. Participants, equipped with sheets of paper containing a blank silhouette of a Barbie-proportioned model, were instructed to first sketch a design atop the template using colored pencils (Figures 8.1a, b and c). Fashion magazines were nearby for inspiration, and the workshop facilitator moved between tables for encouragement and to answer questions. Upon completion of a sketch, participants were invited to select one of the fabric squares to be tailored in likeness of their drawn designs. A template was on-hand as a basic guide for a sleeveless, mid-length dress, which participants could modify and extend to

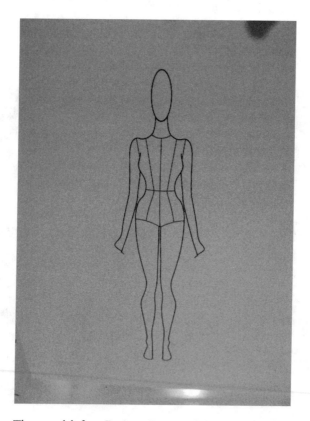

FIGURE 8.1a　Three models from Design a Dress workshop in a museum Barbie exhibit.

FIGURE 8.1b

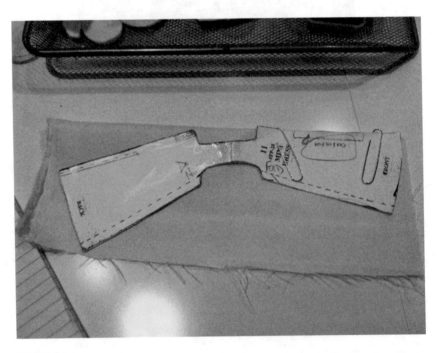

FIGURE 8.1c

align with their drawn designs. Double-sided tape and Velcro were used to suture seams and create fasteners. Finished dresses, which were sized for use on a Barbie doll, could then be taken home. Creating and designing alongside others in the workshop provided participants with a unique perspective into the design process, where young creators could view and compare their designs with others' at each stage of fabrication, as opposed to the more common opportunities to compare works only after completion.

From a smaller range of materials comes a wide margin of variability; indeed, the variety of resulting dresses from each workshop was quite vast (Figures 8.2a and 8.2b). A small tweak to the hemline or neckline in one design could mean the difference between a back-enclosing dress and a front-enclosing jacket. Through these open-ended possibilities of free design, the designer can create multiple identity texts for Barbie, positioning her as a working woman or a Hollywood celebrity through outfits that represent alternative narratives of the designers' choosing. These texts carry with them more of the designers' intentionality and less of what the corporate perspective of Barbie intends for the populace.

FIGURE 8.2a   Range of Barbie designs produced by visitors at museum exhibit.

FIGURE 8.2b

Despite the freedom that free design promotes, all of the raw materials in the workshop, with their chic textiles and feminine colors, lend themselves more easily to designs that promote glamorousness and heteronormativity. For example, there are no one-foot squares of brown corduroy or low-grade denim. In this respect, the aforementioned identity texts that designers could create are somewhat predisposed to fall into those gendered constructions often critiqued by feminist scholars. Furthermore, the objectives of the workshop—the design of a dress, specifically—compound the restrictions placed on any potential identity texts. Surely, the limited design objectives of the workshop are both practical as well as philosophical. Practical, as dressmaking is less complicated than fabricating shirts or pants; philosophical, as Barbie is most famously known for her modeling of dresses more so than other garments.

Barbie is commonly seen as a consumerist-based phenomenon, one that fundamentally promotes the purchasing (and adoption) of upper-middle-class clothing, cars, houses and their accompanying activities and tastes. In contrast, redesign activities allow youth to personally reformulate what Barbie stands for. For instance, the Barbie Basics line (which features dolls in simple black dresses without accessories) empowers young girls to think about designing their own fashions for Barbie, starting with the possibility of not just buying prearranged ensembles. Though less featured in the prominent discourse about Barbie, redesign has been a part of the Barbie culture for generations (Kafai, Peppler, Burke, Moore, & Glosson, 2010), where World War II-era mothers and grandmothers of Barbie owners would design outfits out of scrap fabric, spare buttons and found materials. We imagine opportunities like the Design a Dress workshop as a starting point for today's youth to take up some of the age-old traditions of designing clothing for Barbie, especially in the wake of hugely successful fashion and design media phenomena like the American Bravo Network's *Project Runway*. Barbie represents a range of meanings and potential futures to many girls—she can be blond, Black, young, a software designer or a racecar driver. Fashion creation builds context for this imaginative play and engages girls in fashion design, potentially teaching them grammars important to careers in design, as well as other career paths that value color theory knowledge, fashion and others.

---

o   To what extent is repurposing and remaking commercial Barbie designs possible?

o   What design opportunities and materials are available to children for repurposing and remaking their toys and play materials?

o   What aspects of your students' toys are malleable and open for remaking?

Designing and Selling Dresses in a Virtual World

We turn our attention to design opportunities in Barbie's virtual world, barbie-girls.com. Here, players could design not only clothes but also a Barbiegirl avatar, a digital self perhaps, a proxy that can be maneuvered across screens from closet to bedroom to mall and back again. Designing a personalized avatar was the first step in entering barbiegirls.com. Girls chose from a three-part menu on the avatar screen to select body features and clothing combinations. Avatar design options included 1) body features: skin color, hair color and hairstyle, eye shape and eye color, and mouth shape; 2) clothing choices: styles, patterns, and colors for 'tops, sleeves, and bottoms'; and 3) accessory choices including shoes, jewelry, purses, and hats. Although Barbiegirls players could select items from the three tabs in seemingly endless combinations to create a 'unique look,' the avatars were similar enough to signal a unified Barbiegirl identity and a way of belonging within the Barbie community. Even after designing an avatar, players could return again and again to the avatar screen, creating ongoing opportunities to change clothes, hairstyles, eye and skin color, and so on.

Design opportunities paradoxically incited similar recognition work as players made selections in order to created individual styles and in doing so enacted discourses of competition, individualism, and personal responsibility. At the same time, the designs that girls created were markers of belonging that adhered to peer culture's tastes. Designing clothing and dressing Barbiegirl avatars were among the most popular activities among the five- to eight-year-old girls in the computer club. Girls spent considerable time returning to the avatar design and dress design screens, mixing and remixing elements to try out different looks for their avatars and then calling out to others to 'look at this one,' connecting with other girls in the local peer culture. Players consulted each other on design choices, pointing out which 'bling' or 'decals' were their personal favorites, or simply stating, 'that one's better.'

The emphasis on individual designs that are not *too* individual is consistent with the persona of Barbie as (role) model and fan as fashionista in the brand/consumer relationship created through corporate branding and circulated through Barbie transmedia; the emphasis on personal style is repeated in the online beauty salons and dress shops in barbiegirls and barbie.com. The creation of design by exercising consumer 'choice' in the museum Design a Dress workshop and in barbiegirls.com Dazzling Designs dress shop merges consumerist and post-feminist discourses and identities into inseparable aggregates (e.g., 'avid shopper' and 'cool girl'). Cook (2007) argues that such selections constitute an intransitive empowerment bounded by the parameters of the brand's products and children's ability to consume:

> The universe of options are defined by the brand, by the structure of the promotion or by the context of involvement. Children clearly have more product choices and more commercially relevant choices at their disposal than ever before. If there is a sense of empowerment that is evoked or experienced, [it is] of the intransitive variety as these "options" or "choices" refer back to themselves and encourage identifying the act of making decisions to be coterminous with the semantic universe of a particular product or brand.
>
> *(p. 48)*

But interestingly, there are also numerous learning opportunities in the virtual dress shop for designing and marketing that position girls not only as consumers but as producers and business owners, specifically as designers and retailers, unusual in children's media. The following excerpt from an eight-year-old girl's design play in the Dazzling Designs game demonstrates this producer positioning.

> Simone looks over the black cocktail dress she has just created. She clicks through the confirmation screen, deciding the price of tops, skirts, and dresses relative to the listed cost, which varies depending upon her choices of style, fabric, and ornamentation. Simone adjusts her order, adding and subtracting clothing items until she finally settles on 5 tank tops priced at $24 each, 5 skirts at $26 each, and 5 dresses at $30 each. The shop opens and 45 seconds of hectic selling begins as the shop quickly fills with customers who buy and admire the clothing styles, "I'm lovin' this!". Periodically, Simone re-orders the best-selling items and discounts others until time runs out. A sales summary tallies the number of sales for each design, offering retailing advice about adjusting prices to respond quickly to fluctuations in buyer demand.

---

o   In what way are these doll/clothing texts re-envisioned/redesigned by girl designers?

o   What remakings or replaying of toys are visible among children at play in your school?

Pink Technologies and Playful Pedagogies

In both sites, material and virtual artifacts explicitly target girls as anticipated users through foregrounded design motifs and backgrounded technological uses. Popular culture products intended for young girls are 'often pink and feature icons such as flowers and hearts. "Pink technologies" sometimes offer more limited features than similar hardware aimed at young boys and they shape the construction of technological competence in particular ways' (Marsh, 2010, p. 202). However, we also found affordances in the design technologies that allowed children to make and take dresses, teach peers, create a safe 'girl' space, and learn crafting and retailing skills.

Critical multimodal analysis looks at foregrounded and backgrounded modes to locate tacit aspects of activity to see what constitutes 'natural' and expected ways of participating in a group. In Barbie designs, these back-grounded expectations are the 'non-choices.' The most obvious example is the non-choice body for all avatars with key features made prominent through exaggeration—large eyes, heart-shaped face, slim torso, static frontal view of a model's pose with one arm akimbo—that sends the message that all bodies must conform to the same standard, a pre-decided ideal, fixed and not available for redesign. Similarly, in the Dazzling Designs dress shop and in the museum Design a Dress workshop, it is possible to choose the color, type, patterns, accessories for clothing designs but not the shape of the mannequins that suggest an underlying expectation—the signature Barbie hourglass figure. The modes that are not 'choices' are tacitly given, forming nexus of practice that are naturalized and expected of all members. Nexus are the markers of belonging, in Barbie culture, the use of color, shape, pattern in ways just different enough to be creatively individual but similar enough to be recognizable. Backgrounded modes convey the post-feminist message that there is a desirable body shape, and its posture is designed for maximum display.

> Barbie's transmedia intertextuality revolves around the reproduction and negotiation of 'femininity' as a social construct, more specifically as it relates to notions of "domesticity." . . . Traditional associations between consumption, the domestic sphere and feminine beauty ideals become repositioned in the quasi-public, vicarious space of the virtual beauty salon, where they are not only reproduced within the game's design but also re-enacted by its players.
>
> *(Grimes, 2010, p. 157)*

But the agentic opportunities for redesign are also backgrounded, available through modes, materials, and practices that bring together girls with shared interests. In the two design sites, participants engaged in peer teaching drew upon funds of knowledge (Moll, Amanti, Neff, & Gonzalez, 1992) that linked to craft experiences and sewing skills handed down across generations. Barbie design sites create a space for girls to share their expertise in a girl-privileged space that cordoned off computer spots for girls in the after-school program computer room usually dominated by boys. Importantly, these were safe spaces where girls could play out interests that are often degraded by boys.

Redesigning dolls and their designer/player's identities and imagined futures forms a powerful nexus of semiotic practices that transform the meanings and materials of Barbie products, reconfiguring these artifacts to suit the player/designer's purposes and demonstrating to children in very concrete ways that these media and their messages are malleable. Such 'playful pedagogies' (Buckingham, 2003, p. 317) run on pleasure, emotional attachment, and productive power that allow children to draw on their expertise with familiar resources to make or remix aspects of the design. However, few teachers make space for play or design with popular media, often due to concerns about anticipated objections from administrators or parents or teacher's self-imposed restrictions that popular media is not appropriate for classrooms or even playgrounds (Marsh, 2006).

It may be the case that this resistance would weaken if educators were clearer about the important role such narratives play in children's identity construction. Marginalizing these texts, or banning them outright, serves only to ask of children that they cast off aspects of their identities as they move from home to school.

(Marsh, 2005, p. 39)

Given the learning potential of these sites, how might we incorporate or at least acknowledge the playful pedagogies of transmedia in our classrooms?

Bringing Barbie to School

Recognizing the value in designing and redesigning with Barbie in out-of-school spaces, we echo calls by new literacies and media researchers to infuse literacy curricula with popular transmedia. Dyson (2003), Buckingham (2003), and Marsh (2005), among others, argue that popular media, while problematic, provide a significant site of learning in new literacies and technologies that allow opportunities for productive critique.

We close with suggestions for expanding opportunities for playing and designing with popular transmedia at school:

- **Recognize design and play as literacies.** We need to value children's designs and redesigns as ways to mediate, read, write, reread, rewrite, and artfully reinterpret the world (Wohlwend, Buchholz, Wessel-Powell, Coggin, & Husbye, 2013). This includes adding popular mass-market media toys not only to play centers, but also as resource materials for visual and embodied storytelling, film-making, art classrooms, and art centers in classrooms.
- **Create regular opportunities for child-directed design and play with popular media.** Classrooms need a rich variety of art materials and digital media technologies in addition to picture books, toys, and props for pretending and exploring. In addition to media toys, we should be also making use of the smartphones in children's pockets and backpacks (Shuler, 2009) which provide instant access to intuitive apps and easy-to-operate touchscreens for designing with multimedia.
- **Advocate twenty-first century skills acquisition and new literacies in preference to supporting a minimal curriculum that is focused on traditional basics.** In many classrooms, children's richest learning experiences occur in out-of-school spaces. Bringing transmedia design and play into classrooms allows us to blend out-of-school literacies and art-making with school literacy practices. This approach runs counter to reductive trends that replace the creative production in art-making and play with print literacy skill practice and test preparation.

- **Recognize that play and design allows children to reimagine futures but also opens opportunities to reproduce as well as challenge stereotypes.** We need to avoid dichotomies and mediate children's play and design to help them address exclusionary practices.

References

Brougère, G. (2006). Toy houses: A socio-anthropological approach to analysing objects. *Visual Communication, 5*(1), 5–24.

Buckingham, D. (2003). Media education and the end of the critical consumer. *Harvard Education Review, 73*(3), 309–327.

Carrington, V. (2003). 'I'm in a bad mood. Let's go shopping': Interactive dolls, consumer culture and a 'glocalized' model of literacy. *Journal of Early Childhood Literacy, 3*(1), 83–98.

Chmielewski, D. C. (2010, February 24). Disney hopes kids will take online World of Cars out for a spin, *Los Angeles Times*. Retrieved from http://articles.latimes.com/2010/feb/24/business/la-fi-ct-disney24-2010feb24.

Cook, D. T. (2007). The disempowering empowerment of children's consumer 'choice': Cultural discourses of the child consumer in North America. *Society and Business Review, 2*(1), 37–52.

Dyson, A. H. (2003). *The brothers and sisters learn to write: Popular literacies in childhood and school cultures*. New York: Teachers College Press.

Foucault, M. (1988). Technologies of the self. In L. H. Martin, H. Gutman, & P. H. Hutton (Eds.), *Technologies of the self: A seminar with Michel Foucault* (pp. 16–49). Amherst: University of Massachusetts Press.

Grimes, S. M. (2008). I'm a Barbie Girl, in a BarbieGirls World. *Escapist Magazine*, (165). Retrieved from http://www.escapistmagazine.com/articles/view/issues/issue_165/5187-Im-a-Barbie-Girl-in-a-BarbieGirls-World.

Grimes, S. M. (2010). The digital child at play: How technological, political and commercial rule systems shape children's play in virtual worlds. Unpublished doctoral dissertation, Simon Fraser University, Vancouver, BC, Canada.

Jenkins, H. (2004). The cultural logic of media convergence. *International Journal of Cultural Studies, 7*(1), 33–43.

Jenkins, H. (2006). *Convergence culture: Where old and new media collide*. New York: New York University Press.

Kafai, Y., Peppler, K., Burke, Q., Moore, M., & Glosson, D. (2010). *Fröbel's forgotten gift: Textile construction kits as pathways into play, design and computation*. Published in the proceedings of the 9th International Conference on Interaction Design and Children, Barcelona, Spain.

Kinder, M. (1991). *Playing with power in movies, television, and video games: From Muppet Babies to Teenage Mutant Ninja Turtles*. Berkeley: University of California Press.

Kuenz, J. (2000). Playtime: Toys and the labor of childhood. *Colby Quarterly, 36*(1), 60–76.

Marsh, J. (Ed.). (2005). *Popular culture, new media and digital literacy in early childhood*. New York: RoutledgeFalmer.

Marsh, J. (2006). Popular culture in the literacy curriculum: A Bourdieuan analysis. *Reading Research Quarterly, 41*(2), 160–174.

Marsh, J. (2010). New literacies, old identities: Young girls' experiences of digital literacy at home and school. In C. Jackson, C. Paechter, & E. Reynolds (Eds.), *Girls and education 3–16: Continuing concerns, new agendas* (pp. 197–209). Buckingham: Open University Press.

McRobbie, A. (2004). Notes on 'What Not To Wear' and post-feminist symbolic violence. *The Sociological Review, 52*(2), 97–109.

Moll, L. C., Amanti, C., Neff, D., & Gonzalez, N. (1992). Funds of knowledge for teaching: Using a qualitative approach to connect homes and classrooms. *Theory into Practice, 31*, 132–141.

New London Group. (1996). A pedagogy of multiliteracies: Designing social futures. *Harvard Educational Review, 66*(1), 60–93.

Norris, S. (2004). *Analyzing multimodal interaction: A methodological framework.* London: Routledge.

Orr, L. (2009). 'Difference that is actually sameness mass-reproduced': Barbie joins the princess convergence. *Jeunesse: Young People, Texts, Cultures, 1*(1), 9–30.

Roberts, M. (2007). The fashion police: Governing the self in *What Not to Wear.* In Y. Tasker & D. Negra (Eds.), *Interrogating postfeminism: Gender and the politics of popular culture* (pp. 227–248). Chapel Hill, NC: Duke University Press.

Seiter, E. (1993). *Sold separately: Children and parents in consumer culture.* Piscataway, NJ: Rutgers University Press.

Sekeres, D. C. (2009). The market child and branded fiction: A synergism of children's literature, consumer culture, and new literacies. *Reading Research Quarterly, 44*(4), 399–414.

Shuler, C. (2009). *Pockets of potential: Using mobile technologies to promote children's learning.* New York: The Joan Ganz Cooney Center at Sesame Workshop.

Wilk, R. R. (2000). A critique of desire: Distaste and dislike in consumer behavior. *Consumption, Markets and Culture, 1*(2), 175–196.

Willett, R. (2008). 'What you wear tells a lot about you': Girls dress up online. *Gender and Education, 20*(5), 421–434.

Wohlwend, K. E. (2009). Damsels in discourse: Girls consuming and producing gendered identity texts through Disney Princess play. *Reading Research Quarterly, 44*(1), 57–83.

Wohlwend, K. E. (2011). Mapping modes in children's play and design: An action-oriented approach to critical multimodal analysis. In R. Rogers (Ed.), *An introduction to critical discourse analysis in education* (2nd ed.). Mahwah, NJ: Lawrence Erlbaum.

Wohlwend, K. E., Buchholz, B. A., Wessel-Powell, C., Coggin, L. S., & Husbye, N. E. (2013). *Literacy playshop: New Literacies, popular media, and play in the early childhood classroom.* New York: Teachers College Press.

9

SOCIAL CLASS AND ART ROOM CURRICULUM

Amy Pfeiler-Wunder

This chapter is a partial account of a larger research undertaking, conducted over sixteen weeks in three elementary schools in a single, Midwestern school district serving the children of its 70,000 permanent residents and 30,000 university students. In this chapter, I draw on data from two of the schools—one serving predominantly children living in families in or near poverty and the second serving children whose families are considered upper middle and upper class by the economic standards of the area. There are other important demographics which play a role in my larger findings, including, for example, the rapidly shifting racial and ethnic composition of the area. In this chapter, however, I focus on two issues related to the socioeconomic status (SES) of students' families and how that was reflected in two key ways in the art classrooms I studied.

The first finding I describe involves differences in how the same curriculum is used in the two schools, differences that I argue reflect assumptions about what the children "need" that are grounded in social class discourses. In this sense, we could say that this chapter is a story about *the business of the art room.* I learned about this business during the sixteen weeks I spent in the art rooms not as the teacher, but as an observer. I took field notes and interacted with the students. This was welcomed and encouraged by the teachers. I documented their artwork and some of their dialogue as they worked in the art room. I analyzed and interpreted their artwork and their language as they told stories.

In doing my analyses, I drew from the technique of making the familiar strange (Shklovsky, 1919/1965; cited in Kaomea, 2003). As Kaomea describes, citing Shklovsky, "After we see an object several times, we begin to recognize it. The object is in front of us and we know about it, but we do not see it— hence we cannot say anything significant about it" (p. 15). Analysis and discussion of the data generated in this chapter suggest ways of seeing the work of the art teacher and the artwork of children that go beyond universal ideas of child-hood, developmental age/stage schema for explaining children's interests/artworks, and beyond ideas of children's "natural" capacities for artistry. Rather than questions of "quality", or arguments over the art/craft divide, or the freedom/structure binary, the questions here are around what is produced in the art room. The term "business" suggests the maintenance of opportunities and distinctions related to social class as well as corporate discourses that are currently at play in schools. The "business" hints at a market value language founded on a hierarchical system where individuals in power determine what is given value. The proposal here is that while young children's artwork might be read in any number of ways (e.g., psychology, development, self-expression), it is also possible to read otherwise. Values can also be attributed according to race, gender and, in the stories that follow, through class, or socioeconomic standing. Arts education lends itself to a particular type of "cultural grooming" (Pfeiler-Wunder, in press) which primes a child's understanding of art within particular notions of, for instance, fine art and good art vs. ordinary and everyday.

The second issue I describe calls attention to the familiar and therefore often-unnoticed conversations among the children themselves about money, consumer goods, and expectations for opportunities. One of the most surprising findings of my focused observations was the prevalence not only of talk but also of symbols of wealth in children's artwork. Such talk is particularly enabled in the art room because the ideologies of art curriculum tend to lead to less prescribed and structured curriculum. When discussing a writer's workshop, Anne Haas Dyson (1997) refers to the "official" and "unofficial" curriculum. The official curriculum defines the teacher intentions via her direction of what "should" be going on. The "unofficial" curriculum occurs when students bring into the curriculum their "kid culture", which often demonstrates a disregard for adult norms of what is deemed relevant (Dyson, 1997). Over sixteen weeks, there were numerous conversations, ranging across many topics, and taking many turns. Even the sometimes "simplest" conversation can mark important under-standings of how children were shaping and being shaped by their consumer identity. In the following accounts of some of these conversations, the systems or discourses (Foucault, 1995) that are at play are unpacked. This way of reading the data involved examining the interplay of material culture and the individual experience marked by social construction, and seeing the various "truths" of how class functions in the home, school, and the public arena.

My interest in children's expressions of class and consumer interests began with my own teaching in the art room at my elementary school in this same Midwestern town. A young boy in first grade had boldly drawn floating dollar bills on his "still life" of flowers. He proclaimed, "It's raining money". Reflections on this incident led to a focus on the images and stories that emerged in the art room that concerned issues of class, power and wealth. Later, as part of a larger research undertaking, I arranged to be a "fly on the wall" researcher in other art classrooms in three other schools. In each site, the art room is a space and a time away from the regular "rules" of the classroom. In the art room, it is sometimes possible to hear everyday conversations as children become absorbed with artmaking. In this chapter, I examine the school culture and some of the children's talk that suggested how they viewed themselves, and how children's artmaking was connected with notions of class.

Using a bricolage approach (Kaomea, 2003; Lévi-Strauss, 1966), this chapter sets out the story of the two schools and of two children, Tayshawn and Anson.[1] I place the children and the schools side-by-side for considering the business of art education, and the commodities that are produced and traded in the art room. Finally, some of my own professional history provides the standpoint of the researcher. The teacher's standpoint impacts on children's identities, their artmaking and the art curriculum, and all of these are connected with class issues. As an artist, I work in layers. In my work with collage and bookmaking, I constantly "rest" as glue dries or weights press pages. The narrative I build of these two children, Tayshawn and Anson, is constantly shifting and returning to half thoughts and partially started stories. The stories build in layers, as I shift from one student to the next. In places, I draw connections, and in other places I leave this to the reader to reflect upon. I share my story as teacher and researcher so I might reflect on my own professional identity, and what this means for how I do see and might better see the child and the art room through a lens of class.

Tayshawn and His School

Tayshawn is nine years old and in third grade. He regularly wears black and red tennis shoes, blue jeans, and often a fairly brightly colored shirt covered with designs. His hair is pulled back and twisted into almost shoulder length braids, held with an alternating pattern of white and blue beads. He loves to play video games, often adult rated selections, which he informs me his Chicago father says is "okay". He has an older brother who is fourteen, another who is twelve and one little sister who is two years old. He lives with his mom and her partner, who is the father of Tayshawn's little sister, in a large apartment complex about four miles from school. His mom manages and cares for the family and her partner has a job that Tayshawn was somewhat unclear about. "Sometimes he has to appear at court".

As I drive to Tayshawn's school, I pass the row of simple ranch houses, modestly ranging from around $80,000 to $100,000 in price. They are mostly homes of retirees or are rental homes. The grass is beginning to green up, which gives the neighborhood a refreshed look after the piles of muddy snow have finally disappeared. The neighborhood is adjacent to the historical area of

---

1 Children's names have been changed to pseudonyms.

the city, and has a look reminiscent of the simple suburban homes of the 1950s and 1960s. Just down the street from the school is an older shopping mall. The mall and surrounding area have been recently renovated.

Some children from this working to middle class neighborhood attend Tayshawn's school, but the vast majority of children are from across a busy highway. Crossing the highway yields a different scene: superstores line the highway, mixed with low-income rentals and a neighborhood of low value houses built in the 1970s. The school, which also sits on this side of the highway, is a one-story building that sprawls out along a grassy lawn with a semi-circle drive. Built in the 1970s, the entrance is supported by small metal poles. Aesthetically, the architecture is somewhat non-descript, but the sounds of children on the playground and the presence of a large parking lot easily signal "school yard" to the observer. There are lots of trees and a very large playground features new equipment. The art teacher tells me that initially, the school had difficulty in fundraising for the new play structure. In the end it was the city that helped secure the funding for the project.

During one of my first days at the school, Tayshawn was sitting in the hallway, having been dismissed from the classroom for refusing to do what was required of him. The children in third grade were working on self-portraits and he was not participating. I offered to check on him and stay with him and try to find out what was troubling him. I sat down next to him in the hall and asked: "Would you like to draw for me?" and he began drawing. As he drew, he told me "The Super Bowl[2] is rigged". I was intrigued. Instead of drawing a self-portrait, Tayshawn began by making a large robust looking character, the arms made of sequential bumps, muscles. He informed me the football player he was drawing was Devin Hester, who "moved from the Bears to the New York Giants". A necklace with a small S written on it hung from Hester's neck. Tayshawn informed me it was "a dollar sign". Many of the students in this school actually wore similar large gold chains and medallions. When asked why the dollar sign was in the drawing, he responded, "I like money". In answer to further questions as to why he liked money, he said, "I like to buy things, like Transformers".

According to Tayshawn, his mom moved them to this new, small Midwestern American city because there were a lot of gangs in the large city where he grew up. "They go and shoot around" and "it's not safe to be there". Although his new apartment is several miles away and on the busy highway, his mom walks along an area with few pedestrian sidewalks with his baby sister in the stroller each day to pick him up after school. He informs me that he feels safe in his new home and likes school, the "whole school", "especially PE" (Physical Education).

---

2 The Super Bowl is the American football game, the most important game of each year, that determines the champion team of that year's professional football season.

The teacher and associate at school describe Tayshawn as a "good boy". The teacher spoke about the need to "drill it into him", that he doesn't need to "head down the path of his older brother". The police had picked up his older brother for throwing rocks at an elderly woman's car. As visitor and researcher, I was drawn to Tayshawn and saw him as a really great kid who loved to share stories and enjoyed attention from adults. He came to understand that his artwork could serve as a means to secure my attention. He wants to be "a cop" when he grows up, so he could "chase people down and use taser guns". Tayshawn thought he could be a cop during the day and then play basketball in the evenings. He looks forward to seeing his dad over the summer and spending time in the city.

Tayshawn's school is named after a famous American author, and as you enter the building the focus is around the name of the school. In the hallway, the author's image is painted on the cinder block wall and there are several other art pieces by adults related to this great known author of the nineteenth century. A poster hangs on the door of the art room. It is a close up image of two hands grasped together, one White, one Black, with the caption "Friendship knows no color." Inside the room, a "Chinese motif" engulfs all who enter. There are red Chinese lanterns hanging from the ceiling, and many banners in Chinese calligraphy are hung around the room.

Ms. C, the art teacher, advised that she always begins the year with a "theme" and each grade level works on a project related to a particular culture or time period. She views this strategy as a community building project, providing children with opportunities to view work by other grade levels responding to the same focal point. For example the fifth and sixth graders "googled" to see their name in Chinese and then painted it in calligraphy. Younger students made Chinese lanterns. The third and fourth graders designed and painted kites.

Rules are important at this school and expected behaviors are discussed each time the children come to the art class. There are signs about rules in the art room, as well as signs in the hallways, outlining expected behaviors. For example, hallway signs read:

Responsible

- *Body to self*
- *Follow adult directions*
- *Safe Walking Feet*
- *Clean up after yourself*

Respectful

- *Use manners*
- *Voice level 0 to 1*

Caring

- *Help others in need*
- *Care for property*

The school uses a behavior system to support a positive learning community. In the wider community, the school, which is more racially diverse than many of the schools in the district, has a somewhat negative reputation. The system was titled PBS, or Positive Behavior System. Children are given a ticket for "exhibiting expected behaviors". Then each week the tickets are poured into an empty fish tank on display at the entryway to the school to earn a special school wide reward. The accumulation of tickets is celebrated at certain points throughout the school year. In discussions with the principal and art teacher, the issue of classroom management is frequently referred to as a concern.

Many children and individuals in the community describe the school as the "ghetto school" and 75% of the students receive free and reduced lunch.[3] Many families come from domestic intervention programs, transitional housing or the homeless shelter. The school is a "gap school", meaning it is not meeting certain benchmarks in alignment with No Child Left Behind requirements,[4] so families are allowed to enroll their children at other schools within the district. There is a keen desire from the principal that the community and parents shift from a focus on behaviors to a focus on engaged learning. Enrollments are important to the business of learning, which is a problem for schools constructed and conditioned as lower class in an area with many middle and upper class school options. According to the principal, new visitors often felt that quality learning didn't occur in this space. The business of education here, if based upon the well-maintained dominance of middle class norms and values, seemed to produce a segregated school space.

Anson and His School

A bubbly personality, with a thick somewhat bowl style haircut, Anson is nine years old and in fourth grade. He constantly delights me with his insights, descriptions, and interests. His artwork reflects his descriptive language and his jovial demeanor. His work is colorful, detailed and, more often than not, a narrative accompanies his work. His dress is "clean cut", mostly straight leg jeans or shorts (preferably the kind basketball players wear), jerseys or T-shirts

3 In American public education, the federal "free and reduced lunch" program provides school lunches to low income families. Thus to name the school's percentage of children on free and reduced lunch is how the socioeconomic status of the school's community is marked.

4 See http://www2.ed.gov/nclb/landing.jhtml

from the chain stores in town. Tennis shoes complete the ensemble. One day he wears a jersey with the local university mascot emblazoned on the front, with matching shorts. I ask him if he knows the team player the number six represents, and he says, "It's just a number".

Anson has an older teenage brother, and his mom manages the household, while his dad is the president of an engineering company. Anson informs me his dad would prefer a job that is more fun, and wants to work at a marina. This would be a future "starter off job" for Anson, when he turns fourteen. Beyond his future aspirations, he tells me that Mario and Sonic are his video games of choice and football and soccer are his favorite sports. He has traveled throughout the United States, and enjoys weekends and the summers at his family's lake house to "see people we see every year". Anson is comfortable talking with adults, and often mentions the close friendships of the adult circle his family participates in. They had just moved to a bigger house up the street, because they were surrounded by what his family had described as "life long friends". Beyond friendships, sports and his love of school, Anson has two goals in life: to be an Olympic gold medalist, and to go to Australia. The "School Hall of Fame" showcased in the school's front hall testifies to the accomplishments of its graduates, and is a daily reminder to Anson and his schoolmates that anything is possible.

As I drive to Anson's school, I wind past a few hotels and then down a sloped street past a new golf course. The rolling hillsides and undeveloped areas are a reminder of the corn and soybean hills that dominate the landscape outside the town limits. The hilly countryside adds to the peaceful sense that you are moving away from the heart of the town. Houses range from $500,000 to millions of dollars, and they spot the landscape with manicured lawns. Pre-fabricated children's play structures often stand in the backyards. Here, 5.3% of the students receive free and reduced lunch. In many of the homes, garages are another focal point, met by long cement driveways and occasional basketball hoops. I leave the school around 3:30 on my research days, and often see only one or two children playing in their driveway basketball courts. As documented in Annette Lareau's (2003) *Unequal childhoods*, children here match the middle class and upper middle class practice of sending them to spend afterschool hours in structured activities or attend afterschool programs.

The street to the school is nestled around the golf course and a wooded area. I cross a quaint bridge with tall black streetlights reminiscent of the styles of the 1930s and 1940s. Around a slight bend sits the one-story school. Sprawled against a flat stretch of landscape, the school itself was built in 1998 and is well kept. In the spring, daffodils bloom profusely and large Spiraea bushes spring up in perfectly manicured rows against the streamlined school. The building is made of brown brick with two large atriums forming sloped roofs on the building. In the library, the atrium brings a soft light to the space. The library is quite cozy, even featuring a live bird house.

As you enter the school, a large glass case is filled with children's art. Vibrant creatures and heads stare at you from within the glass. Third grade Oaxacan-inspired creatures are constructed with small wooden boxes, beads, bits of wood and old golf tees. Amusing faces, often with large googley eyes, are also in the case. Children in the sixth grade used a subtraction method, and twisted and formed a block of clay into a person or character of choice. Throughout the school, the halls are adorned with examples of the children's artworks: oil pastel drawings of flowers, obviously inspired by the work of Georgia O'Keefe; Mola paper cuttings that "describe a life experience"; and jungle paintings by children in the second grade. The Mola designs are based on a traditional handcrafted textile piece created by the Kuna women in Panama. Colorful fabrics are layered in a reverse applique technique.

On the door matted and laminated in green construction paper the school mission statement reads:

> [The school is] *committed to serving the whole child. We acknowledge that each student's physical, social, and emotional well being is integral to learning. The individual needs of all unique learners are accepted, fostered and challenged, promoting life long learning in a safe and nurturing environment.*

Next to the art room door, a sign reads:

> *"Art is not a frill; it is an essential language that makes it possible to communicate feelings and ideas words cannot express."*

> (Ernest Boyer)

The art room is well lit and large. Hanging from the ceiling are two large butterfly kites and a puppet. The classroom is dotted with "artifacts" and trinkets from various parts of the world. There is a large carpet where children can gather. Bulletin boards in the room highlight particular lessons students are working on and art is hanging throughout the space. For the first few months of my visits, the large bulletin board in the room featured a winter day scene made through a first and second grade collaboration project.

The art room functions around a philosophy of independence, and "inspirational phrases" are little treasures found throughout the room:

> *"I'll give you independence if you give back responsibility"*
> *"Don't just make it okay—make it great, make it art!"*

Before reading the next section, reflect and respond to the following questions:

> o   What do you think the business of art education should be from your perspective?
> o   What do you think is the business of the art room from the child's perspective?
> o   What do you think is the business of the art room from the teacher's perspective?
> o   What do you think is the business of the art room from the administrator's perspective?

Class and the District Art Education Curriculum

Without question, the experience of entering Anson's school was a more distinctly pleasing aesthetic one than entering Tayshawn's school, and each time I entered either, I felt "class" wash over me. Even my field notes reflect that I wrote more "poetically" about the neighborhood as I approached Anson's school—e.g., "rolling hills". There were both hidden and overt markers of class at each school. The neighborhoods had a distinct difference related to the size and price of homes. Rules and structure were aspects of each school environment but behavior was a larger concern at Tayshawn's school. Even afterschool pick-up from the school was marked by class. At Tayshawn's school, many children walked home with parents who had walked to meet them at the end of the school day. At Anson's school, parent pick-up was highly structured. At the end of the day, a long line of cars snaked around the driveway. Children waited in the gym and an intercom system was used to announce which car was pulling up, so children could get into their car and avoid any weather conditions. The art teacher described this as "valet" parking. Class *was* present.

American schools make little claim of equality of facilities or provisions for students. The *No Child Left Behind* (NCLB) legislation demands the laudable goal of equitable education outcomes for all American children. And yet, NCLB does nothing to address the fact that school funding, which is tied to local taxation and local property values, produces year-per-pupil spending ranging in 2012 from $6,064 in Utah to $18,667 in Washington D.C. (CNN, 2012). Even within districts where funding per student is equal, differences in amounts spent and how money is spent emerge—both as a reflection of parents' abilities to fundraise on behalf of their child's school and because of differences in the status and power of parents and their ability to influence how money is spent. In Anson's school, where the art program was understood as part of the class cultivation of the children, the art room budget was larger than at Tayshawn's school.

One way the district in my study attempted to guarantee that the class and race differences clearly visible from school to school did not produce different outcomes for the children was through the provision of a single curriculum to all schools. The governance of the arts curriculum in the USA rests with state departments of education which define content expectations and assessments. Both schools described in this chapter were legislated to provide art education. The school district then has the responsibility to develop curriculum using the national art standards as guidelines. In this mandated curriculum provided to both schools, the Visual Art Program Philosophy states:

> *The [. . . District] Art Teachers believe that each student is a creating, thinking and responsive being with something significant to contribute to society. Through a variety of art experiences, students build self-esteem, technical skills, perceptual skills and critical thinking skills by making art, studying art and appreciating art. [. . .] We believe that art is essential to each student's education. It confirms the individual's uniqueness, encourages creativity, promotes higher order thinking skills and builds a better understanding of our world.*

The curriculum even specifies themes for organizing content for each year level:

* *Kindergarten: "I am an Artist"*
* *First/Second: "Self/Others"*
* *Third/Fourth: "Community"*
* *Fifth/Sixth: "I know . . . I Wonder"*

In spite of this veneer of sameness, administrative interpretations of curriculum and families' expectations for what it means to "be an artist" play a large part in what happens in the art room. The day-to-day activity is designed, implemented and evaluated by the teacher. The children's experiences are therefore imbued, to varying degrees, with the teacher's professional identity and expectations about how best to adapt the provided curriculum to her perceptions of student needs and experiences. This is another place where class re-enters the picture. Critiques of education approaches highlight that teachers are generally middle class and White (Newman, 1998), and this has a roll-on effect when it comes to arts education. Choices for art appreciation are shaped by teachers' knowledge, leading to the reality that White middle class teachers frequently teach about "dead White males", upholding Eurocentric canons and customs that distance, dislocate, underrepresent, and misrepresent "Others" (Brantlinger, 2003; Kozol, 2001; Spivak, 1988, 1994). Recent calls for more issue based teaching (Gaudelius & Speirs, 2001), have been put forward in response to such critiques. More recently, arts educators in the field have promoted the use of more contemporary artists (Freedman, 2003; Gaudelius & Speirs, 2001), or using Big Ideas (Walker, 2001) connecting ideas to children's lived lives.

Issue based approaches to art education emphasize contemporary art and contemporary issues, and claim teaching as a space where an understanding of difference and desire for equity emerge (Gaudelius & Speirs, 2001). "This approach to content seeks to include diverse perspectives and understandings of the ways in which knowledge is constructed and used. The many knowledges that students bring to the classroom are valued, as are their everyday lives and experiences" (Gaudelius & Speirs, 2001, p. 1–2). This has meant an increase in attending to women artists, multiculturalism education, and a broader view of what defines art. However, it can still be easy to create "Other" as one attends to the complex issues surrounding how art is defined historically, culturally, and philosophically.

In Tayshawn's case, this could possibly mean the difference between his being invited to produce a self-portrait, and an investigation of the body, muscle-building, or even corruption in the Superbowl. However, this is not just a simple matter of switching content, and "freeing up" the curriculum is not without its problems. When the structure of curriculum is less prescribed, more "localised", with the teacher afforded more choices, then the teacher's class and culture might be said to be even more influential. In addition, viewpoints and expectations of artmaking differ according to school cultures, which in part are shaped by parental expectations. Even the liberal middle classes manifest far more respect for the "fidelities of tradition" than they believe, or at least claim (Olssen, 2005). In the scenario previously described, Tayshawn is asked to make a self-portrait, but he prefers to draw his favorite football player, and ponder on whether the Super Bowl is being "rigged". When it comes to the children, their education might be aimed at not so much critically informing their minds, or engaging in reflective practice but rather, "protecting" their minds and adopting "appropriate" middle class values (Olssen, 2005, 374–375). A form of cultural grooming is often entrenched in the art curriculum, and partly due to the influence of middle and upper middle class families, who understand "fine art" as hand in hand with notions of what is "good" and "valuable". Tayshawn struggles with this. He wants to be a cop by day, and a basketball player at night.

Curriculum and Class

Central to the "educational enterprise" is the curriculum used in "defining the forms of thinking that are likely to be promoted in the school" (Eisner, 2002, p. 148). Curriculum often functions in order to maintain the status quo. In both Anson's school and Tayshawn's, differences in administrators', teachers', and families' viewpoints of art and the goals of the art classroom can be seen as closely related to cultivating particular class values. The following observations go some way to explaining the similarities and the differences apparent in the two different schools, which might be explained by class.

At Anson's school, the principal highlighted that families held a particular viewpoint of what art education and art products should look like. Parents viewed art as a product and expected a specified purpose, rather than seeing art as a means for expression. The parents expected that some projects in the art room were made to support the school—for example, making cards for a fundraiser during the holiday time. The principal felt parents placed a high level of emphasis on academics. Art is appreciated, but not the main focus. They want their children to be high achievers in all subject matter and art is seen as something to be achieved. The art teacher noted the strong attendance at the annual art show, and how parents enjoyed matted and framed artwork along with descriptions of projects on the backs of each piece.

In contrast, the administrator at Tayshawn's school, Ms. H, put emphasis on the individual child, cautioning against a view that suggested socioeconomic status was strictly the cause of difference between outcomes in art education for students at her school and other district schools. When discussing the possibilities for home visits due to low attendance, Ms. H insisted that homes were not to be framed as "deficit". She saw this as illustrative of non-cultural bias. This focus on the individual child, while often seen as aligned to progressive education, in this school yielded concerns with behaviors as a major issue. The positive behavior system already accepted and in use by teachers (if not family members) in Tayshawn's school would eventually be mandated to be implemented district wide. Anson's art teacher expressed concern over this universal mandate, since she felt the students in Anson's school "knew how to behave in school" because the expectations in place at home matched what was expected at school.

In Tayshawn's art classroom, one of Ms. C's struggles was implementing the curriculum due to what she saw as time constraints often pushing in on the projects. She commented on the students' levels of engagement in the activity and how that slowed the work down. Ms. C also taught art at another school, which she compared with Tayshawn's school, and she saw a number of differences. When asked, "Do you see a difference in how you present lessons, in outcomes?" she was definite that she "noticed different outcomes", and firstly she referred to the children:

> I do see a difference, I think at both schools the kids love art and they know to do their best work . . . I think with more life experience, my kids at my other school having more opportunity to travel with their family . . . makes a difference.

These two responses demonstrate the conflicting discourses and discomfort the teacher and administrator felt over describing the differences they saw between the children at Tayshawn's school and in other schools in the district. In the first instance, the teacher locates the problem in the children's locus of control. She qualifies this by assuring me that a love of art is common to all children, and she goes on to assert that it is the differences in the children's life experiences that lead to different outcomes of arts education.

Ms. C did not initially mention differences in pedagogy as a potential factor in the different experiences and outcomes in the two schools. However, her pedagogies were different at her two schools. When pressed, Ms. C described that at Tayshawn's school, unlike her other school, she did not put a firm due date for projects. She preferred an open timeline because it often took her more time to present lessons, or for students to complete the project.

> *Well different because of a number of reasons, different* [at Tayshawn's School] *because of behaviors, difference because of actual abilities. If I give a big packet on Egyptian life, it might take longer, we might take turns reading . . . sometimes I will scale a lesson back. It is not because I have different expectations but sometimes reading levels . . . it's just different.*

So here, it is the teacher's expectations that are different. Because of what she has come to know about behavior and student abilities, she presents lessons differently, and has different expectations for outcomes. She allows more time for each project, because of disruptions, and what she judges as ability levels, and overall experiences of the children. Broader school policies included smaller class sizes to accommodate the high needs of students and a more transient population. These also have direct impact on how much is covered in a given class period.

Ms. C struggles to explain "difference" and appears to baulk at recognizing or naming social class as a possible explanation. We discuss the impact of socio-economic status, and I ask if any considerations are given to this when planning the curriculum. Ms. C is most offended by the smaller budget for Tayshawn's school when compared to other schools in the district and feels her students deserved the same opportunities, if not more, than the children in other schools who had more advantages. She says she doesn't feel she considers socioeco-nomic status in her teaching, but her other responses seem to highlight that SES does indeed impact her decision-making. This is not necessarily a conscious choice. However, her adaptation to the curriculum illustrates conscious choices in meeting the needs of her students.

Even though the mandated curriculum suggested project outcomes and prescribes to the level of naming the "focus" for each year level, the curriculums unfolded quite differently. For example, Anson's school has a generous budget for art education while Tayshawn's does not. The budget discrepancies created limitations for achieving the curriculum and expected student outcomes. The principals from each school value the philosophy of the art teacher and are supportive of the program but their expressed reasons for supporting the arts differ. At Anson's school, the principal referred to the parents' expectations and outlined a particular viewpoint that she attributed to families—how they thought art education and art products should look. These families expected success in all areas of academics. Here, art served as an indicator of academic success, acted as a fundraiser, and was something for the children to experience.

In Tayshawn's school, art seemed connected with concerns over behaviors, and time constraints and demands. Here it seemed that art was appreciated in the school, but it was the perception of school personnel that there were so many other aspects competing for the parents' time and resources, that art was not a strong focus for the families. In Tayshawn's school, toy objects, beads, and other trinkets were presented as rewards. In spite of common belief that the art room is a space that is different, that may enable some freedoms and affordances not available elsewhere in the school environment, in Tayshawn's school the art room was like the other school spaces in at least this regard—it was a space where market value was given to "good behavior" through a rewards system for behavior management.

○ Describe your school culture through the lens of class. Do you feel your school maintains a middle class ideology? How could this be disrupted?

○ What language do you use when talking about visual art? Do you give credit to fine art, craft, outsider art, and folk art . . .?

Consumed . . . Children's Talk, Class and Consumerism

Balls of brightly colored yarn were strewn in boxes across the floor at Anson's school. Categorized by hues, the students would meander from their tables to select a color from the monochromatically organized boxes. Students were busy creating a double-sided woven pattern on a cardboard loom. The warp and wefts of intricate relationship would eventually form a pouch. Weaving pouches was outlined in the curriculum under "Third Grade" or "Year #1 for 3rd/4th". Year #1 indicated the suggested activities if it was a third and fourth grade combination classroom. The curriculum suggested a focus on the art of the Navajo by creating woven pouches. These activities were "suggested" and it was common practice for individual art teachers to create their own adaptations within the curriculum. During the creation of the weavings, I was curious to learn what the children might place in their pouches. In what seems to be a simple exchange about pleasures in consumerism, my attention was drawn to the signs and symbols of wealth and power as objects were used as markers of identity, as the children chatted while making their art task.

When asked what might be contained in their pouches, some responded "rocks", others said "cell phones", "iPods" or "spare change". I asked what they might buy with the spare change, and they simultaneously responded: "CANDY!!" This started an animated conversation:

Heather: My mom makes me buy things I want but we don't need.

Annabel: That stinks.

Anson: I get things on special occasions, like birthdays, but then sometimes every fourth month my mom buys me a random thing like Legos . . . I am literally obsessed with Legos.

Laurie: Me too.

 Laurie goes on to describe the extensive Lego neighborhood she has created in her basement and how she finds further inspiration by accessing the lego.com website, and watches animated Lego comics.

Anson: I want to be an architect when I grow up. It all started from Legos, probably when I was two.

While making the textile pouches, using one of the oldest technologies for weaving, the children's conversation made an interesting contradiction. They are part of a "plugged in" society of instant information and access through YouTube, radio, music and podcasts on a regular basis. A bleak reading of this conversation sees the children as reproducing the adult world of consumerism, and in turn, this consumer society produces children "as what the whole has made them" (Horkheimer & Adorno, 2002, p. 101). The consumer is the duped buyer in light of modern technologies.

> The power of industrial society is imprinted on people once and for all. The products of the culture industry are such that they can be alertly consumed even in a state of distraction. (Horkheimer & Adorno, 2002, p.101)

However, erasure of human capacity might not be the only way to read the children's talk. Certainly, with "Google access", the need to remember the name of a once popular song, or directions to the airport, has become practically obsolete. At the same time, though, we might see new possibilities due to the easy availability of information. Laurie's connection to information might produce an individual with more power, able to click on a button and be inspired with design ideas from lego.com. Or the site might work against the aims of quality arts education, limiting performance and innovation from the individual. Even if the children were "playing" with the pouches, and designing them for their operation of cell phones from their observation of the adult world, it is possible to give credit to the creative thinking of children, and see them as producing "their own small world of things within the greater one" (Benjamin, 1978, p. 69).

As I continued to observe the various children and their activities and interactions in the art rooms, I wondered about the significance of the objects that "consumed" many of their lives. One day a conversation about Anson's grandmother sparked this conversation:

Grace: *My grandma is always buying me things I really don't know what to do with!*

Anson: *Do you believe in Santa Claus?*

Grace: *No, not really anymore.*

Anson: *My mom has kind of messed things up, [but] I pretend to believe so she gives me stuff!*

Grace: *You will never believe what my grandma bought me . . . a Barbie blanket.*

Julie: *Oh, my gosh!*

Anson: *This year I am only asking for a couple of things . . . scooter, DSI, or a Xbox5 . . . oh, yeah and a lava lamp and air soft shot gun.*

Mike: *They'll only bruise you but not kill you . . .*

Jennifer: *I don't really ask for things, my mom just gets me things.*

Things did seem important, both here at Anson's school, as well as at Tayshawn's. For all the children, money was delightful, not only for what it could buy, but also for what they *imagined* it could buy. Even when Anson is wanting only a "couple of things," the short-list would tally to an expensive bill. These objects also seemed to qualify as status symbols. In market terms, some are worth more or less in the social and economic rewards they bring, (e.g., the Barbie blanket) or, in Bourdieu's theories of social capital, some objects "also take on their own value within local social settings" (Lindqvist & Seitz, 2008, p. 151). The Barbie blanket was labeled as absurd against the more grown up toys of video games and play guns. Individuals mark themselves by their buying power and the classroom is not exempt. As the children discussed their toys or made references to clothes, often these could be read as simply conversations around their relationship to objects and things in their lives.

The social and relational spaces of school and home both intersect and maintain a particular notion of class. At Anson's school, conversations in the art room were regularly about the status of objects in children's lives. The children's talk often centered around their understanding of wealth, as understood in their home. Excess was a concern. "My grandma is always buying me things I really don't know what to do with!" Toys dominated their discussions, and could be understood as indicators of middle class values of how children should spend their time—such as constructing Lego cities and having a familiarity with technology.

In Tayshawn's school, children would adorn themselves with the beads gained for good behavior as they left the art room, and they were a mark of status and value. Status was also demonstrated through the material culture of the children's clothes. They marked themselves through expensive tennis shoes and often a variety of gold necklaces. Money symbols were also additions to artwork, in the form of necklaces. Tayshawn's favorite objects included video games and X-men characters, which found their way symbolically transferred in his artwork. He and the other children talked simultaneously about the lack of things they had, and their desires, such as cars. Children wanting or desiring things appeared to be present, regardless of class standing—but from their casual conversations it was easy to understand that what they *received* was different.

Desires to be part of organized activities were different for Tayshawn than in Anson's case. When Tayshawn carefully carved his self-portrait into his clay, he "dressed" himself with a basketball uniform. When I asked if he played on a team, he said "Not yet, but I have been practicing". I asked if he was part of the afterschool program for basketball. He told me he had attended last year, but then his parents said it cost hundreds of dollars and took him out of the program. Although I can't generalize on the opportunities for outside activities, I did know from conversation with the art teacher that the majority of Tayshawn's "outside" school experiences occurred because the paraeducator treated him to these events (such as trips to the races, McDonald's, etc.).

Lareau (2003) discusses how in middle class families, it is common for parents to "follow up on children's interests, often by enrolling them in organized activities" (p. 82). As she further describes, "Parental involvement is a key component of the child-rearing strategy of concerted cultivation. Lareau described concerted cultivation as a style of parenting that involves deliberate attempts to foster children's talents, interests, and tastes through deliberately incorporating organized activities such as sports or arts programs. One result of concerted cultivation is that middle class children gain a sense of being "*entitled* to have adults focus on the minute details of their lives" (p. 82). Additionally, children expect adults to listen to their opinions and desires. When Anson was given a part he did not like in a Christmas play, he was allowed by his parents to choose not to participate.

Lareau describes the daily life of children from poor and working class families as typified by a much different parent–child relationship. Parents' words are taken as final and children "do not pressure adults to cater to their wishes" (Lareau, 2003, p. 83). It seemed, in Tayshawn's nonchalant response to my questions regarding afterschool activities, that *not participating* in some organized activity was his "normal". Instead of a summer filled with numerous camps or vacations mentioned by many of the children in Anson's school, Tayshawn looked forward to visiting his father and seeing the individuals his father hung out with.

The signs and symbols pertaining to money and wealth in the art room are both fluid and powerful. In both schools, a type of social capital operated in shared values systems, and the currency was in the objects they possessed. For the children in Anson's school, objects were highly valued and expensive and worked to establish their lifestyle within the one shared class status. At Tayshawn's school, the value of money was afforded through such things as clothing, expensive tennis shoes, and personal adornment, but this was in contrast to their home life. Their homes often lacked technology, food, and transportation options. In both these schools, self-expression through clothing might be read as disrupting a particular way of seeing class, or establishing it.

○ What type of toys and objects do children in your classroom value? Are these valued by monetary worth or by status among the children, despite market value?

○ How does class mark toys?

○ How might toys construct a notion of the child as middle class? Prestigious? Wealthy? Powerful? Poor?

Amy, the Teacher—My Story

Particular situations "prime" us for acting out particular ways of being (Gladwell, 2005). How do educational spaces such as the art room prime a child to maintain particular class status? The conversations about "things" show the "business" of education, specifically how children mark and are marked through their socioeconomic status (SES), and how the art room can sit in the intersection of social spaces and the relationships which mark children's experiences in school. This entanglement occurs through the intersection of school, home, family, teacher, community, society and culture. These social and relational spaces act in forms of replication and tension. Replication of class notions can occur when middle class ideals are maintained, at the points of intersection of school and the relational spaces surrounding the school experience. Tensions might arise when this predominant system is pushed against. The children are marked by class. What of their teachers?

Historically, the goal of some curriculum writers has been to make the curriculum "teacher-proof" (e.g., Montessori). In this account of two schools in a single district, both are governed by the same curriculum which seeks to institute the same expectations and outcomes for all children. In the many ways teachers can position the child artist, which ones does the teacher knowingly and not so knowingly use to describe her/his students? How does the governance (surveillance by parents, administrations, other teachers) silence the interests and voices of students or direct the work of the art teacher? How does the teacher's identity, including class, change or affect the way students are viewed? Foucault's discussions of the self draw attention to the importance of dissecting one's own lived life to understand the conception of self. Care of the self has two purposes, to bring about and maintain greater freedom for the individual and to give due concern and respect to others by attending to their needs (Infinito, 2003). This overcomes the myth of locating our true selves, because we are in constant formation.

"Copy it," stated my second grade teacher. Staring at me was Renoir's *Girl with a Watering Can*. The little girl with golden blonde hair was mesmerizing. She was adorned in a pristine blue dress lined with lace and accentuated by bright gold buttons, and I remember a feeling of bliss as I observed the image by Renoir. Copying a "real" artist felt authentic, in comparison with the mimeographed worksheets that filled my school lessons. I felt exposed to the "finer things" of life.

At the same time, I wondered what this pristine little girl possibly had in common with how I viewed myself—a somewhat geeky, good-humored farm girl in my Catholic school uniform. I couldn't wait to emerge from the confines of the school bus and change into my hand-me-down play clothes in order to explore the 380-acre playground of my family's farm. In retrospect, I believe there was a disconnect between the image and my experience. I now read the use of the fine art reproduction and assignment a form of "cultural grooming" (Pfeiler-Wunder, in press), a notion and belief that the "natural" child artist should be exposed to the "finer things of life". Surely, as a young farm girl, my experiences with fine art and music were limited. It is quite possible that the teacher felt my ideas and experiences of aesthetic appreciation were lacking. These images of the great masters and fine art prints had worked as a form of "cultural grooming" (Pfeiler-Wunder, in press), and I suspect may have discounted my own experience related to the visual arts as a child of working class parents. The art of my life was experienced through the landscape of Middle America; rolling green hills, patchwork quilting, and folk art.

My research into the art classroom is driven by many curiosities—and these curiosities are filtered through my childhood experience of class. Class is a sensitive topic. Growing up in a working class family affects my teaching and how I view my students. Particular to this chapter is my curiosity about how a common curriculum becomes interpreted in school cultures, when viewed through the lens of class. In the art room, professional identity impacts on curriculum, and is subject to the expectations of others (families, teachers, administrators), and can shape and be shaped by curricular tools.

In the following conversation a simple mark made by the teacher took on new meaning in the culture of the art room. As the class at Anson's school was finishing for the day, one student asked me to write on the back of the loom her teacher's initials, SH, which served to identify which class the work belonged to. The warp and weft threads had consumed a large area of the cardboard and she was finding it difficult to write the initials. Glancing at my writing:

Amelia remarked: I like your money symbol.
Amy: *Money symbol?*

> *When I wrote the SH I must have melded them together and it appeared to be a dollar sign.*

Amy: *Why do you like my money symbol?*

Amelia: *Because it is money.*

> *Several students joined in the conversation at this point.*
> *"She likes money".*
> *"She was the mayor of our class and her dad likes money. He is a banker."*

As the dialogue continued, I observed how money and the conversations surrounding it acted as a form of cultural capital. The ideas surrounding money frequently emerged in children's conversation, like the time I routinely asked Riley what he wanted to be when he grew up. This seemingly basic question elaborated into a lively discussion and debate between the students at the table.

Joe: *Did you know the senate is trying to close the banks?*

Jane: *I'm pretty sure some people want the government to control the banks which is sort of weird.*

Jill: *Why?*

Janet: *But the government is smarter than the banks.*

For me, listening to young children discussing politics was fascinating. At the dinner table of my childhood, conversation revolved around the events of the day and politics were never discussed. A "normal" conversation or even the absence of conversation[5] in the art room, then, can mark and be marked by class, relating to the children and the teacher. So too these matters can shape the curriculum. According to the findings in Brantlinger's (2003) research, teachers who came from working class backgrounds often focused less on the rigors of the academics and more on the social and moral agency of their students. Teachers of affluent background often promulgated a more "academic" agenda, continuing a particular status quo and hierarchy in social class. Curriculum is not teacher proof, and "children learn to perform the academic knowledge imparted by their teachers who are also performing it. Exclusively school curricula and the teacher's lesson determine what they say and do" (Garoian, 2002, p. 122).

---

5 In this chapter, there is no documentation of direct conversations in Tayshawn's classroom, for a number of reasons. First and foremost only two forms were returned from parents, giving consent for me to include these children as participants in my research undertaking. (According to the teacher, it was often difficult to collect forms returned from parents.) In addition, much of my time with Tayshawn was spent one-on-one, since he was often sent to work alone because of his behavior.

- o   Tell the story of how you became an art educator.
- o   Now, critically reflect on the language you used to describe this experience.
- o   How does the language you used position yourself in relationship to your students? To yourself?

The Final Layer: Reflections . . .

When I walked into the art classrooms in Tayshawn's and Anson's schools there were many similarities. The rooms were filled with interesting art objects including artifacts from other cultures. Shelves housed paper, markers, scissors, glue, and many other materials indicative of artmaking. The sounds of children filled the rooms and pictures of children's art were on display in the hallways and art room. At Tayshawn's school, the caterpillar images by Kindergarten children and abstract cray pas line drawings shape ideas of what is aesthetically pleasing, "typical and normal" child art. Across the district, Anson's cut paper mola and weaving, also aesthetically pleasing, colorful, and delightful to observe, do the same work, and say as much about "culture" or "product" as they do about "children".

In this chapter, I propose that these images cannot be fully understood, nor fully appreciated, until we consider the impact of class on the culture of the school and how that acts upon the artmaking of children. When I first began spending my days visiting the schools, I found it difficult to put into words the ways in which class was present in the school cultures. I felt it wash over me when I entered the school, but I was reluctant to go along with the stereotypes that were already floated within the community on the "reputation" of particular schools. But class was present. Not only in story, but also in the infrastructure of schools, the art teachers' relationship to schools, and how the art curriculum was implemented. Class also acted as a force shaping my reading of the schools, and my abilities to recognize and articulate differences.

The children in these art rooms are traversing boundaries every day. They do this through the signs and symbols they employ in their work, the meaning of objects (including toys) in their daily lives, and the complexities of language learned and exchanged within their (childhood) cultures—and these boundaries are crossed in both the *official* and *unofficial* work of the curriculum (Dyson, 1997). As children negotiate their social and relational spaces, my questions are about the business of art education, and how class shapes the ways in which school culture works.

This chapter provides partial accounts of two children, Tayshawn and Anson, and their school experience, specifically examining their interactions with the unfolding art curriculum. Through listening closely to their talk amid other children's voices, it is possible to notice how the impact of class intersects with school culture in the art room. The use of narrative as a "fundamental process of human research and development" (Rolling, 2010, p. 6) has enabled a "*re-search*" (Wilson, in Rolling, 2010, p. 6), to look again at art and how it works.

Class is sometimes the "silent" topic in education. Informed dialogue situated around the experiences of others, combined with a careful reflection of one's own positioning, can trouble "previously conceived facts and beliefs" (Freedman, 2007, p. 216), shedding new light on practices that have become taken-for-granted. Social and relational spaces can intersect and tangle with class, and it is important to take into account how this can affect how teachers view children, how children see themselves, and the ways in which curriculum maintains or pushes on these spaces.

The stories and vignettes collected in this chapter illuminate the children's conversations about their wants and needs while they were working in an art class. Their dialogue and behaviors in the art room highlighted how class and family set the stage for particular understandings of power and wealth. In these young children, money was understood both physically and psychologically. It is not always easy for teachers to critically reflect on their own professional identities and particularly how these are tied to class. Equally, it is not always easy to dissect the everyday and mundane conversations which unfold in the art room. However, through examination of what feels "ordinary", it becomes possible to attend to place, language, story and the types of identities that are shared and hidden within sites such as the art room, and through stories.

There are those who will deny the workings of class in so called democratic schools and classrooms. The notion of education as a child's means to create a sense of autonomous self (see Olssen, 2005), to *become* an individual who has freedom to actively engage in the world, is understood in many countries as an important goal to strive for. In the art room, it is appealing to view the space as a site that celebrates self-expression, as being more centered on becoming an autonomous self. But these notions do not stand up to close scrutiny. In this chapter, the stories go some way to capturing ways in which class acts, not only on children, but, perhaps more importantly, on our own professional identities (our own sense of an autonomous self as educators) and on how we view the school and the child.

References

Benjamin, W. (1978). One way street (selection). In P. Demetz (Ed.), *Walter Benjamin: Essays, aphorisms, autobiographical writings* (pp. 6–96). New York: Schocken Books.

Brantlinger, E. (2003). *Dividing class: How the middle class negotiates and rationalizes school advantage.* New York: RoutledgeFalmer.

CNN (2012, June 21). Which places spent the most per student on education? CNN. http://Schoolsofthought.blogs.cnn.com/2012/06/21/which-places-spent-most-per-student-on-education/

Dyson, A. H. (1997). *Writing superheroes: Contemporary childhood, popular culture, classroom literacy.* New York: Teachers College Press.

Eisner, E. (2002). *Arts and the creation of mind*. New Haven, CT: Yale College Press.

Foucault, M. (1995). *Discipline and punish: The birth of the prison* (A. Sheridan, Trans., 1977). New York: Vintage Books.

Freedman, K. (2003). *Teaching visual culture: Curriculum, aesthetics and the social life of art*. New York: Teachers College Press.

Freedman, K. (2007). Artmaking/troublemaking: Creativity, policy, and leadership in art education. *Studies in Art Education, 48*(2), 204–217.

Garoian, C. (2002). Children performing the art of identity. In Y. Gaudelius & P. Speirs (Eds.), *Contemporary issues in art education* (pp. 119–129). Upper Saddle River, NJ: Prentice Hall.

Gaudelius, Y., & Speirs, P. (2001). *Contemporary issues in art education*. Reston, VA: National Art Education Association.

Gladwell, M. (2005). *Blink*. New York & Boston: Little Brown.

Horkheimer, M., & Adorno, T. W. (2002). *Dialetic of enlightenment*. Stanford, CA: Stanford University Press.

Infinito, J. (2003). Ethical self-formation: A look at the later Foucault. *Education Theory, 53*(2), 155–171.

Kaomea, J. (2003). Reading erasures and making the familiar strange: Defamiliarizing methods for research in formerly colonized and historically oppressed communities. *Educational Researcher, 32*(2), 14–25.

Kozol, J. (2001). *Ordinary resurrections: Children in the years of hope*. New York: HarperCollins.

Lareau, A. (2003). *Unequal childhoods: Class, race and family life*. Berkeley: University of California Press.

Lévi-Strauss, C. (1966). *The savage mind*. Chicago: University of Chicago Press.

Lindqvist, J., & Seitz, D. (2008). *The elements of literacy*. New York: Longman.

Newman, K. (1998). *Falling from grace: The experience of downward mobility in the American middle class*. New York: Vintage.

Olssen, M. (2005). Foucault, educational research and the issue of autonomy. *Educational Philosophy and Theory, 37*(3), 365–387.

Pfeiler-Wunder, A. (in press). Understanding and using case study informed by auto-ethnography. In M. Buffington & S. Wilson McCay (Eds.), *Practice theory: Seeing the power of teacher researchers*. Reston, VA: The National Art Education Association.

Rolling, J. H. (2010). Art education at the turn of the tide: The utility of narrative in curriculum-making and education research. *Art Education, 63*(3), 6–12.

Spivak, G. C. (1988). Can the subaltern speak? In C. Nelson & L. Grossberg (Eds.), *Marxism and the interpretation of culture* (pp. 271–313). Urbana: University of Illinois Press.

Spivak, G. C. (1994). Bonding in difference. In A. Arteaga (Ed.), *An other tongue: Nation and ethnicity in the linguistic borderlands*. Durham, NC: Duke University Press.

Walker, S. (2001). Publications *Teaching meaning in artmaking*. Worcester, MA: Davis.

10

CHILDREN'S CONCERT EXPERIENCE

An Intercultural Approach

Jan Sverre Knudsen

Introduction

The gym of the small rural school in south-western Norway is packed with children. Indian Kathak dancer Mahua Shankar, in a bright orange and yellow traditional dress, is pirouetting across the floor to the accompaniment of Mitilesh Kumar's whirling tabla beats. As she stops turning and starts to imitate the drum beats by pounding the floor with her own bare feet, something happens among the younger children seated on mats and low benches at the front of the audience. A pair of small feet start tapping the floor, immediately followed by others, and in a matter of seconds, foot-tapping, stepping and waving has spread to all the first and second graders in the front rows. While a couple of the teachers seem to be on the verge of interrupting the spontaneous reaction, the performers make encouraging nods and gestures, inspiring the children to continue as the performance builds up to a chaotic climax of sound and movement.

The description above is based on an observation from one of many school concerts with professional Indian musicians in rural areas in the county of Rogaland, Norway. For six years, selected public schools and municipal music schools in the region have taken part in a comprehensive cultural interchange program involving the state-funded organization Concerts Norway, various public schools and music schools in the area, and the Indian school concert promoter SPIC MACAY (Society for the Promotion of Indian Classical Music Amongst Children and Youth). The program also involves sending Norwegian musicians to India to play concerts of various genres for Indian schoolchildren.

The aim of this chapter is two-fold. First, it seeks to explore some key issues regarding young children's experiences of and reactions to the concert event. What associations do they make and how do they respond? How should we understand their reactions? Are there any particular considerations that should be taken into account when presenting children with music that they have no previous knowledge of? Second, the chapter raises issues concerning concert promotion in view of the prevailing ideologies of the cooperating organizations. The concluding discussion departs from the understanding that these two areas are intimately connected, that is, that successful concert promotion to young children in an intercultural setting depends both on an awareness of children's meaning-making strategies and on an understanding of ideological aims, knowledge and practices.

The Concert Experience

The school concert may be understood as a "ritual in social space" (Small, 1995, 1998). Although the concert experience itself is always strictly personal and therefore can be infinitely varied, affect and meaning are constructed socially and reflexively through various aspects of the ritual and the discourses that surround it. School concerts involve practical organization and preparations, as well as artistic and educational negotiations on various levels, ranging from discussions concerning the choice of musicians and their actions on stage to the ways in which the teachers prepare children by "tuning them in" to the concert event. All of these factors influence the concert ritual and the individual experience of every child attending the performance.

Music exists through social construction and creates meaning through social interpretation. Experiencing any music event initiates a series of *interpretive moves*: categorizations, evaluations, associations, imagery and reflections; consciously or unconsciously linking music to our previous experience (Keil & Feld, 1994). Interpretive moves are socially and culturally connected. After hearing only a few bars of music we instantly locate it within the framework of our cultural soundscape, placing it in relation to our concepts and categories as well as to our personal preferences and conceptions of value. This process is basically what renders our experience of sounds intelligible and decodable in a particular way. Interpretive moves are carried out by children and adults alike, although the associations, evaluations and categories employed by children are designed and structured in accordance with the particular modes of reception and interpretation prevailing in the children's culture they are part of.

In the psychology of music, various studies deal with how our relationship to music changes with different stages of life (Gembris, 2005; LeBlanc, Sims, Siivola, & Obert, 1996). Empirical research on music preferences suggests that the level of interest in and openness towards a variety of musical styles varies through childhood and adolescence. A general observation is that children in preschool and the lower grades are more receptive than adults, and have a more open attitude to the unknown. According to LeBlanc et al. (1996), this openness more or less seems to follow a U-shaped curve: while children in the lower grades are open to a variety of music genres, the degree of openness declines during grades six, seven and eight, before rising slightly again during high school years.

Experiences from intercultural music projects in Norway clearly support observations identifying a greater openness to unfamiliar music in early childhood, as well as a tendency towards more closed or restricted attitudes in adolescence. Such observations have been highlighted in research focusing on music projects with explicitly anti-racist goals, such as the ambitious "Resonant community" project. The author of a report on this project asserted that it was crucial to reach children with positive images of "foreign" music at an early age "before prejudicial attitudes are internalized" (Skyllstad, 1993, p. 5).

Musical preferences and value hierarchies are to a certain extent always culturally learned. We inevitably place what we hear within the context of our previous listening experience and the prevalent cultural frames in our societies: "We learn how to feel and how to deploy particular emotions in various ways and contexts which are appropriate to our situation" (Finnegan, 1989, p. 183). Children are exposed to cultural learning from an early stage through the expression of likes and dislikes among people in their surroundings. The greater openness observed among young children is apparently attributable to their lack of fixed—or at least their less developed—categories into which different types of music can be placed. The complex hierarchies of taste and value that permeate, structure and divide the cultural world of adults have yet to be developed in the minds of young children. Additionally, it may be argued that musical genres are not as closely linked to personal identity for young children as they are for older children and adolescents.

Thus, one of the things that both research and common knowledge tell us is the quite unsurprising fact that young children experience music in different ways than adults. However, the crucial point to investigate more precisely with regard to concert promotion to children is just what these differences consist of, how they can be understood, and what implications they may have for our thinking concerning children and the arts. The intercultural setting is particularly interesting because children will be exposed to unfamiliar music styles, presumably reducing the influence of pre-existing attitudes and value judgements.

---

o   In what ways do young children's concert experience and concert behavior differ from those of adults? Illustrate with examples from your own experience or your own work with children.

o   What factors should be taken into consideration when presenting young children to music from unfamiliar cultures? Are there any particular challenges or advantages?

Context

The methodological approach underlying this chapter is basically child-centered with a focus on children's own perspectives and meaning-making strategies. It recognizes that children are capable of contributing to discussions concerning their own reception and understanding of culture. Through verbal as well as non-verbal expressions children themselves can provide ". . . expert testimony about their experiences, associations and lifestyles" (Thomson, 2008, p. 1). The methodological challenge consists in offering good opportunities for children's "voices" to be heard and acknowledged, and to be aware of the various modes of expression particular to children's culture.

The field research occurred over a two year period in the county of Rogaland, where several municipalities in rural areas have been involved in the Norwegian–Indian exchange project. The main focus was the children's concert experience, observed through their physical and verbal responses. Two different school concert productions featuring Indian classical and semi-classical music were studied: "A meeting with Indian masters" (*Indisk mestermøte*) with Sunanda Sharma (song), Jai Shankar (tabla) and Mukesh Sharma (sarod); and "Dance me all the way to India" (*Dans meg helt til India*) with Mahua Shankar (Kathak dance), Mitilesh Kumar Jah (tabla) and the Norwegian storyteller Ylva Sjaastad, who also served as an interpreter. Research data consists of field observations at 12 different concerts in Rogaland, ten group interviews with child audiences, observations of post-performance question-and-answer sessions with children and performers, plus interviews with teachers, musicians and organizers. Observations were primarily directed towards the child audience, with a special focus on their responses, during and immediately after the concert event. The first year's tour involved children in all the primary years of schooling. The second year had a particular focus on the younger children (aged 5 to 8). All interviews were recorded digitally and relevant selections were transcribed. Observations and interviews were also carried out at public concert events featuring the Indian musicians organized in cooperation with local municipal music schools. In order to gain an understanding of Indian concert promotion, observations at similar school concerts organized by SPIC MACAY in India were carried out at the beginning of the second year of the study, and for comparative reasons, two concerts with a Norwegian program for kindergartens were studied in June 2011.

Observations and Results

Young children will rarely sit motionless for an entire 40-minute concert, even though they may concentrate deeply during parts of it. As the observation introducing this chapter suggests, there is a lot going on in a school concert audience at a performance of Indian music. The urge to move while attending a live performance is for many children an integral part of the experience, and cannot be constrained by norms regarding concert behavior. Concerts of the kind discussed here will always include some type of interaction between the musicians and the audience. Indeed, such interaction is strongly encouraged by Concerts Norway during the process of concert production. The Indian performers invited their audiences to sing Indian scales or engage in organized physical movement. For example, they might ask the children to clap at the beginning of each rhythmic cycle in the music.

Lively and energetic music and dance also tends to inspire a lot of movement that is more spontaneous in nature, particularly in the lower grades. Many such physical responses can be characterized as *imitation*. Lacking their own instruments, children watching the tabla player would drum with their hands on the floor, the benches or the mats they were sitting on. Children inspired by the Kathak dancer would stamp their feet or mimic the intricate movements of her hands and arms. And when Sunanda Sharma sang the classical Indian scales while making the traditional hand movements corresponding to the particular notes, she was immediately copied both orally and physically by children in the audience. On one occasion a girl adopted what looked like a lotus position, similar to the performers in front of her. Children also copied each other's body movements, resulting in a contagious imitation that spread like wildfire.

In early childhood, the act of physical imitation is fundamental to intersubjective communication and learning (Trevarthen, 1993; Trevarthen, Kokkinaki, & Fiamenghi, 1997). Imitation is a complex behavioral competency with various underlying mechanisms. A basic matching of body movement appears practically from birth, whereas more precise physical mimicry develops during the second year of life (Jones, 2007). During the childhood years, the practice of imitation is essential to the informal music learning of children's culture. In many traditional music cultures around the world, the main vehicle for the transmission of musical culture is imitation. This is certainly true of Indian classical music training of which the guru–shishiya (master–apprentice) relationship is a fundamental element (e.g., Grimmer, 2011). Recent research in

FIGURE 10.1   Boys imitating tabla drumming.
All photos courtesy of Jan Sverre Knudsen.

Western music education also emphasizes the role of imitation in learning processes, particularly in popular music (Green, 2002, 2008).

Besides observing physical reactions, the study included conversations with children. Immediately after each performance, the children were allowed to ask the performers questions. Later, interviews were conducted with selected groups of children, usually in their own classrooms. Open-ended questions were used in order to find out about the children's experiences and what interpretive moves they were employing: What was going on in your head during the concert? What kind of mood were you in? Conversations were lively, often spinning off in directions that apparently had little to do with Indian music and dance.

Talking about music with children has its challenges. The ability to convey a concert experience in words is a culturally learned skill which requires the ability to separate, order and "translate" experience to the realm of verbal language. There is a great deal of variation in the degree to which children are accustomed to reflecting verbally after a performance. Generally speaking, young children rarely possess a "developed" vocabulary for talking about musical experience. However, as exemplified later, they will employ metaphors, fantasies and body language relevant to their own culture of childhood.

Children attending a school concert observe intensely, and may direct their attention and concentration towards any visual or aural aspect of the event. According to Tia DeNora, "[m]usic affords concentration because it structures the sonic environment, because it dispels random or idiosyncratic stimuli,

FIGURE 10.2 Sunanda Sharma and Jai Shankar.

aesthetic or otherwise" (DeNora, 2000, pp. 60–61). The children in Rogaland were attentive and curious, noticing a wide range of different aspects of the performance: sounds, clothing, instruments and gestures.

As many of the responses from the children could suggest, their attention was primarily caught by the performers' appearance and actions rather than the musical sound. The children were curious about these unusual and colorful performers, especially as most of them had never encountered Indian performers before. The child audiences had minimal cultural predispositions regarding the music presented. Their knowledge of India was sparse and often limited to certain stereotypes. Their first questions and comments focused particularly on aspects of the performance that were unfamiliar; the strange, the different and the extraordinary: "Why do you have a red mark on your forehead?", "Why are you dancing barefoot?", "Why are you wearing those bells on your feet?", "Do you have to wear all that jewelry?".

A concert experience stimulates the production of mental imagery. The children's comments gave an impression of their pre-existing images of India, as well as centering on difference and the exotic. There were many associations to elephants, holy cows, turbans, colorful dresses, gods, temples and palaces— even giraffes and pyramids. Images of India frequently referred to poverty: "They dance barefoot because they have no shoes", "They have houses that fall apart easily". Interestingly, the children observed in India also frequently resorted to prevalent images and stereotypes in their reflections. Following a concert with the Norwegian jazz band Dabrhahi at Tagore International School in Delhi, a second grader related that listening to the "Norwegian music" made her imagine ". . . people dressed in red, with long caps, walking arm in arm in the streets,[. . .] singing happily". Evidently, the understanding that this was a Norwegian band had made a deeper impression than any associations to the Latin Jazz they were playing.

A focus on *difference* also characterized many of the introductions made by concert hosts in Rogaland. One headmaster introduced Mahua Shankar and Mitilesh Kumar as "exciting visitors" from a culture that is "very different", playing instruments that are "very unfamiliar". Still, in many of the concert presentations there was also an emphasis on the benefits of intercultural encounters. One concert host spoke of how music of different kinds could go well together, and at an evening family concert in cooperation with the local music school the venue was decorated with national flags and symbols of both Norway and India (the Taj Mahal and Norwegian mountains and fiords).

The concert experience provides a space in time and place for associations and reflections. As Tia DeNora argues ". . . musical affect is constituted reflexively, in and through the practice of articulating or connecting music with other things" (DeNora, 2000, p. 33). While difference and novelty obviously attracts attention, some of the *interpretive moves* employed by the children suggest a need to anchor the experience by connecting it to something familiar and secure. Many of the younger children would refer to people they knew or to some previous experience: "My cousin went to India", "I've got a book about India at home", "I've got a drum like that". Such comments can be characterized as "*me too*" statements, which are very common among young children vying for attention. Following a concert that has been the focal point for an entire class, these statements can be understood as expressing a wish to enter into this positive focus and share some of the status the concert ritual endows on the performers.

Sometimes children's associations may take off in unexpected directions. One boy in first grade started out by telling us that he had seen something similar before, a dance performance from Thailand that he had attended with his father and his father's Asian girlfriend. He continued by explaining that the family didn't go to these "boring" events anymore because his father had quarreled and broken up with the woman and that he "thought her children were not very nice". This association could of course have been dismissed as being of little relevance to experiencing Indian music. Still, it can be argued that this kind of "off-task" association from a young child is also a valid response worthy of our attention (Sipe, 2002, p. 481). For children and adults alike, the concert experience provides an entry point for any personal association, often initiating chains of thought that go their own surprising ways. While children in safe and supportive surroundings easily verbalize these thoughts, adults' responses will generally be more restrained by norms and conventions. If a child's mind is brimming with complicated or difficult thoughts, the concert experience may afford an occasion for letting those thoughts surface. Moreover, being given the opportunity to talk about such thoughts in a secure setting may even provide a beneficial emotional release.

It has been argued that music is experienced and expressed holistically in children's lives (Bjørkvold, 1992). Simply put, music is not only something you listen to, it is something you engage with both mentally and physically. Studies of children's spontaneous vocal and instrumental improvisations emphasize the all-inclusive role of music in their daily life: as communication, emotional expression and accompaniment to physical action (Campbell, 1998; Knudsen, 2008; Young, 2004). Other studies show how children attending interpretive performances such as kindergarten read-alouds will engage by mentally "inserting" themselves into the performance (Sipe, 2002, p. 478). Many of the children at the school concerts not only responded physically, but would also imagine themselves within the frames of the performance, reflecting upon how their own minds and bodies would experience taking part in the music and dance: "It made me want to dance", "I wanted to try the instruments", "If I were to dance in a dress like that I would sweat a lot", "It would hurt my fingers to play the drum that fast", "Dancing like that would make me feel dizzy". When invited to talk about what the performers had been doing, verbal responses would often be supplemented by body language to illustrate the point. Some younger children would simply say: "They did like this!", and start stamping their feet or drumming on the floor. Physical demonstration was apparently more relevant than words.

The children were obviously impressed by the virtuosity of the Indian performers. They were fascinated by the pirouettes of the Kathak dancer and the speed of the tabla drumming. Traditionally, an Indian instrumental *raga* develops slowly and gradually through the *alap-jor jhala-gat* structure. It starts with a rhythmically free exploration of the particular melodic mode of the raga (*alap*), then develops steadily through the gradual addition of a pulsating rhythm (*jor*), increases in speed and intensity with the addition of tabla accompaniment (*jhala*), before ending in a climax of speed and rhythm-oriented virtuoso improvisations (*gat*) (Wade, 1980). Since the duration of a raga performance can vary from 10–15 minutes to an hour or more, a 40-minute school concert obviously requires a lot of adaptation. The improvised pieces tend to be shortened, and the highlights are more frequent. The performers in Rogaland tended to emphasize their technical abilities and virtuosity. Jai Shankar demonstrated that he could play 40 drum beats in a second, and Mahua Shankar made the children count her 21 consecutive pirouettes across the floor. Comments from the children included: "They played very fast", "I was, like, shocked that they could play so fast", "I can't understand how they do it".

A notion common to both Western and Indian philosophy of music is that experiencing music influences our feelings or state of mind, and may have the capacity to "transport" us from one emotional state to another, like a cultural

FIGURE 10.3 Mahua Shankar making pirouettes.

vehicle that can be "ridden like a bike or boarded like a train" (DeNora, 2000, p. 7). When children were prompted to talk about their emotions during the concert, some would resort to images of being in a different place: "I felt like I was in a spa", "I became hyper, as if I was at a party", "I felt like I was flying", "I felt like I was inside a pyramid". Others would relate their feelings to their bodies: "When he was playing drums I felt a banging inside my head", "There was, like a jumble inside my head" or "It made me sleepy". There were also many accounts of feeling happy "Like hip hurrah to watch!", or feeling sad when the concert ended too soon.

Question-and-answer sessions after the concerts would usually start with the children asking the performers quite personal questions: "How old are you?", "How long have you been playing?", "Where do you come from?" and "Where did you get that dress?" According to Christopher Small, a concert can be understood as ". . . an encounter between human beings that is mediated by nonverbal organized sounds" (Small, 1995). The human encounter is, of course, a major benefit of the live music experience of a school concert. Apparently, the children reflected upon the concert more as a meeting with people than as a meeting with sound. They never described musical sound without being prompted to do so. The ability to describe sound detached from the performers' actions requires a certain conceptual separation, in addition to training and familiarity with a whole set of appropriate expressions. As adults we often describe musical sound metaphorically, as soft or hard, dark or bright, high or low, heavy or light—or use words that reflect ways in which music engages our emotions: peaceful, melancholy, disturbing or exciting. When the children were asked "What did it sound like?" they would use imaginative terms relevant to their own childhood world: the richly ornamented vocal improvisations of Sunanda Sharma were described as "a curly sound", and the sound of Jai Shankar's tabla drumming was "funny", "bubbly", or "like thunder".

---

o   How would you encourage children to talk about their concert experience?

o   How would you talk to children about your own concert experience?

o   How can teachers enhance children's concert experience?

Organizing Concerts for Young Children

The children's experiences at concerts featuring Indian music raise various issues of general importance to music education and our understanding of the role of the arts in early childhood. The cooperation between two organizations with different histories, goals and intentions also raises intriguing issues. Accordingly, a brief presentation of Concerts Norway and SPIC MACAY is necessary before the final discussion, which relates the research findings to ideologies of concert promotion furthered by these organizations.

Concerts Norway is a government-funded cultural organization that comes under the auspices of the Norwegian Ministry of Culture. It was established in 1968 with the main purpose of making ". . . live music of high artistic quality available to all people in the country" (Rikskonsertene, 2009a). Concerts Norway engages more than 800 artists annually, performing a total of 9,947[1] concerts in all the country's 433 municipalities. The great majority of these are school concerts (8,997), while the rest are concerts for kindergartens (632) and public concerts (318), mostly for adult audiences. The result of this remarkable cultural program is that every Norwegian child during school hours gets to attend at least two free concerts a year with professional musicians. Concert promotion also involves the development and distribution of resource material, information and recordings, so teachers can prepare for and follow up the event with the children.

Concerts Norway presents a great variety of music genres, from classical to popular. The profile of the organization's programming reflects its egalitarian philosophy. As an official report stated: "On the artistic level, there is no logical or value-based justification that some genres are superior to others"[2] (Rikskonsertene, 2009b). However, among the wide variety of music promoted, there is a clear emphasis on non-commercial genres, such as jazz and traditional music. In particular, music from developing countries is noticeably well repre-sented. Since 2000, collaborations with the Ministry of Foreign Affairs have resulted in a wide variety of musical exchanges and school concert tours, with performers from countries such as China, Palestine, Pakistan, Nepal, South Africa and India.

SPIC MACAY, the Society for the Promotion of Indian Classical Music And Culture Amongst Youth, is a non-profit organization that aims to promote Indian classical music, classical dance, and other aspects of Indian culture. The society has over 300 chapters in India and around the world and each year hosts more than 2,000 concerts, lecture-demonstrations and seminars. The SPIC MACAY website states that the aim of the organization is to:

> . . . introduce traditional Indian culture to the youth of this country with a hope that the beauty, grace and wisdom embodied in it will become an integral part of his life, whatever his dreams and ambitions may be. Classical Indian music and dance, carrying with them generations of wisdom dating back to antiquity, become the chief medium for creating awareness in students.
>
> *(SPIC MACAY, 2011)*

---

1 All statistics are from 2009.

2 Author's translation from Norwegian.

While Concerts Norway is a state-sponsored organization with relatively predictable funding, SPIC MACAY is largely dependent on donations and the efforts of innumerable volunteers. The organization reflects the visions and ambitions of its founder, Kiran Seth, a US-trained engineer who has chaired the executive board since 1977. Today Kiran Seth is an inspirational presence within the organization who continues to exert considerable influence over its artistic ideals and strategies. SPIC MACAY's concert programming clearly signals a hierarchy of music genres, with Indian classical music firmly at the top. According to Kiran Seth, music must be "abstract, subtle, inspiring and mystical" if it is to have the capacity to "uplift the soul".[3] While he recognizes that certain music in various other genres—Western classical or rock—may also have this capacity, he makes a clear distinction between music that is "only entertainment" and music that "goes deeper". According to SPIC MACAY's underlying philosophy, Indian classical music has, by far, the greatest potential for reaching the ultimate goal of "creating awareness" (Jain, 2010).

Over the years, both SPIC MACAY and Concerts Norway have gathered considerable experience in the field of music education and have developed highly successful models for promoting concerts for children. While the two organizations share an overall aim of presenting high-quality live music, there are important differences in their ambitions and strategies. Each organization justifies the presentation of music to children in different, sometimes contrasting, ways.

In my opinion, it is relevant to consider the practices prevailing in these organizations as reflecting different ideologies of music promotion. These ideologies influence a wide range of discourses within both organizations: legitimacy and authority, myths and emotions, values and habits. While an organization's ideologies will to some extent be revealed in its formal plans and programs, a full understanding will require an examination of prevailing tacit knowledge, that is, the many aspects of an organization's practice that are taken for granted and rarely, if ever, discussed.

Strictly speaking, both Concerts Norway and SPIC MACAY are not educational institutions but cultural and artistic organizations whose activities are directed towards children and adolescents. While the concerts discussed above clearly included educational aspects—not least influenced by the fact that they took place within a school setting—education is not the dominant *raison d'être* of either organization. Both consider the experience of music as valuable and enriching in itself—something that every child in Norway and India should have the right to enjoy. SPIC MACAY highlights music's ability to "uplift the soul" and "create awareness", while Concerts Norway aims to produce

---

3 Interview with Kiran Seth (January 23, 2011).

concert experiences that "surprise, move and excite" the child audiences. These ideological guidelines inevitably lead to an experience-based, largely non-instrumental discourse of justification; the value of a concert is not judged on the basis of what the children might *learn* when it comes to musical skills or cultural knowledge, it is simply considered valuable for them to listen to and engage with music and dance of high quality.

Such justifications for concert promotion can be linked to various discourses in both Indian and Western thinking. According to *Rasa* thinking, which is the classical Indian theory of aesthetics, the value of musical reception derives from the ways in which particular pitch combinations, rhythms or *ragas* produce corresponding human emotions in the listener (Ruckert, 2004; Wade, 1980). The primary value of music is ascribed to the experience in itself, rather than any educational or social goals that go beyond it. This kind of non-instrumental, experience-based rationale for promoting music might also be linked to ideas of cultural rights, such as those presented in the United Nations Convention on the Rights of the Child which states that children have the right to ". . . participate fully in cultural and artistic life" and to enjoy ". . . equal opportunities for cultural, artistic, recreational and leisure activity" (United Nations, 1998). Experience-based rationales can also be understood as an approximation to how concert experiences are regarded in the adult world. Obviously, as adult consumers of culture we are rarely confronted with questions like "what did you learn?" or "do you remember the names of the instruments?" after enjoying a concert experience. Rather, the value assigned to the concert is understood in terms of our personal appreciation of the event as it is unfolding.

As the observations and results from this project demonstrate, children experience a concert event in a great variety of ways. While musical reception and the ritual of the school concert to a certain extent are culturally learned and passed down by adults, young children evidently have ways of experiencing, associating and reacting physically that are particular to being a child. Recognizing these particularities raises key questions concerning the production and promotion of art to children. Since children experience the arts differently, should we also adapt and adjust the focus and format of concerts to address these differences in a relevant way? To what extent and in what ways should this be done?

In this regard there are interesting differences between the promotional ideologies and practices of Concerts Norway and SPIC MACAY—differences that ultimately have to do with views on children and childhood. Across Scandinavia, the notion of a particular "children's culture" has had a major influence. In Scandinavian early childhood research there is a strong tendency to focus on children's subjectivity and social participation rather than on formal learning (e.g., Kjørholt, 2001). A pioneering Norwegian project aimed at developing concerts for infants recommended concerts to be produced "on the conditions of children's culture", paying attention to "children's listening preferences" (Valberg, 2002). For Concerts Norway, these dominant ideas have influenced the focus and format of concert productions, particularly in the new concert programs for kindergartens. Concerts include a great deal of interaction with the audience, as well as playfulness and humor. A theatrical style of performance is common—adults take on roles, often entering a childlike mode of acting and communicating with the audience. In the case of the concerts discussed here, Concerts Norway encouraged the Indian performers to adopt some of these ideas. This required the performers to make some adjustments to their usual performances in order to take account of the Norwegian mode of concert presentation.

For SPIC MACAY there is a different kind of seriousness surrounding music. Their programs mainly consist of Indian classical and semi-classical music, which traditionally is performed for adult audiences who sit motionless for hours without interacting much with the musicians. Even young children are expected to be able to benefit from listening to music in much the same way as adults, without the performers employing any special adaptations or "tricks". Adapting performances for school concert formats in India evidently involves some abbreviations, alterations and explanations, but there is never any significant departure from the traditional concert format. Unsurprisingly, tensions have arisen when SPIC MACAY organizers and performers have been confronted with certain expectations from Concerts Norway. Some comments from the Indian side suggest that Concerts Norway do not treat music seriously enough and underestimate children's ability to experience the "depth" of music. The Norwegian approach is occasionally seen as causing music to become "only entertainment", with performers resorting to "the red nose effect" to catch the children's attention. Still, in both Norway and India there are differences of opinion and ongoing discussions surrounding these matters. Several Norwegian performers have been praised for their "playful" approach by Indian teachers. For example, the principal of a Delhi school was extremely enthusiastic about the Norwegian jazz group Dabrhahi who visited her school: "They showed an amazing kind of playfulness. They were obviously having fun, and that caught on with the children". She added: "Maybe in India, in our times, we are too ambitious [. . .] We are suppressing childhood".[4]

Two of the *interpretive moves* documented in the conversations with children are especially worth noting: first, connecting to the different "other", on a personal level; and second, drawing associations with your own life world by placing the experience within pre-existing frames of understanding. While these *moves* are an important part of children's strategies for making the concert experience intelligible and understandable, they also imply a challenge for any

---

4 Interview with Ms Rekha Bakshi, Vasant Valley School, Delhi (January 20, 2011).

intercultural program aimed at children. A meeting with the "other" that fails to connect to the child's own life experience can easily remain simply an enjoyable and entertaining happening. After several years of cooperation, there is a common understanding within both Concerts Norway and SPIC MACAY that there is a need to reach further. There is a wish to create a deeper, more lasting impression. More ambitious approaches have been tried out in Rogaland over the past few years in the form of intensive two-to-four-day workshops involving Indian musicians, Norwegian music teachers and pupils at municipal music schools, plus music and dance students from Stavanger University. The workshops have culminated in public performances at local cultural venues, involving various organizations and local artists. Similar activities have been carried out with Norwegian musicians visiting India.

These wider-ranging "hands-on" events have obviously contributed to bringing performers and pupils closer, reducing the perceived distance to the "exotic" visitors. Being taught by professional Indian musicians working alongside your own local music school teacher for several days makes a strong—and presumably more lasting—impact. This kind of work seems highly relevant in view of Concert Norway's efforts to strengthen cultural diversity by creating ". . . mutual understanding, knowledge and respect across cultural and geographical borders" (Concerts Norway, 2011). However, such close cooperation also involves a number of challenges, and a fair amount of negotiation is required to deal with the meeting between different practices and ideologies of music education. When Mukesh Sharma started to introduce Norwegian guitar pupils and their teachers to the traditional melodic lines of the *sarod*, there were some quite desperate attempts to "translate" the music into the more familiar Western notation and guitar scales. Similarly, Norwegian music teachers attending Sunanda Sharma's class in the oral tradition of Indian song had their pens and paper ready, eager to write it all down in an understandable way. While these responses were clearly meant to facilitate learning and provide references for future use, it can still be argued that they are not in line with fundamental aspects of the teaching of this form of traditional Indian music.

As mentioned earlier, the conversations with the children often started out with an open question like: "What was going on in your mind during the concert?" On a few occasions a child would give an answer like: "nothing", "only grey", or "just empty". While it would be easy to regard such answers as an expression of shyness, or as uninteresting and beside the point, I would argue for an understanding that calls for particular attention in the intercultural setting discussed here. All musical cultures are linked to more or less dominant, and more or less rigidly understood, norms concerning preferred modes of musical reception, as well as particular norms concerning children's musical reception. This not only concerns views as to what is acceptable behavior at a musical event, but actually touches upon ideas as to how one should react mentally to music. For example, in the early childhood music education of

Western cultures, children are often encouraged to visualize and fantasize when listening to Western classical music. In contrast, in the classical Indian tradition and the music education promoted by SPIC MACAY, there is a strong focus on spirituality in musical reception. This spirituality is not strictly religious, but is more a general human spirituality linked to the idea that certain music has the capacity to enrich our lives by "uplifting the soul". It could appropriately be summed up in the concept of "the blank mind", which is found in SPIC MACAY's music promotion, as well as in the children's conversations about music. A fourth grader at Tagore International School in Delhi gave this explanation in a group conversation following a school concert: "Basically, when you are hearing Indian music and you close your eyes, your mind goes blank. You can't think of anything except what the musician is playing". The idea of a "blank mind" should not be understood as an "empty mind", but rather as a state of being totally open in the sense of one's mind being exclusively directed towards the music, devoid of any thoughts and associations. According to this conceptualization, any association or visualization will present an obstacle to ideal or "pure" musical reception. Parallel ideas can be found in the Western philosophy of aesthetics, particularly in Kant's influential—and much contested—idea of the *disinterested interest* in which art is to be enjoyed for its own sake, not for any benefits that it confers on the observer (Kant & Walker, 2008).

The school concert programs arranged in cooperation between Norway and India involve a mutual process of learning. Two ambitious organizations

FIGURE 10.4 What is going on in their minds?

working together will inevitably face challenges when getting involved in each other's practices, strategies and ideals. Being confronted with different views on concert promotion, education and childhood can be an eye-opener leading one to reflect on fundamental aspects of one's own approach. Cooperating on an organizational as well as a practical level involves becoming acquainted with formal plans and programs as well as the entire corpus of tacit knowledge and taken-for-granted assumptions that govern everyday practice. Hopefully, the issues raised here based on research into children's own concert experience can add to the understanding of the intercultural concert experience while also providing a challenge to general ideas concerning music reception, music education and concert promotion to children.

References

Bjørkvold, J.-R. (1992). *The muse within: Creativity and communication, song and play from childhood through maturity*. New York: HarperCollins.

Campbell, P. S. (1998). *Songs in their heads: Music and its meaning in children's lives*. New York: Oxford University Press.

Concerts Norway. (2011). *Rikskonsertene* [website]. Retrieved December 2, 2011, from http://www.rikskonsertene.no/no/no/English/.

DeNora, T. (2000). *Music in everyday life*. Cambridge: Cambridge University Press.

Finnegan, R. (1989). *The hidden musicians: Music-making in an English town*. Cambridge: Cambridge University Press.

Gembris, H. (2005). Musikalische präferenzen. In R. Oerter & T. H. Stoffer (Eds.), *Spezielle Musikpsychologie* (Vol. Bd. 2, pp. 279–341). Göttingen: Hogrefe.

Green, L. (2002). *How popular musicians learn: A way ahead for music education*. Aldershot, UK: Ashgate.

Green, L. (2008). *Music, informal learning and the school: A new classroom pedagogy*. Aldershot, UK: Ashgate.

Grimmer, S. (2011). Continuity and change: The guru–shishya relationship in Karnatic classical music training. In L. Green (Ed.), *Learning, teaching, and musical identity: Voices across cultures* (pp. 91–108). Bloomington: Indiana University Press.

Jain, A. (2010). A holistic education. *Sandesh—National newsletter of SPIC MACAY, 16*(1), 8.

Jones, S. S. (2007). Imitation in infancy: The development of mimicry. *Psychological Science, 18*(7), 593–599.

Kant, I., & Walker, N. (2008). *Critique of judgement*. New York: Oxford University Press.

Keil, C., & Feld, S. (1994). *Music grooves: Essays and dialogues*. Chicago: University of Chicago Press.

Kjørholt, A. T. (2001). "The participating child". A vital pillar in this century? *Nordisk Pedagogikk, 21*, 65–81.

Knudsen, J. S. (2008). Children's improvised vocalisations—Learning, communication and technology of the self. *Contemporary Issues in Early Childhood, Special issue: Children and the Arts* (Ed. Felicity McArdle), *9*(4), 287–296.

LeBlanc, A., Sims, W. L., Siivola, C., & Obert, M. (1996). Music style preferences of different age listeners. *Journal of Research in Music Education, 44*(1), 49–59.

Rikskonsertene. (2009a). *Bruk konserten!* Oslo: Rikskonsertene.

Rikskonsertene. (2009b). *Høringsuttalelse vedr. Dift-rapport 2009:3 "Nye tider—nye takter?" En gjennomgang av Rikskonsertene.* Oslo: Concerts Norway.

Ruckert, G. E. (2004). *Music in North India: Experiencing music, expressing culture.* Oxford: Oxford University Press.

Sipe, L. R. (2002). Talking back and taking over: Young children's expressive engagement during storybook read-alouds. *The Reading Teacher, 55*(5), 476–483.

Skyllstad, K. (1993). *Summary report. The resonant community—Fostering interracial understanding through music.* Oslo: Norwegian Concert Institute.

Small, C. (1995). *Musicking: A ritual in social space.* Retrieved December 1, 2011, from http://www.musekids.org/musicking.html.

Small, C. (1998). *Musicking: The meanings of performing and listening.* Hanover, NH: University Press of New England.

SPIC MACAY. (2011). *Society for Promotion of Indian Classical Music And Culture Amongst Youth.* [website]. Retrieved December 1, 2011, from http://spicmacay.com/.

Thomson, P. (2008). Children and young people: Voices in visual research. In P. Thomson (Ed.), *Doing visual research with children and young people* (pp. 1–20). London: Routledge.

Trevarthen, C. (1993). The self born in intersubjectivity: The psychology of an infant communicating. In U. Neisser (Ed.), *The Perceived Self* (pp. 121–173). Cambridge: Cambridge University Press.

Trevarthen, C., Kokkinaki, T., & Fiamenghi, G. A. (1997). What infants' imitations communicate with mothers, with fathers and with peers. In J. Nadel & G. Butterworth (Eds.), *Imitation in infancy* (pp. 127–185). Cambridge: Cambridge University Press.

United Nations. (1998). *Convention on the rights of the child.* New York: United Nations.

Valberg, T. (2002). *Vidunderlige, deilige, grensesprengende opplevelser til gode: Utviklingstrekk ved konserten—med særlig øye for konserten som arena for musikkformidling til barn.* Kristiansand: Høyskoleforlaget i samarbeid med Høgskolen i Agder.

Wade, B. C. (1980). Some principles of Indian classical music. In E. May (Ed.), *Musics of many cultures: An introduction* (pp. 83–110). Berkeley: University of California Press.

Young, S. (2004). Young children's spontaneous vocalising: Insights into play and pathways to singing. *International Journal of Early Childhood, 36*(2), 59–75.

11

THERE'S MORE TO ART THAN MEETS THE EYE

A Series of Provocations from Unit X

Felicity McArdle

Background

In the land that has come to be known as Australia, traces of ochre images have been found, painted on rock walls, possibly as long as 35,000 years ago. The people who made those marks speak to us across time. Through their marks, we have learned some things about one of the most ancient cultures on Earth, a culture that is still alive and flourishing today. Are those images art? And are the people who painted them artists? Is art painted, or painting?

Like the chapters that have gone before in this book, this final chapter is an invitation to ask new and different questions—about art, teaching art, and teaching art with young children. There are those who would call those ancient ochre images 'rock art', but this would be the result of constructing the images in a particular way. There are those who would see something else entirely—possibly as records of scientific knowledge, geography, astronomy. How we see and think and speak 'art' is sometimes contentious and always contingent. Why were the images painted on the rock walls? What do/did the images do? Who painted them? Did children paint on the rock walls?

The focus of this chapter is on preparing teachers who will be working with young children. In 1999, Paul Duncum listed what he considered generalist teachers needed to know in order to teach art well. He listed a number of strategies for making and responding to art. More than ten years later, there is still the pressing need for teachers to consider the *what* and the *how* of the art they teach. This chapter is a partial account of the design and conduct of a unit of study in a Bachelor Degree. Unit X is part of the curriculum studies for preparing early years teachers in one university in Queensland, Australia. Unit X is a 13-week program of study offered in the first year of a four year program in the teacher education course. It was built on a major scholarly undertaking (McArdle, 2001), and is designed to introduce students to foundation discipline knowledge in the arts, as well as pedagogical strategies for effective arts education with young children. Unit X is currently in its 8th iteration.[1] It is continuously changing, and it will never be 'finished'. The thinking in this chapter draws from some of the data generated, in various forms, throughout the past seven years of 'doing Unit X'. The pedagogy is a deliberate attempt to disrupt the color-by-numbers approach to teaching and learning at university level, and this disruption works for better and worse. What follows is a collection of five provocations for those who are preparing to teach young children.

In the current climate with unprecedented intrusion of national agendas (McWilliam & Taylor, 2012), there is an assumption that the way to better test results is through teacher improvement, which apparently comes through the standardization of teacher learning. With the best of intentions, the prescribing of 'Professional Standards' can have the effect of de-professionalization, taking away teachers' capacities to make informed judgments. Ironies abound when a place must be found for the arts, in a regime that produces standardized tests, national curriculums, measurements and benchmarks. In my home State of Queensland, the first national, standardized tests for literacy and numeracy were introduced in 2008, and 2009 was declared the Year of Creativity.

This insistence on standardization and creativity is only one example of the confusing mixture of 'how to's' when it comes to preparing teachers for arts education. Despite years of critique and alternative learning theories, many teacher education institutions remain bastions of developmental psychology. Links between psychology and modernist art have had the effect that 'natural unfolding' is the best way for young children to learn about art and therefore teachers should avoid 'teaching'. The assumption is that given an attractive array of resources and an 'appropriate' environment, children will naturally progress along a linear sequence of stages in their developing artistry, theoretically, to eventual mastery. Nothing could be simpler!

As a general rule, preservice art education students start with simple teaching tasks, and are taught to carve up learning into grids, boxes, phases and steps. Eventually, the thinking goes, they will learn to put all this together. Learning to teach-by-numbers, like learning to color-by-numbers, produces a deceptively over-simplified impression of the task. In reality, many of these students encounter so many contradictions and inconsistencies when they graduate into the 'real world' that they leave the profession, having spent less time teaching than they spent being trained (Darling-Hammond & Bransford, 2005). Keeping it simple is not always the best way to approach learning about a process that is complex and complicated.

---

1 For more on this, see an earlier account: McArdle (2012).

The provocations in this chapter borrow from Lather's (2006) arguments for multiplicities in the teaching of research. The field of arts education is one of 'wild profusion' (Lather, 2006), not a neat, gridded rubric of staged learning. It is this complexity that Unit X attempts to capture and convey to art education students. In Unit X, the starting point for the students is an introduction to the persistent and ongoing debates and ambivalences that characterize the field of arts education, and the arts. Second, Unit X promotes the idea that if they are to learn to teach art, art educators must learn to welcome error (Claxton, 2005) and the learning possibilities that come from making mistakes. Some students have a lot to un-learn. Others re-learn. It would be too tidy to suggest a direct relationship but it is possible that, in Unit X, those who risk most, learn most. The trouble with this is that existing university systems of assessment and grading fail to recognize much of what is involved in this approach to teaching and learning. So, thirdly, students of Unit X must learn to appreciate differences—not only differences across people, cultures and countries, but differences in ways of thinking, knowing and being.

The risk, in this climate of university funding tied to student ratings, is that teaching becomes more about students' 'enjoyment' levels, and this is understood as that the learning they experience should be 'fun and easy'. Rather, what they *can* experience is the 'pleasure of learning—a pleasure gained from wrestling with ideas and problems, knowing confusion, and coming out the other end' (McWilliam & Taylor, 2012). The assumption in Unit X is that the complexity of the arts makes it a useful thing to think with. Making art can be useful for helping students work against technical formulae for thinking and doing. Unit X is designed as an Ouroboros, the snake swallowing its tail, a metaphor which captures the cyclical and self-reflexive nature of the learning. The students learn about art through doing art, and they learn about learning through doing art, and they learn about the teaching of art through their learning as they do art.

This chapter is likewise meant to prompt a wrestling with complex ideas, an opportunity to work through confusion and arrive at new ways of seeing. What follows is a bricolage, a term used in this case to denote a playful sense, and another way of knowing, through placing ideas side by side, leaving space for the reader to make sense. Sometimes, the introduction of a new thought can contradict, change or effect the idea that precedes or follows. Overlap and overlays, connections and disconnections, stand alone ideas, provocations, questions, stories. For Deleuze, philosophy is productively disoriented by uncontainable difference (see Grosz, 1994). Some of the ideas have been hinted at in earlier chapters in this book, others have been dealt with in greater detail but in different contexts, and some are newly raised in this final chapter. How the reader 'sees' this bricolage will depend on what the reader brings to the assemblage of ideas. The purpose of this final chapter is to produce new thought, new questions, new ways of seeing arts and teaching and learning.

. . . on Embedding Indigenous Knowledges

The first lecture of Unit X begins with acknowledgment of the original custodians of the land, and students are introduced to a number of ways of thinking about art. Australia has a sorry history of its treatment of its Indigenous people, and sadly, many first year students enrolled in a teacher education program would be more likely to recognize and name the Mona Lisa and Leonardo da Vinci than any painting by an Australian Aboriginal artist, past or present.

Until fairly recently, if anything was taught in Australian schools about Indigenous art, it would have been fairly restricted to references to the 'rock art'. Even then, mention was limited to the stencil outlined marks of hands preserved on rock walls by a technique that involved blowing ochre/paint from the mouth, over the hand and arm, leaving an outline. This 'rock art' is now known to also feature more complex and distinct images, like the 'X-ray' style images of Barramundi, and special dreaming spirits, including the Wandjina, Mimis, and Quinkins. To those who know what to 'read' in these images, it is possible to connect country (place) with story and particular knowledges. Somehow, describing this as 'rock art' has the effect of reducing complex forms of knowledge (science, astronomy, conservation, caring for country, geography) to 'primitive' and obsolete, even extinct—and the same understanding is often applied to those people associated with producing the images.

In Australia, one of the most remote and fragile continents, much of the traditional Indigenous art could be said to depict a 'mapping' of the land, the places of water, and the animals, plants and landforms that belong in the land. Contemporary Indigenous artists have enjoyed international success and the artworks from some, such as the Papunya Art Movement, have become central to Australian art. Contrary to popular understandings, 'dot paintings' are fairly recently popularized on canvas, and widespread interest in contemporary Aboriginal art was generally regarded as only spawned in the 1970s. Artists such as Clifford Possum Tjapaltjarri and Kaapa Tjampitjinpa produced works that have become international sensations. Emily Kame Kngwarreye's painting *Earth's Creation* was the first Indigenous artwork to sell for more than $1 million, in 2007. Other contemporary Indigenous artists, such as Richard Bell, Tracey Moffatt, and Gordon Bennett, address social and political issues more 'literally' through their art, commenting on questions of identity, race, and power. Australian Aboriginal art is unique, intriguing, varied, and captivating.

Most first year university students are unable to name Clifford Possum Tjapaltjarri or Emily Kngwarreye, much less recognize their works. In the 1970s, when Geoffrey Bardon began working with the Papunya Tula artists, Aboriginal children were still being taken from their families,[2] and most

2 See *Bringing them home: The 'Stolen children'* report (1997). http://humanrights.gov.au/social_justice/6th_report/index.html/

non-Indigenous Australians were oblivious to these government sanctioned policies and practices. Arguably, it is at least partly through the arts that consciousness has been raised, and Australians have accessed Indigenous cultures, histories and knowledges. Through music, dance, paintings, weavings, carvings and other artforms, most Australians can now appreciate that there is more to the culture of the Indigenous peoples of their land than ancient rock paintings and so called 'primitive' beliefs.

There are those who will argue that Australia is now a multicultural country, and that the children in almost any day care center or classroom are likely to bring a range of cultural backgrounds with them. This is not disputed, but if classrooms are to recognize these many differences beyond the token 'fried rice day for China', then this work begins with paying respects to the traditional custodians of the land. Dreaming Stories are an important part of the cultural heritage of Australia's original people. They are sources of knowledge and wisdom for everyone. They can be used to introduce children to many concepts including science, cultural diversity, emotional literacy, communication and the arts (see Connor, 2007). In Unit X, we begin with recognizing the stories, artworks, music and dance of the original peoples of the land, and pay our respects to their continuing contribution to our culture and communities. It is the power of the arts to communicate these ideas that provides the starting point for the semester. This is one of the core learning objectives for the Unit. Art as culture is one of the dominant discourses explored in Unit X. Students are prompted to consider how, in any culture, past and present, it is the dance, music, images, that can convey the histories, beliefs and stories of the land and the people, and communicate these across borders and barriers, including time, space and language.

But, when it comes to a culture's rock paintings, carvings, weavings, dance (see Sansom's chapter in this book for her story of the haka) . . . is it 'Art'?

Provocation 1: How/Why is Indigenous knowledge embedded in the arts curriculum for teacher education?

. . . on Questions

It would be a mistake to simply collapse all art into a category of 'culture', just as it is a mistake to continue a binary logic that separates master/primitif, art/craft, gallery/cave. These are not 'opposites' and in some cases, they are unrelated. To isolate Aboriginal 'art' and certain symbols from the Aboriginal people's wider world views, beliefs and knowledge systems is a product of colonialism (Bolt, with Martin, 2001). 'Reality is not dialectical, colonialism is' (Hardt & Negri, 2000, p. 128, in Lather, 2006). The second provocation in this chapter, mirroring the movement in Unit X, sits alongside the first, but works against some of the presumptions. New questions about art, knowledge and artists make new thinking possible.

The next move in Unit X is to rupture a neat and colonial dialectical way of thinking about art. One way to 'switch on' students' interest in Indigenous culture is to display spectacular and famous Indigenous artworks. However, to read all of these works using a white European 'Art History' template can work for better and worse. The students can stay 'safe' and 'appreciate' the art, but at the same time, miss the opportunity for more profound learning. Picasso sent out travellers to bring him back masks and carvings from so called 'exotic' distant lands. While these masks were considered 'primitive artefacts', Picasso's copies of them were called 'masterpieces'. Are the spears, boomerangs and throwing sticks used in traditional and historical Indigenous ways of being understood by the students as 'primitive tools' and 'artefacts', or are they technologies for living? The point of provocation here is how images are 'read' and understood.

The issue with these questions around Indigenous art is more than simply a matter of words and naming. In traditional rock art, there are profound differences in the nature of image and imaging (Bolt, with Martin, 2001). The presumption is that images are representational, and this way of thinking lies at the heart of the curriculum in Australian arts education. In their exchange over pre-conceptions of art education in Australia, Bolt and Martin go into a question of reading the images as not representation, but rather, more a case of representationalism—a mode of thinking in which humans set the world before themselves and in relation to themselves (see Heidegger, 1977). This way of seeing the world might itself be understood as a form of colonialism, figuring every thing as an object or resource for use by man-as-subject (Bolt, with Martin, 2001). In MacRae's chapter earlier in this book, she refers to her earlier research undertaking that examined the effects of Euclidian geometry on how we see the world (see MacRae, 2008). This is similar to the question posed by Bolt and Martin—*what effect does art have?*

The performative function of image is invisible to the 'enlightened' subject of Western modernity, who doubts anything that can't be seen. Words like 'magic' and 'voodoo' are called upon for expressing the inexpressible. Representationalist preconceptions about the nature of the image and imaging have us analyzing 'representations' as 'objects' rather than entities with forces and effects. Tools and materials of practice are understood as resources at 'our' disposal to make artworks. The artwork itself becomes an object or resource caught up in an economy of cultural exchange (both symbolic and currency) (Bolt, with Martin, 2001). It is very difficult to think outside the paradigm of representationalism.

But there are other ways of understanding the image. Performance is 'an act of concurrent actual production' through which embodied knowledges and effects are produced (Carter, 1996, p. 84). Instead of images being 'signs' or standing in for or signifying concepts, ideas or things, they produce social meanings and material effects. Meaning is not revealed or clarified, but it is through the performance of the image that embodied situated events are produced (Carter, 1996). In this understanding, imaging produces real material effects. For example, in the performance of language, dance, painting, singing and other rituals, the emphasis is not on what the dance/song/painting represents, but rather on what it can do and what effects it will have (Bolt, with Martin, 2001). The word 'art' is commonly used to separate a particular 'activity' from 'everyday' life, whereas the connectedness of Aboriginal ontology and art makes art as much of the world as people are (Bolt, with Martin, 2001). When Indigenous Australian 'productions', 'manifestations' and 'showings' operate according to a performative principle rather than a representational one, then this is a very different economy from representation (Jones, 2000).

When it comes to the arts and young children, a non-representational principle and a productive materiality can help to at least begin to question some entrenched taboos in early childhood arts education that make young children's artistic efforts almost critique-free. Being with children as they make their paintings and drawings can show a teacher many different ways of understanding and supporting young children in their day to day living and learning. In the following story of Melissa and 'the darling', rather than stopping with her 'reading' of the underlying psychological 'meaning' of the painting, it was also helpful for Melissa's teacher to think about what the process of painting the picture did for Melissa.

> *Melissa and her mother arrived together at kindergarten every morning, and regularly exchanged excited stories about "the darling" who was "growing inside mummy", and who would soon be arriving in to their family. There was much talk about how much Melissa loved "the darling", and how she couldn't wait for the darling to arrive, and how she would play with the darling, and cuddle the darling, and welcome the darling into her life.*
>
> *One day, after her Mum had left, Melissa spent some time on a painting. She drew herself walking along beside her mother, holding her hand. Her mother had a big tummy, and they were both smiling. In the sky were dark storm clouds, and out of one of the clouds came a streak of lightning. The lightning arched in a sweeping line, and went straight to Melissa's mother's tummy, and Melissa showed the drawing to her teacher and said "oh dear!"*[3]

---

3 Thanks to Lyn Kafoa who shared this story when coordinator of Family Daycare Scheme Pine Rivers.

Melissa's teacher, Rebecca, was alerted to the notion that perhaps all was not so sweet and light around the arrival of 'the darling'. As a consequence of Melissa's painting, Rebecca made sure she spent some extra time with Melissa, listening and learning with her as they worked alongside each other over the next few weeks. If the painting is seen for its performative function, then Melissa's act of painting has effect and can achieve something for Melissa (and Melissa's mum, and 'the darling'). There is obviously no need for a sensitive teacher like Rebecca to offer to scribe a story about Melissa's painting, or ask her to 'tell me about your picture'.

Likewise, the practice of super-imposing layers on images on rock walls is better understood when the image is understood as performative. Recognizing the performative function of art is not confined to Indigenous and/or ancient peoples. Marcel Duchamp's shocking graffiti on the Mona Lisa was a reference to the bogus religiosity attached to art in European galleries (Berger, 1981). In her chapter on dance in this volume, Sansom shows how the haka can have direct and tangible effects on the thousands of spectators as well as the players. Knudsen raises some similar possibilities in his discussion of the music in the schools, and in his earlier research into young children and their musicality (see Knudsen, 2008). In Shakespeare's *Hamlet*, drama is used to 'out' the murderer: 'the play's the thing, wherein I'll catch the conscience of the king'. Perhaps examples for the 'performing arts'—dance, music, drama—make it easier to grasp the performative function.

However, as the New London Group wrote in 1996, we are surrounded by visual imagery, much of it more powerful than any other source of information. And these images are acting on us. Historically, religious art was produced with express purposes for effecting the behavior of those who viewed it—lifting hearts and minds to a higher plane, providing aspirations, and the means to meditative and contemplative states of mind. More than in any earlier times, it is important now that children learn that images are produced and that they have effects on us. Understanding this performative function of art can provide different frames for understanding young children and what they are engaged in when they draw, paint, dance, sing, play. In Chapter Two, Knight explores the performative function of drawing, and, in her earlier study (2009), describes how her daughter Hannah proceeds to cover Linda's drawing with her own marks. Knight goes on to analyze this as a moment in which Hannah works through power imbalances she experiences every day as a child in her relationships with adults.

Provocation 2: Don't ask: *'What is it?'* Ask: *'What can the painting do?'* and: *'What effects will the painting have?'*

. . . on Baggage

This third provocation is a direct response to the previous one, but the focus now shifts from young children to teacher education, as an illustration of the power of the arts. In answer to the question of what art can do, every year that Unit X has run, undeniable evidence demonstrates how, like super powers in the comic books, the arts can work for better and for worse.

When it comes to preparing 'quality' teachers who will deliver 'quality' arts education, we have our work cut out for us. It is possible that many students who enroll in university studies are products of poor quality arts education themselves. After twelve years of schooling, it is not uncommon for students to arrive in the Unit X workshops and not know that mixing white with a tiny bit of red will make pink. Worse still, it's not simply that nobody has taught them anything, although all too often, this is the case. In addition, many students need to un-learn much of what they bring with them to the university class-room. They have baggage (National Review of Visual Education, 2009). The following excerpts are extracted from students' reflections generated over the seven years of Unit X and they remain uncannily similar each year, with each cohort of students:

> Not too sure how I'll go as I really am not that artistic.
>
> (Tony, 2004)

> Whereas, previously the thought or mention of the word art made me cringe and feel inferior as I did not think I was capable of producing a "work of art" that was viewed as a "work of art" by others.
>
> (Marie, 2006)

> I have not drawn for years and have relied on templates for class displays.
>
> (Jennifer, 2005)

> [visiting gallery] . . . because I didn't know the language of art, couldn't read the abstracts about the artworks and consequently felt extremely uncomfortable.
>
> (Theresa, 2008)

> When I painted a picture my Grade 3 teacher got cross for "wasting paint" as "the picture wasn't up to the level my age group should be producing". I was devastated and I still say to people "I am not artistic" when in truth I haven't really attempted art since. After the teacher's comments, I never liked painting from then as it repre-sented how childish my art efforts were. I believed I was not artistic. Today many people describe me as artistic but this is not a natural state for me and is something I have had to work very hard at.
>
> (Elizabeth, 2010)

I have not experienced art since I was 13. I am finding it very relaxing.

(Shauna, 2010)

This week I attempted a lino cutting. I never even knew this sort of medium existed.

(Shauna, 2010)

These sentiments and experiences are relayed repeatedly by students in Unit X, and those who teach in the Unit are no longer surprised. But this is not simply a matter of 'therapy' for addressing earlier hurts. It is possible to locate a number of discourses at play here. Theresa's feeling of inadequacy because she does not have access to the 'language' of the gallery can point to the art-as-language discourse, and the literacy arguments around empowerment (New London Group, 1996). Being 'illiterate' at the gallery prevents Theresa from feeling comfortable enough to learn. It appears that Tony sees artistry as a personal trait (Wright, 2012), an identity factor, and one that he lacks. Jennifer might be indicating here that she 'knows' that relying on templates is somehow breaking a 'rule' but nevertheless has her reasons for breaking that rule (Foucault, 1983). And Elizabeth draws from another available discourse to qualify her being described by others as 'artistic'. She refuses this way of being, since it appears she has a strong understanding that 'being artistic' is a 'natural state' possessed by others, but not by her (McArdle & Piscitelli, 2002).

These excerpts were selected as typical, and it is safe to say that the larger proportion of students, on commencing Unit X, have a low opinion of themselves and their artistic capabilities. And yet, at the same time, these art education students often come to the program believing that 'not knowing' about art is OK. For some students, not knowing is a reasonably safe disclosure. There is a discursive construction of art that allows for this—'I don't know much about art, but . . . I know what I like/my 2-year-old could do that/I don't get it'. Coming into the art education program, these students test the story about art that has worked for them thus far. The first few weeks of the Unit are characterized by a general feeling of high anxiety coming from the students, frequent and repeated questions and queries around every aspect of the Unit, and various attempts to manoeuvre and negotiate ways of avoiding actually having to engage in art production.

In some cases, the arts have had such powerful effects that a 13-week semester is not enough to un-do what effect a seemingly small and insignificant act, such as Elizabeth described, can have. With respect to the discipline of psychology, a deal of sensitivity is called for, especially in the early weeks of the semester. It is important to avoid any amateur 'pop-psychology' therapy sessions. At the same time, it remains important that students become aware of the power in these experiences, the folly of a thoughtless teacher/curriculum/ other and, more importantly, that they resolve to not re-visit such an effect on the young children with whom they will work.

Evidence of the effectiveness of the planned learning in Unit X has been measured by a number of success factors, not the least being the changes in students' attitudes towards the arts at the end of the semester. In one year, quantitative data (survey, n=56) demonstrated that student perceptions of their artistic ability changed positively as a result of their experience in the program. In response to the statement 'I consider myself artistic', there were no longer any students who strongly disagreed (originally 10%), and at the end of semester more than half the students considered themselves artistic, to some degree (from 35% to over 60%).[4] In 2008, students were asked to add to a 'graffiti wall' in the final lecture, and one student wrote:

> *This unit has opened my eyes, opened my imagination, opened my thoughts, introduced me to artists, mediums and textures I was unaware of.*
>
> (Kathy, graffiti wall, 2008)

Unit X is not a neat story of success nor the recipe for the 'proper' way to prepare teachers for arts education. Simplistic analysis and interpretations of data can easily reinforce beliefs and the anticipated goals, and any number of factors can change the story of Unit X with each iteration. The 'good student' (Llamas, 2006) might know how to write a self-assessment in a reflective journal in a way that will please the instructor. Self-reporting on one's attitudes and beliefs can be fluid. Nevertheless, over a number of semesters, and through a number of data sources, it is possible to make some claims to successes in turning students around when they arrive with an accumulation of negative arts baggage.

The point here is that the questions asked about teacher education are as much about attitude as content, and the effect of art on teachers is as important as the effect of art on young children. If students complete Unit X with an appreciation for the importance and power of the arts, then the chances are that they will at least include the arts in their planned curriculum for young children. In order to be able to support children's artistry, their teachers must be able to draw on their own arts-related knowledge and knowledge of related pedagogical practices (Eckhoff, 2011). And they must see the need for the arts in the curriculum.

Provocation 3: What effects might dance/song/painting have on those who teach the arts?

---

4 For more on this, see McArdle, 2012.

. . . on Not Making it Simple

Of course, this approach has risks, and teaching Unit X is not for the faint hearted. But neither is teaching young children. Preparing teachers means preparing for diversity—of opinions, beliefs, practices, people, and places. And the answer is not to 'make it simple to begin with'. The fourth provocation in this chapter turns from discourses of art to discourses of pedagogy. This is no longer a matter of choosing between paradigms. Instead, teaching for the future requires capturing the play of knowledges (Lather, 2006)—hands off teaching, hands on learning, structure, freedom, creativity, skills and techniques, cultural, social, political, Indigenous, digital, networked, graffiti, high art, low art, anti-art. The object is not to reach consensus, but rather, to deal with multiplicity.

To begin with, in the first part of Unit X, the students are provided with a map of the field—the debates, the contradictions, the ambivalences and the overlaps. Students are invited to locate themselves in the tensions that characterize the field of arts education. Data suggests that students work with the complexities. Suzanne demonstrated her willingness to engage the contradictions:

> *Predominantly the process is if you enjoy the process but aren't happy with the result the enjoyment of the process will inspire you to keep trying until you are happy with the product. However, if you are never happy with the result you will eventually stop trying thus the product is also important.*
>
> (Suzanne, 2009)

Another student demonstrated her willingness to embrace contradictory thinking, not confined to her artistry:

> *I am extremely confident as I had to become independent at a young age yet I suffer greatly from lack of self esteem.*
>
> (Anna, 2009)

At the heart of the design of Unit X is the principle that the students will learn through doing. If students are to understand the effect of the arts, then Unit X must teach for the effect, as much as for the content. Drawing on Claxton's call to teachers to build on the learning power students bring, the underlying pedagogical strategies for Unit X are for the teachers to 'stop explaining' and to teach their students to 'welcome error' as a learning opportunity (Claxton, 2005). Complex and unclear is OK, and struggling with problems brings pleasure, when students know confusion and come out the other side (McWilliam & Taylor, 2012). Unit X is not 'teaching by numbers', or rubrics, or grids, or proformas. Not all students embrace this approach to learning and teaching.

Four weeks of the semester are given over to an extended block of time working in an art studio with a practising artist. Students who choose to learn frequently request extra time in the studio, outside their classes, and conduct sustained research into skills and techniques that become essential to the successful completion of their artworks. Resisting the pressure to dumb down the curriculum, expectations in risk-taking and innovation are increased, while high levels of support are maintained (McWilliam & Taylor, 2012). The studio block of four weeks signals a move away from a narrow format of lecture/tutorial, and towards an investigative workshop, where 'serious play' (Grieshaber & McArdle, 2010) is legitimate and a way of learning.

To choose to learn means choosing the discomfort of the unfamiliar and the 'not yet' (McWilliam & Taylor, 2012). This does not come easily to all students, particularly those who are the products of the rubrification (Quinn, 2010) of education—where learning is tidied into grids and indicators, and judged by standards that are spelled out in minute detail.

My preconceived beliefs about myself not being able to draw artistically inhibited me from trying out new modes of thinking and working.

(Anna, 2009)

Anna recognizes what she does not know. According to Leadbeater (2000), this ignorance can be useful for learning. If Anna were to know all the 'rules' for drawing (e.g., eyes at halfway point, width of mouth aligned with center of eyes, and so on . . .) this could prevent her from taking risks, experimenting, and creating new effects. A degree of ignorance about drawing can lead to finding new and original ways of seeing and drawing. It is what Anna 'knows' (her preconceived beliefs) about drawing that prevents her from taking risks. Ignorance of drawing 'rules' and expectations could prove more useful. Creativity can come from constraints.

This same 'useful ignorance' might be as true for teachers and parents as it is for children. When we 'know' about effective teaching or parenting, we are less likely to move away from these certainties. To take risks or experiment in ways that appear to deviate from what we know to be true is not always easy, nor comfortable. However, comfort, security, and easy success, low level clerical work in low challenge classrooms, is no preparation for the confusions and complications of real learning (McWilliam & Taylor, 2012). Teachers of the future need a broad set of creative capabilities that heighten their ability to select, shuffle, re-combine, or synthesize existing facts, ideas, faculties and skills in original ways. They need to welcome error-making as opportunity to learn, rather than simply 'playing safe' through passive imitation and memorization (McWilliam & Taylor, 2012).

If the success of Unit X comes down to student satisfaction scores, then to cause discomfort through challenging problems, minimizing explanations, and presenting uncertainties will be risky. On the other hand, it is possible for more nuanced readings of success, including asking the question of what effect the Unit has. In one particular year, answers to the question 'What have you learned in Unit X' included the following:

> *Seeing what other students did [. . .] there are so many more ideas out there than what you did.*
>
> (Kath)

> *I learned that it is OK to have many trials and errors before you achieve that special "work of art". From these trials and errors you problem solve, learn and develop your artistic abilities.*
>
> (Peter)

> *The girls at my table and I are all working on the lino cuttings together, feeding back to each other and exploring different things we can do with the lino together. This has been a great team building experience too, even if we are all doing things totally different.*
>
> (Catherine)

> *I have found an inner peace inside myself, a time when I'm immersed in an art activity I'm quiet and calm. I have found this unit, especially the classes with [artist] to be fulfilling, interesting, stimulating. And very enjoyable. I plan to venture into other art classes in the community.*
>
> (Roberta)

> *I trust I can be a teacher with an open minded approach to children's art.*
>
> (Pia)

> *I needed some tangible processes to draw on, giving me some guidance on how to proceed and overcome challenges in my thinking.*
>
> (Fran)

What is particularly important in these extracts from reflective journals is that the students have articulated a range of learning outcomes, not confined to 'content' so much as concepts and capacities that will prepare them for their future teaching. Through a process of mapping key words as indicators of particular discourses in play, it was possible to identify a number of important teaching and learning principles in the students' thinking—not just in the arts, but broader understandings about learning. The getting of ideas can be collaborative, not solitary (Kath, Catherine). Errors are part of learning, and achieving something 'special' comes through experimenting, failing and trying again (Peter). Catherine and Roberta both notice the importance of relationships in the processes, albeit experienced very differently. It would seem that Catherine's learning has been like the peloton (team building exercise), and the result of her feeling part of a group (the girls at my table). Roberta's words, on the other hand, suggest a more solitary arts experience (inner peace inside myself), but also acknowledges the importance of her relationship with the artist/teacher. Fran appears to have learned about learning through her own self-reflective processes. And Pia's words might be a suggestion that something in Unit X has changed the way she sees children's art and that she can imagine possibilities for the teacher she might become.

What can art achieve in a 13-week semester? The first few weeks of semester are generally intense, with a seemingly endless barrage of questions from students, generated by the 'uncertainties' in both content and delivery of the unit. But, the experience of not knowing, of staying in the grey, of the discomfort of taking risks, experimenting, failing and coming back up again, of imagining possibilities—all of these attributes will be important to the teacher who is going to teach in a classroom like the one described in Chapter Five by Sherbine and Boldt. Teachers who welcome 'wild profusion' will be able to negotiate the constantly changing landscape of education, far beyond the application of technical methods and procedures (Lather, 2006). They have experienced the pleasure of learning, and not through staying safe and 'satisfied'. Rather, they have produced and learned from ruptures, failures, breaks and refusals (Lather, 2006).

This is no neat story of absolute excellence, all learning outcomes achieved, and a new model of excellence in teacher education produced. On the contrary, Unit X is not everyone's cup of tea, and for some students, resistance is the path they choose. Leaving aside analysis of strictly higher education issues for another discussion, the biggest disappointment is when persistent discourses prevail, and the evidence shows that, at the end of semester, some beliefs and practices remain unchanged for some students.

> *To make sure my pedagogy includes self expression and non restricted, non directed art programs.*
>
> (Rhonda. Journal 10.)

In early childhood arts education, the discourses of freedom, self-expression and no-structure have a long history and are particularly enduring. Here, Rhonda has completed her 4-week studio module with an artist. Students were provided with a detailed brief that, to most eyes, would appear quite restrictive and directed. They were to construct a 'self portrait', and it must contain an image of themselves. And yet, Rhonda has learned to aspire to a pedagogy that is 'non restricted, non directed'. This is a mystery. Either the structure and direction provided was invisible to her, or she is reacting to what she considers the undesirable level of restrictions she experienced, and is vowing not to do this when it comes to her own approach to teaching.

In one year of our Unit X teaching, the question of the role of the teacher seemed to remain unchanged over the course of the semester. Approximately 30% of students believed, at the beginning of semester, that 'teachers should not interfere with children's art' (McArdle, 2012). At the end of the semester, when it was hoped that students would have problematized the 'hands off' mantra (McArdle & Piscitelli, 2002) and learned that intentional teaching and support on the part of the teacher is helpful, the number who continued to believe in 'hands off' actually increased marginally (approximately 37%).

It would appear that some pedagogical strategies, for some students, may prove to be counter-productive and serve to reinforce rather than disrupt entrenched beliefs. As Foucault wrote: 'nothing is innocent and everything is dangerous' (1983, p. 343). But just because something is dangerous doesn't mean it can't be used. The puzzling points of resistance or rupture mark the need for constant updating and improvements to the pedagogical strategies used in Unit X, and the need to constantly seek out and evaluate formal and informal feedback from students and colleagues (McWilliam & Taylor, 2012). Just as for the students enrolled in Unit X who are preparing for teaching, similar principles apply for those who teach about arts education: not knowing can be a good thing; the benefits of knowing confusion and coming out the other end are well worth the discomfort; and improvising and possibility thinking produce creative and innovative effects, and pleasure in learning and teaching.

> Provocation 4: Teach the pleasure of learning: stop explaining, welcome error, support students in their experience of knowing confusion and coming out the other end.

. . . on Not 'Doing Reggio'

Finally, the last provocation is prompted by a concern over how this chapter is taking shape. Unit X, like all teaching, is situated in a particular context, culture and historical time—marked by multiplicity and competing discourses that do not map tidily onto one another. It is not described (partially) here as a model for all teacher education when it comes to the arts. Simply put, in Unit X, some things are working, but the unit is constantly in need of revisiting, and revising. Preparing teachers to expect a job that requires nothing more of them than to teach-by-numbers prepares them for failure, disillusionment, and worse. The appeal of the teach-by-numbers manual is its packaging as a solution.

Historically, in early childhood education, an enduringly attractive package is the 'model'. The irresistible pull of the model of excellence answers that endless search for that imaginary teacher who is teaching 'properly'. Along with this belief in a 'proper' way to teach must come the realization that, although this might be an ideal to strive for, the more likely end to the search for the one best way to do early childhood art education is that the notion is an 'impossible fiction' (Walkerdine, 1992). The final provocation in this chapter, then, is to the fervor that has arisen for engaging young children in the arts through 'doing Reggio.'

When I first began to hear early childhood teachers speak of 'doing Reggio', I confess to looking forward to hearing more about what I mistakenly believed to be this charismatic Italian educator whose name was Reggio, who had cracked the code to teaching 'properly'. To be fair, the educators in the Italian municipality of Reggio Emilia (there is no person called Reggio) are the first to say that it is erroneous for teachers to say they are 'doing Reggio' (see McLure, 2008). Nevertheless, my own participation in an official 'Study Tour' in 2010 did little to convince me that this was not a package, being somewhat aggressively marketed. I was reminded of another equally glamorous and appealing product from a European country—IKEA. Like IKEA, Reggio has been taken up in any number of countries around the world. But unlike IKEA, Reggio is not portable furniture; it is a system for education, and the degree of portability of models of education is what is in question here (Johnson, 1999).

In his 2011 address at the American Educational Research Association (AERA), Allan Luke posed the questions around how well policy crosses borders. He gave examples of the movement of educational innovation and educational science from one cultural context to another, from one nation to another, from one jurisdiction or system to another. The function of localized generation of knowledge can easily be subsumed or overshadowed by the 'representation' of the model. But like IKEA, there is always the disappointment when the piece is brought home and assembled, and is never quite as glamorous as it looks in the showroom, or there is a piece missing, or it doesn't go with everything else in the house (Ariely, 2010).

It is not my purpose to critique the approaches or teachers of Reggio, many of whom have been constant in their continuous generation of knowledge about their practices, the children with whom they work, and making children's capacities visible. The presence of an artist as a staff member in Reggio inspired child care centers has an obvious effect on the children's developing artistry, and there are few who could fault an approach to pedagogy that encourages thoughtful selection of abundant resources, scaffolding of children's constructions of knowledge, and the active listening and relationships on which this particular approach to pedagogy has been built.

For some, this is simply 'good art education' (New, 1994). A key feature of the centers in the municipality of Reggio Emilia is the collaboration between arts educators, early childhood educators, community artists, and community-based arts organizations (Lim, 2008).[5] Echoing MacRae's work in her chapter

---

5 Interestingly, at the time of my visit to the Reggio Emilia Study Tour, the artist (atelier) was no longer to be a permanent member of the staff at a number of the centers for the younger children . . . due to funding cuts.

in this book, in the Reggio approach, a flexible curriculum is planned around careful choices of inspirational objects (Fredriksen, 2010). The proliferation of sales of 'light boxes' as featured in the centers in Reggio might be linked to efforts to attend to the aesthetics of the carefully planned learning environments. More nuanced understandings, though, of aesthetics would have that the aesthetics of a classroom relate more to what the children do there than any particular resources or 'styles' (see Lewin-Benham, 2011).

The emphasis on the arts and the presence and status of artists is sometimes lost in translation when the Reggio approach is transported elsewhere. Historically, the featuring of the arts in curriculum for young children has varying roots across borders. Just as Malaguzzi rode his bicycle into the district of Reggio Emilia after the Second World War, Viktor Lowenfeld was also troubled over the horrors of that war. He saw children as the future, and believed that the way to a peaceful world was through their arts education—the teachers were to keep their 'hands off' children's art, lest they inhibit their 'natural' goodness and innocence, and visit neuroses and pathologies on them. Children's art was to be about freedom, non-intervention, self-expression, and natural development. And, for still others, what the children in the Reggio centers do is not so much about art as design, which makes sense when considering the geography of the district of Reggio Emilia and its proximity to world famous design centers. The distinction between various discourses of art alone can produce clearly different understandings of what the children in Reggio Emilia centers are doing when they draw, paint, construct.

In their ten year content analysis of the *Early Childhood Education Journal*, Walsh and Petty (2007) analyzed the content of 492 relevant publications, and found six approaches to early childhood education most commonly mentioned—three from the US (Head Start, Bank Street and High/Scope), and three from Europe (Reggio Emilia, Montessori, Waldorf). Perhaps this tells us simply the models that are most researched, most studied, and most visible. Notwithstanding, it is interesting to imagine all those that do not make it to this list. In my home country of Australia, I live in the State of Queensland, and on the outskirts of the capital city is a smaller city called Ipswich. In the district of Ipswich, a small network of early childhood educators have recently embarked on an extended program of professional development. The program included educators from various early years settings (long daycare, after-school hours care, and family daycare). They met regularly over a period of 12 months, and together, they theorized, reflected, discussed and developed a range of excellent, cutting-edge practices. My question is: 'Why are we not all talking now about "doing Ipswich"?' Students in Unit X would be much more likely to talk about the practices of the teachers in Reggio Emilia than to know anything about the practices of that group of educators in Ipswich, Queensland, Australia.

Why Reggio? And why now? Even a quick and cursory search of the early childhood literature will show Reggio is being adapted, adopted, brought home, and applied in the US, Australia, the UK, the Scandinavian countries, Hong Kong, Singapore, Thailand, Canada, and now mainland China. One possible explanation is the attraction of a model that speaks back to current policy emphasis. Across OECD countries, comparable approaches have been developed that are aimed at expanding the 'professionalization' of early childhood workforces (Tobin, 2005). These policies have come to be enacted through increasing surveillance mechanisms, such as licensing and accreditation of programs and facilities, and performance measures in the allocation of funding (Luke, 2011). Understandably, a system of education that has, so far, managed to avoid such an agenda has its attractions.

One way of describing the Reggio approach is as an exemplar of progressive, child-centered education (Edwards, 2003). The ideology is explicit, and children are positioned as intelligent, creative, whole persons. Not unlike Montessori, another Italian educator, in the Reggio model, learning is understood as enabled through the provision of carefully prepared aesthetically pleasing environments. Parents are partners with the teachers in their children's education. It is important to note, at the same time, that notions of the 'whole child' and parents as partners are not universal truths. The whole child who grows up in Reggio Emilia, for instance, is surrounded by Italian architecture, monuments, churches, piazzas, not to mention the beliefs and practices of their parents and extended families. The whole child who grows up in Cochiti Pueblo society, to take Luke's reference to the work of Romero-Little (2010), grows up in an 'intricate and dynamic socialization process' which has been 'shaped by Indigenous languages and guided by Indigenous epistemologies for thousands of years' (p. 12).

In the so called Reggio-inspired classroom, whether in US, UK or PRC, children are encouraged/taught/trained to exchange their ideas through discussion rather than passively absorb knowledge from the teacher (Kim & Darling, 2009). But here is one of those points at which the IKEA-disappointment factor might be most likely to occur. Education is part of a total cultural, social, and political economic settlement and part of the agenda is to produce a certain type of child (Simola, 2005). Reforms are produced and work in situ (Luke, 2011). Matters of culture, ideology and political economy are not incidental. And to adapt particular Western/European based approaches that 'culturally model' (Lee, 2001) community interaction, learning, and vernacular language practices (consider: atelier, piazza, and even documentation) ignores the contingencies of culture and context.

This comes full circle to the initial points made at the beginning of this chapter, about the importance of knowing history and culture. The possibilities for a principled policy/practice borrowing begin from an understanding of cultural and historical context (Luke, 2011). Perhaps it is this that the centers in Reggio Emilia best exemplify. As opposed to standards-based curriculum, imagine implementing a culture-based curriculum that draws upon Indigenous knowledge, traditions and language (Yazzie-Mintz, 2011). While not a blueprint that is portable and a ready-to-assemble kit that can be transported globally, the best lesson to be learned from Reggio Emilia might be to note the depth of connection between education and the culture, politics and history of place.

Provocation 5: Culture, politics, ideology and the economy are not incidental to the arts. Is creativity culture-free?

End Note

The work of this chapter is to bring this book to a close, and it is the hope of all who have contributed to this book that we have created a space that can enable ways of working through those 'uneasy moments' (Luke & Gore, 1992) and places in present practices where we all get stuck. We share the desire to move on from competitions between paradigms and situate our efforts within contemporary knowledge problematics (Lather, 2006).

Our questions come from all over, and regardless of any particular artistic or pedagogical persuasion, we all do our work within frames of certainty and uncertainties, consensus and dissensus, modernism and postmodernism, and a proliferation of data, information, theories and methods. We work in climates where national agendas for education are increasingly influenced by corporate discourses of competition and measurables, and . . . where words like 'inclusive education' are used in relation to those who are excluded, and . . . where projects for professionalizing the workforce actually have the effect of de-professionalizing the teacher in the classroom, and . . . where raising the standards has actually led to a 'dumbing down to excellence' (McWilliam, 2009).

This book is a prompt to re-think what is thinkable and not thinkable, sayable and not sayable, when it comes to the work of teachers who will be working with young children. Is it possible, for instance, for a teacher to say: 'I'm not very book-ish. I don't really get reading. The children in my class this year won't get much reading. They will have to wait until next year, when they go to Ms Warhol'. Or is it possible for a university student to say: 'Instead of a 2,500 word essay, could I show you what I know about this through making a YouTube short film, and linking that with my study Blog and my Facebook page?' Or could parents, looking for guidance on where to enroll their children, look up a 'MySchool' website that scores every school in the country on the children's artistry and creativity, and where success is attributed to those schools that dedicate substantial time in the curriculum to nurturing children's creativity and imagination?

When it comes to the arts, smart teachers understand how policy and pedagogy shape students' perceptions of art, and how the relationship between culture and learning for all students can be embraced (Smith, 2008). Attempts to shut down and narrow the curriculum are best met with a proliferation of possibilities.

References

Ariely, D. (2010). *The upside of irrationality: The unexpected benefits of defying logic at work and at home.* New York: Harper Collins.

Berger, J. (1981). *Ways of seeing.* London: BBC and Penguin Books.

Bolt, B., with Martin, K. (2001). The unremarked representationalist pre-conceptions of western art education in Australia. *Australian Art Education, 24*(1), 18–21.

Carter, P. (1996.) *The lie of the land.* London: Faber and Faber.

Claxton, G. (2005, July). Learning to learn: The fourth generation. Paper presented at the Twelfth International Conference on Thinking, Melbourne.

Connor, J. (2007). *Dreaming stories: A springboard for learning* [Book and DVD]. Research in Practice Series, *14*(2). Watson, ACT: Early Childhood Australia.

Darling-Hammond, L., & Bransford, J. (2005). *Preparing teachers for a changing world: What teachers should learn and be able to do.* San Francisco, CA: John Wiley & Sons.

Duncum, P. (1999). What elementary generalist teachers need to know to teach art well. *Art Education, 52*(6), 33–37.

Eckhoff, A. (2011). Art experiments: Introducing an artist-in-residence programme in early childhood education. *Early Child Development and Care, 181*(3), 371–385.

Edwards, C. (2003). 'Fine designs' from Italy: Montessori education and the Reggio Emilia approach. *Montessori Life, 15*(1), 34–40.

Foucault, M. (1983). *The Foucault reader* (Paul Rabinow, Ed.), New York: Vintage.

Fredriksen, B. (2010). Meaning making, democratic participation and art in early childhood education: Can inspiring objects structure dynamic curricula? *International Journal of Education through Art, 6*(3), 381–395.

Grieshaber, S., & McArdle, F. (2010). *The trouble with play.* New York: McGraw-Hill Open University Press.

Grosz, E. (1994). A thousand tiny sexes: Feminism and rhizomatics. In C. V. Boundas & D. Olkowski (Eds.) *Gilles Deleuze and the theatre of philosophy.* New York: Routledge.

Heidegger, M. (1977). *The question concerning technology and other essays.* (W. Lovitt, Trans.). New York: Garland.

Johnson, R. (1999). Colonialism and cargo cults. *Contemporary Issues in Early Childhood, 1*(1), 61–78.

Jones, R. (2000). Transformations. *Hypatia, 15*(2), 151–159.

Kim, B., & Darling, L. (2009). Monet, Malaguzzi, and the constructive conversations of preschoolers in a Reggio-inspired classroom. *Early Childhood Education Journal, 37*(2), 137–145.

Knight, L. (2009). Mother and child sharing through drawing: Intergenerational collaborative processes for making artworks. *International Art in Early Childhood Research Journal, 1*(1), 1–12.

Knudsen, J. S. (2008). Children's improvised vocalisations—Learning, communication and technology of the self. *Contemporary issues in early Childhood, Special issue: Children and the Arts* (Ed. Felicity McArdle), *9*(4), 287–296.

Lather, P. (2006). Paradigm proliferation as a good thing to think with: Teaching research in education as a wild profusion. *International Journal of Qualitative Studies in Education, 19*(1), 35–57.

Leadbeater, C. (2000). *Living on thin air: The new economy.* New York: Viking.

Lee, C. (2001). Is October Brown Chinese? A cultural modelling system for under-achieving students. *American Educational Research Journal, 38*, 97–141.

Lewin-Benham, A. (2011). *Twelve best practices for early childhood education: Integrating Reggio and other inspired approaches.* New York: Teachers College Press.

Lim, N. (2008). Enriching the context for musical learning. *Arts Education Policy Review. 109*(3), 27–36.

Llamas, J. (2006). Technologies of disciplinary power in action: The norm of the 'good student'. *Higher Education, 52*(4), 665–686.

Luke, A. (2011). Generalizing across borders. Policy and the limits of educational science. *Educational Researcher, 40*(8), 367–377.

Luke, C., & Gore, J. (Eds.). (1992). *Feminisms and critical pedagogy.* New York: Routledge.

MacRae, C. (2008). Representing space: Katie's horse and the recalcitrant object. *Contemporary Issues in Early Childhood (Special Issue), 9*(4), 275–286.

McArdle, F. (2001) Art in early childhood: The discourse of 'proper' teaching. PhD thesis, Queensland University of Technology.

McArdle, F. (2012). New maps of learning for quality art education: What pre-service teachers should learn and be able to do. *Australian Educational Researcher, 39*(1), 91–106.

McArdle, F., & Piscitelli, B. (2002). Early childhood art education: A palimpsest. *Australian Art Education, 25*(1), 11–15.

McLure, M.A. (2008). *Building theories: Play, making, and pedagogical documentation in early childhood art education.* Pennsylvania State University. ProQuest Dissertations and Theses: 3414376. Retrieved July 2012, from http://gradworks.umi.com/34/14/3414376.html.

McWilliam, E. (2009). Teaching for creativity: From sage to guide to meddler. *Asia Pacific Journal of Education, 29*(3), 281–293.

McWilliam, E., & Taylor, P. (2012). *Personally significant learning.* Retrieved September 13, 2012, from http://www.ericamcwilliam.com.au/personally-significant-learning/.

National Review of Visual Education (NRVE). (2009). *First we see: The National Review of Visual Education.* Retrieved July 20, 2009, from http://www.australiacouncil.gov.au/_data/assets/pdf_file/0003/36372/NRVE_Final_Report.pdf.

New, R. (1994) Reggio Emilia: Its vision and its challenges for educators in the United States. In L. G. Katz & B. Cesarone (Eds.), *Reflections on the Reggio Emilia approach* (pp. 33–40). Eric/EECE Monograph Series.

New London Group. (1996). A pedagogy of multiliteracies: Designing social futures. *Harvard Educational Review, 66*(1), 60–93.

Quinn, M. (2010). 'Ex and the city': On cosmopolitanism, community and the 'Curriculum of Refuge'. *Transnational Curriculum Inquiry, 7*(1). Retrieved May 2011, from http://nitinat.library.ubc.ca/ojs/index.php/tci.

Romero-Little, M. E. (2010). How should young Indigenous children be prepared for learning? A vision of early childhood education for Indigenous children. *Journal of American Indian Education, 49*, 7–28.

Simola, H. (2005). The Finnish miracle of PISA: Historical and sociological remarks on teaching and teacher education. *Comparative Education, 41*, 455–470.

Smith, J. (2008). Art education in New Zealand: Framing the past/locating the present/questioning the future. *Australian Art Education, 31*(2), 100–117.

Tobin, J. (2005). Quality in early childhood education: An anthropologist's perspective. *Early Education and Development, 16*, 422–434.

Walkerdine, V. (1992). Progressive pedagogy and political struggle. In C. Luke & J. Gore (Eds.), *Feminisms and critical pedagogy* (pp. 15–24). New York: Routledge.

Walsh, B. & Petty, K. (2007). Frequency of Six Early Childhood Education Approaches: A 10-Year Content Analysis of Early Childhood Education Journal. *Early Childhood Education Journal, 34*(5), 301–305.

Wright, S. (2012). *Children, meaning making and the arts (2nd edition)*. Frenchs Forest, NSW: Pearson Education Australia.

Yazzie-Mintz, T. (2011). Native teachers' beliefs and practices: Choosing language and cultural revitalization over uniformity and standardization. *Contemporary Issues in Early Childhood, 12*(4), 315–326.

CONTRIBUTORS

Eeva Anttila is Professor in dance pedagogy at the University of the Arts Helsinki/Theatre Academy, Finland. She is widely published in the field of arts education, including the *International Handbook for Research in Art Education, 2006,* co-edited by Liora Bresler and Christine Thompson. Her research interests are particularly in dance education, as well as the arts, aesthetics, and learning.

Gail Boldt is Associate Professor at The Pennsylvania State University, USA. She is a theorist with interests in the affective worlds of children in schools, literacies, elementary and early childhood education, identity (including gender, sexuality, and race), the politics of educational reform, and cultural studies. She works from post-structural and psychoanalytic perspectives. She is widely published in literacy, early childhood, and childhood studies. Her most recent publications include *Challenging the Politics of Teacher Accountability: Toward a More Hopeful Educational Future* with William Ayers; *Reading 'A Pedagogy of Multiliteracies': Bodies, Texts and Emergence* with Kevin Leander; and *Moments of Meeting: Learning to Play with Reading Resistance* with Billie Pivnick.

Linda Knight is Senior Lecturer, Queensland University of Technology, Australia. As well as being an academic and member of a number of community and curriculum committees, Linda is a practising artist who has exhibited nationally and internationally. She leads and coordinates the *International Drawing on Knowledge Research Network,* and she is particularly interested in researching drawing and collaborative drawing with young children.

Jan Sverre Knudsen is a professor at the Faculty of Education and International Studies, Oslo and Akershus University College, as well as lecturer in world music at the Department of Musicology, Oslo University. He is also a trained music therapist. His research and publications focus on musical expressions in early childhood, and on issues related to multicultural music education and the music of immigrant communities. His website is http://home.hio.no/~jansk/.

Christina MacRae is currently working as a full time nursery school teacher in the UK. She has worked on research projects at a number of universities, including most recently the Manchester Metropolitan University. From 2006–2008, she worked with Maggie MacLure and Liz Jones on the funded project that investigated 'Becoming a problem: how and why children acquire a reputation as "naughty" in the earliest years at school'. Her interests are in the arts and young children, as well as the ethnographies of classrooms, and she has published in books, journal articles, and practitioner publications.

Felicity McArdle is Associate Professor at Queensland University of Technology, Australia. Before coming to QUT, she worked for over fourteen years as a classroom teacher, in a range of contexts, including urban, rural and remote settings. Her research interests are in arts education and teacher education, and she was a member of the consortium that wrote the first national curriculum for the early years, Early Years Learning Framework (EYLF). Her recent publications are focused on teacher education and the place of creativity as well as The Trouble with Play, Open University Press, 2010 co-authored (with S. Grieshaber).

Kylie Peppler is currently an Assistant Professor at Indiana University and received her Ph.D. from the University of California, Los Angeles, USA. She was awarded the Indiana Governor's Award for Tomorrow's Leaders in 2009, and has also been recognized for her work in new media, computers, arts and education. Her recent publications include examinations of creativity, gaming, collaborations and social media environments, and she co-edited (with Y. Kafai & R. Chapman) a volume titled, The Computer Clubhouse: Creativity and Constructionism in Youth Communities, NY: Teachers College Press, 2009.

Amy Pfeiler-Wunder is an Assistant Professor at Kuztown University, Pennsylvania, USA. She has worked extensively as a K-6 elementary art teacher, and in 2007 was awarded NAEA Western Region Outstanding Elementary Art Educator award. In addition to her own creative works, Amy's publications include: Let's Play: Dewey, Aesthetics and the Elementary Art Room, which was published in the Journal of the Philosophy Society of Australasia, 2007. She also works closely with Dr Marilyn Stewart with The Dinner Party Institute focused on feminist pedagogy, and serves in leadership roles within the National Art Education Association.

Adrienne Sansom has a Ph.D. from the School of Educational Leadership and Cultural Foundations, and an MA in Dance, both from The University of North Carolina at Greensboro. She is a senior lecturer in the School of Curriculum and Pedagogy at the Faculty of Education, The University of Auckland. Her particular area of teaching is in the field of dance and drama education, specializing in early years pedagogy. Adrienne's pedagogy and, thus, philosophical beliefs, are embedded in the principles and practices of early childhood education. Current research focuses on the body and embodied knowing. Adrienne is currently Chair of Dance and the Child International.

Kortney Sherbine is a doctoral candidate at the Pennsylvania State University. A former classroom teacher in a public elementary school, Kortney currently teaches language and literacy education courses in the teacher education program. She draws on the philosophies of Gilles Deleuze and Felix Guattari to consider pedagogy as well as children's fanaticism.

Christine Marmé Thompson is Professor, School of Visual Arts, Pennsylvania State University, USA. She taught at the School of Art and Design, University of Illinois at Urbana-Champaign, from 1985–2001. She was awarded the June King McFee Award, Women's Caucus, National Art Education Association, 2005, and is widely published in journals and books on arts education in early childhood. She co-authored, with Liora Bresler, *The Arts in Children's Lives: Context, Culture and Curriculum* (2002).

Karen E. Wohlend is an assistant professor in Literacy, Culture, and Language Education in the School of Education at Indiana University. Her research reconceptualizes play as a literacy for reading and writing identity texts and as a tactic for participating and learning in early childhood classrooms. Wohlend is the author of *Playing Their Way into Literacies: Reading, Writing and Belonging in the Early Childhood Classroom* as well as numerous articles and chapters that provide a critical perspective on children's play and new literacies, popular media, gender, and identity.

INDEX

NOTE: Page numbers in *italic figures* refer to illustrations.
In the interests of clarity the term *socioeconomic status (SES)* has been used throughout the index instead of *class*, using the word *class* in its educational context.